Contents

Santa Catalina, Arequipa

Llamas

Chilean Flag

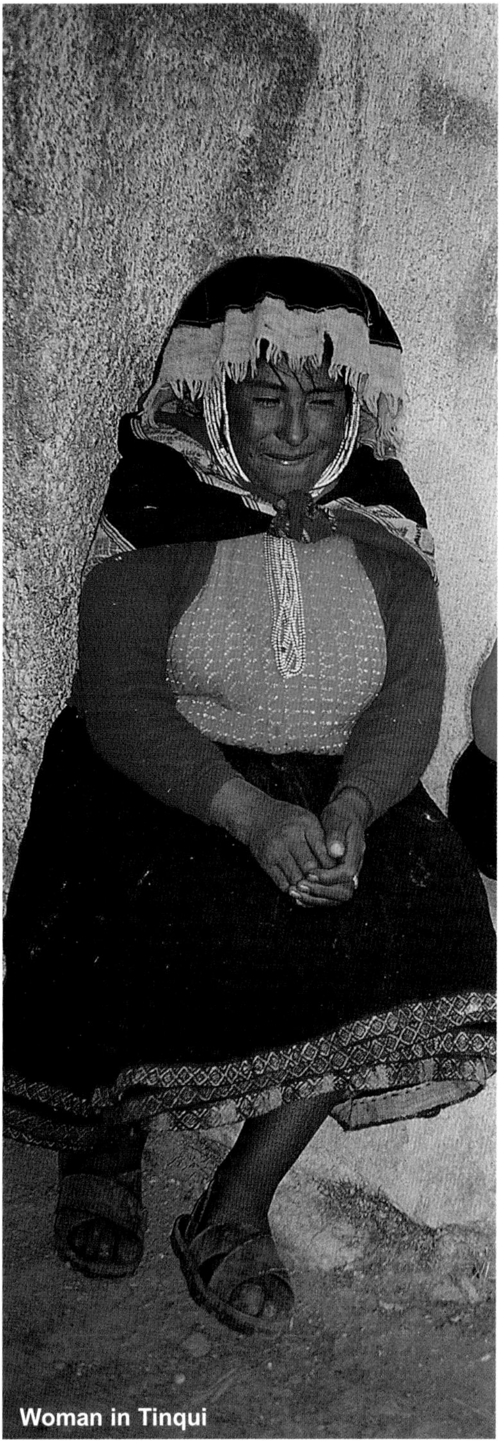

Woman in Tinqui

South America - The Andes

Venezuela
Unusual flora and accesible mountains in the Sierra Nevada
S. N. de Santa Marta
Caracas
Sierra Nevada
Colombia
Some of the most beautiful scenery in the Andes
S.N. del Cocuy
Bogota
Los Nevados
Equator
Quito
Cotopaxi
Ecuador
The famous Avenue of the Volcanoes
Northern Peru
Peru's most dramatic peaks
Brazil
Cord. Blanca
Huaraz
Cord. Huayhuash
Lima
Cuzco
Cord. Vilcanota
Cord. Real
Southern Peru
Wonderful ruins at the heart of the old Inca empire and the worlds deepest canyon
Arequipa
La Paz
Bolivia
Wild desert scenery and steep jungle treks
Cord. Occidental
Paraguay
Sao Paulo
Rio de Janeiro
Calama
Tropic of Capricorn
Salta
Puna de Atacama
The High Andes
The highest peaks in the Andes rise above desert landscapes
Aconcagua
Mendoza
Santiago
Uruguay
Buenos Aires
Chile
Argentina
The Lake District
Mellow scenery, snow-capped volcanoes and lush forests
Bariloche
Patagonia
Spectacular rock spires and glaciers
Los Glaciares
Torres del Paine
Rio Gallegos
Punta Arenas
Tierra del Fuego
Isla Navarino
0 500 1000 1500km

Summary of the main treks and walks

	WHEN TO GO	DURATION	TERRAIN	EFFORT	PAGE
VENEZUELA	NDJFMA				
La Culata		3 days	No path	Moderate	28
La Travesia		2-3 days	Technical	Moderate	31
COLOMBIA	NDJFM				
Santa Marta Circuit		5 days	Rough path	Moderate	37
Cocuy Circuit		6 days	Technical	Difficult	39
Los Nevados Traverse		5 days	Rough path	Moderate	42
ECUADOR	JJASONDJF				
Antisana to Cotopaxi Trek		4-5 days	Easy path	Moderate	48
Inca Trail to Ingapirca		2-3 days	Easy path	Easy	50
NORTHERN PERU	MJJASO				
Quebrada Los Cedros		7-8 days	Easy path	Moderate	57
Quebrada Santa Cruz		4 days	Easy path	Moderate	60
Olleros to Chavin		3 days	Easy path	Easy	62
Huayhuash Circuit		10-14 days	Easy path	Difficult	64
Ticlla Circuit		5-6 days	Rough path	Difficult	70
SOUTHERN PERU	AMJJAS				
Inca Trail to Machu Picchu		3 days	Easy path	Easy	76
Ausangate Circuit		6 days	Easy path	Moderate	80
Colca Canyon		5-6 days	Easy path	Moderate	85
Misti Circuit and Ascent		3 days	Rough path	Moderate	87
BOLIVIA	AMJJASO				
Illampu Circuit		7 days	Rough path	Difficult	93
Taquesi Trail		2-3 days	Easy path	Moderate	97
Choro Trail		4 days	Easy path	Easy	99
Cordillera Apolobamba		7-8 days	Rough path	Moderate	101
Pomerape Circuit		4-5 days	No path	Moderate	105
THE HIGH ANDES	NDJFM				
Licancabur Ascent		3-4 days	No path	Difficult	111
Nevados de Cachi		4-5 days	No path	Extreme	113
High Puna Traverse		7-8 days	No path	Extreme	115
Aconcagua Treks		3-6 days	Easy path	Moderate	119
Aconcagua Ascent		10-16 days	Rough path	Extreme	122
del Plomo Ascent		5 days	Rough path	Difficult	124
Marmolejo Traverse		4 days	Technical	Extreme	126
THE LAKE DISTRICT	NDJFMA				
Antuco Circuit		3 days	No path	Moderate	131
Villarrica Traverse		5-6 days	Rough path	Difficult	133
Paso de las Nubes		4 days	Rough path	Moderate	137
Nahuel Huapi Traverse		4 days	No path	Moderate	140
PATAGONIA	NDJFMA				
Fitzroy Semi Circuit		4-5 days	Easy path	Moderate	146
Ice-cap Circuit		6 days	Technical	Extreme	150
Torres del Paine Circuit		5-6 days	Rough path	Difficult	153
Valdivieso Circuit		4 days	No path	Extreme	159
Isla Navarino Circuit		4-5 days	No path	Difficult	162

Introduction

This book is a guide to the best multi-day walking opportunities in the Andes, whether trekking or backpacking. A selection of single day walks are also included for each area, as are ascents of easy peaks where these fit nicely into an itinerary.

Many people are at first wary of travelling to South America because of the problems experienced in Peru and Colombia in recent years. Though parts of Colombia are still not a good place to travel, Peru is now much safer than it was in the early 1990's. Other parts of the continent have never been at all dangerous - comparing Patagonia to Colombia is a bit like comparing Norway to Afghanistan.

There is a tremendous variety of mountain scenery in the Andes. This is not surprising given that they are the worlds longest mountain chain at over 9000km. There are areas where steep 'Alpine' mountains rise from some of the wettest tropical forest on earth, places where steaming volcanoes stand in solitude above the worlds driest deserts and areas where improbable rock spires rise from thick temperate forest or icy glaciers. Much of the Andes is still very remote, but other areas now have good tourist infrastructure. While many of the treks in the Andes are at high altitudes those in Patagonia are mostly at or near sea level.

All areas of the Andes have superb mountain scenery and people that speak Spanish, but there are huge cultural differences between the different Andean nations. If you want to see llamas, traditional costumes, fascinating archaeology and bustling markets then you'll need to go to either Peru, Bolivia or Ecuador. In these countries you'll have to put up with generally poorer health and sanitation than you get in Europe or North America. If you prefer to visit a relatively clean and modern country, with good roads, air-conditioned buses and big supermarkets then you should choose either Chile or Argentina. Venezuela and Colombia are somewhere between the two extremes. Of course everywhere in South America is a bit of a mixture between the old and the modern.

The variety of climates throughout South America ensures that the weather will be good somewhere on the continent at any time of year.

Trekking or Backpacking

Throughout this guidebook trekking is taken to mean an extended multi-day walk through the mountains where pack animals (or very occasionally porters) are available to carry all your equipment. Backpacking is taken to mean an extended walk where you will have to carry all your own equipment.

TREKKING

Easily the most popular adventure holiday in South America is a trekking trip in the Andes. On all of the treks featured here you'll see some great scenery and colourful local people while mules or donkeys will do the hard work. Trekking still involves some moderate exercise, but with pack animals or porters to carry all your equipment most active walkers will cope with all the treks featured here. Most treks in the Andes last less than a week and can be easily combined with time spent pursuing other adventure activities or just sightseeing. Peru and Bolivia undoubtedly have the best of the trekking in the Andes. Indeed they have some world famous treks, such as the circuit of the spectacular Cordillera Huayhuash, the Quebrada Santa Cruz trail in the Cordillera Blanca and the descent to Coroico in the Cordillera Real. However many of the more famous treks are now busy and under quite considerable environmental pressure, while many of the less well known treks featured in this guidebook are no less rewarding and will be found much quieter.

BACKPACKING

In Chile, Argentina, Colombia and Venezuela there are fewer facilities set up for trekkers and most multi-day walking trips will involve at least some backpacking. Some previous experience of short backpacking trips is recommended before trying one of these wilderness walks. A bit more fitness is needed to carry everything you need for up to a week on your back, but the rewards are certainly worthwhile. Best examples of backpacking trips are the spectacular and famous circuit of the Torres del Paine, the Villarrica traverse in the Lake District and the traverse of the Sierra Nevada in Venezuela.

WALKING AND HIKING

The terms walking and hiking are used variously through the text and mean only travel on foot, with no reference to whether you are trekking or backpacking.

Using This Guidebook

GRADES

A dual grading system is used to cover two principal factors, the difficulty of the terrain encountered and the amount of effort required to complete the route. These grades are given as averages for the whole route, but individual sections may be harder or easier.

TERRAIN GRADES

The routes are given an overall grade for the difficulty of terrain encountered, the difficulty of route finding and the extent of any hazards such as sections of scrambling, glacier or river crossings. An average overall grade for the whole route is given in the summary and specific sections of the walk may also be graded within the text. A four point scale has been used as follows

Easy Path - Most of the route will be on easy paths with no significant obstacles.

Rough Path - Sections of the route may be quite rough e.g. river crossings, steep scree, fallen trees, but there will still be a reasonably easy to follow or well marked trail.

No Path - Most of the route will be over unmarked terrain with rough ground and route finding difficulties.

Technical - The route will include serious sections of scrambling, glacier crossings or serious river crossings as well as difficult navigation. A rope and/or ice-axe and/or crampons may be required.

EFFORT REQUIRED

A separate indication of the effort you'll have to put in (and therefore the fitness you'll need) is also given. This takes into account the total distance and height climbed, the type of terrain encountered, how sustained the walk is and in particular whether you'll be backpacking or trekking. If you are backpacking a route described as 'trekking' then you should add an extra effort grade to that given in the text. A four point scale is used again.

Easy - The easiest treks, generally at reasonable altitudes (up to 4000m) and on good well marked paths.

Moderate - The easiest and shortest backpacking routes and treks which are more sustained or at higher altitudes.

Difficult - The longest, hardest treks involving over a week of sustained effort and backpacking routes of considerable length and difficulty in possibly adverse weather.

Extreme - The very hardest and longest backpacking routes, all of which will involve difficult weather and ground conditions and considerable ascent.

TIMES

The days required are those for a reasonably quick but not hurried completion of the route, by a party fit enough for the terrain. These allow perhaps 6-8 hours of walking per day and therefore some spare time at camps in the evenings. All treks could be done quicker but this would spoil some of the enjoyment. Unfit, unacclimatised or inexperienced parties will certainly take longer. No allowance is made for side-trips or ascents even though these are described in the text.

Timings given in bold type for individual sections of the route generally follow the same principles but do not include any time for meal stops, viewpoints etc. These timings are cumulative. Times not in bold are for navigation purposes only and don't contribute to the daily total.

DISTANCES

The distances quoted have generally been measured directly from a large scale (1:50,000 or 1:100,000) map, so the actual distance walked will be somewhat longer, depending on how many zigzags there are on the trail and how good your navigation is!

TOTAL ASCENT

This has again been estimated from large scale maps and so does not take into account the many little ups and downs of around 10-20m that are found on many paths The ascent of any peaks is not included. Total descent is also given in the few cases where this is significant.

TREK PROFILES

Each trek has a trek profile, a graphic indication of height versus distance, showing the overall nature and altitude of the trek. The heights of passes, campsites etc. can be quickly seen. These profiles are not intended for use in route finding.

TREK MAPS

The sketch maps are intended for planning and comparison purposes only and they should not be relied on for navigation, for which an accurate topographical map should be bought (see Map to Use). The red letters and numbers used on the maps refer to sections of the trek or walk as described in the text.

MAP TO USE

The map listed under the heading **Map to Use** (at the start of each description) is the best readily available map for doing the walk. These are usually published by the national Instituto Geografico Militar (IGM) for the country concerned. These maps are usually topographically quite accurate (i.e. contours and rivers are correct) but roads, towns and villages may be inaccurately marked or very out of date. These maps will almost never have the exact trail marked on it, and a reasonable skill in map reading may be needed to follow the route, particularly on routes rated as **No Path** or **Technical.** An indication is given in the text if a particularly high standard of navigation is required.

Cuzco

The Andes - A Quick Tour

The Andes are the world's second greatest mountain range after the Himalaya/Karakoram system in central Asia. In both height and extent no other range rivals the Andes for second place. The Andes run down the west side of the South American continent through the countries of Venezuela, Colombia, Ecuador, Peru, Bolivia, Chile and Argentina to the land that has been called the uttermost part of the earth - Patagonia.

From north to south the Andes are over 8500km in length, but rarely over 250km wide. (At the widest in southern Bolivia the Andean plateau is only 500km wide) For most of this distance the Andes are not one continuous chain of mountains but a high plateau (generally 3000-4000m) from which rise many isolated ranges, commonly known as Cordilleras or Nudos.

In **Venezuela** and **Colombia** (pages 25-44) the Andes rise directly from the palm fringed shores of the Caribbean. Several mountain ranges reach over 5000m, just high enough to catch a wee bit of snow. There are several good treks and backpacking trips here, with unusual vegetation and wonderful forests. However the climate can be a bit damp even in the November to January dry season. Further south in **Ecuador** (pages 45-52) the landscape is more plateau-like with a number of large snow-capped volcanoes including the famous Cotopaxi rising from this plateau. There are some good treks across the high plateaux between these volcanoes which have become popular in recent years, but again the weather is a little unpredictable.

Perhaps because it was the heart of the Inca Empire, **Peru** (pages 53-88) is the country which has shaped most people's image of South America. It is certainly the country with most to offer the trekker interested in the culture and history of the area they are visiting. There are still many impressive Inca archaeological ruins to be seen, such as the fortress city of Machu Picchu near Cuzco and in the highlands there is also still a rich native culture, complete with llamas, ponchos and panpipes. Finally, Peru's mountains are without doubt the most spectacular and majestic in the Andes. The Cordillera's Blanca, Huayhuash and Vilcanota are the most impressive in the country with some of the best high altitude trekking on the continent.

Bolivia (pages 89-108) is a lesser known landlocked country lying south of Peru, with which it has much in common. The Cordillera Real offer good trekking around 6000m peaks and you can enjoy all the colour and buzz of South America in the nearby capital of La Paz. On the Chilean border the volcanic Cordillera Occidental offer easy volcano ascents and some interesting wildlife.

South of Bolivia, the high peaks of the Andes form the long boundary between **Chile** and **Argentina**. This remote area, covered in our High Andes chapter (pages 109-128) is known as the Puna de Atacama. Although it contains the highest concentration of 6000m peaks in the Andes, the walking opportunities are rather limited due to the lack of water in many areas.

Further south still is Aconcagua, at 6959m the highest peak in the Andes. This massive mountain lies entirely in Argentina but is only 120km from the Pacific Ocean, from where it can be seen on clear days. There are also some very wild mountain areas nearby where many exciting and exploratory backpacking routes are possible.

South of Aconcagua the Andes become much lower. In the **Lake District** (pages 129-142) of Chile and Argentina the highest peaks are snow capped volcanoes and these are surrounded by beautiful forests of beech and monkey puzzle which provide more good walking and backpacking. The Lake District has also become one of the biggest centres in South America for other outdoor sports such as rafting and kayaking. This is a great part of the Andes for a mellow walking holiday spent just enjoying the scenery and tea-rooms, though there are some pretty tough longer backpacking routes too.

At the extreme southern end of the continent is the great wilderness of **Patagonia** (pages 143-164) where gales blow in frequently from the icy waters of the Antarctic Ocean and often bring rain. The rewards of enduring this weather (which is nearly, but not quite, as bad as a Scottish summer) are great - when the clouds part the stunning granite needles of Cerro Torre, FitzRoy and the Torres del Paine are revealed. These peaks are great challenges for the best mountaineers and create great views for the rest of us to admire.

Vilcanota kids

How to Travel

There are basically three different ways of arranging your trekking or walking holiday.

1. You can organise everything yourself; from flights to South America, to hotels in your destination city, to donkeys in some remote Andean village. This is certainly the most difficult option for travel, but it is also the cheapest and can be very rewarding. You need to speak some Spanish if you're going to travel this way anywhere in the Andes. Total cost, including flights, for a typical three week trekking holiday in Peru could be as little as US$1200 per person. A three week backpacking trip in Patagonia will be closer to US$1600.

2. As a sort of half way house you can book your own flights, buses and hotels but use a local tour operator to sort out your trek or adventure trip. This is a little more expensive than going it entirely alone, but also a little less hassle. There are plenty of tour operators in Cuzco, Huaraz, La Paz and the other main tourist centres in the Andes who can organise treks and other adventures. Total cost including flights will be about US$2000 per person for a typical three week trek in Peru, up to US$2500 for a trip to Patagonia of three weeks.

3. Finally you can go with a home-based tour operator, who will organise everything for you. There is a huge choice available these days (see list below) with many companies specialising in trekking, climbing, rafting etc. This is undoubtedly the easiest way to travel and can be a good idea if you're planning to travel alone as you'll end up in a group of like minded individuals. The hardest decision you'll need to make in South America is where to buy your next beer! The downside is that this is the most expensive way to travel to South America, with a three week trek in Peru costing up to US$3000, and a three week Patagonian trip costing up to US$3700.

UK Trek and Travel Operators

Specialist tour operators in the UK offering trekking in the Andes include

Andes. A small Scottish company run by the authors of this book, who offer treks, climbs and ski trips to South America, tel. 01556 503929 john@andes.com

Andean Trails. A small Scottish company, specialising in Peru and Patagonia, tel. 0131 663 4063 info@andeantrails.co.uk

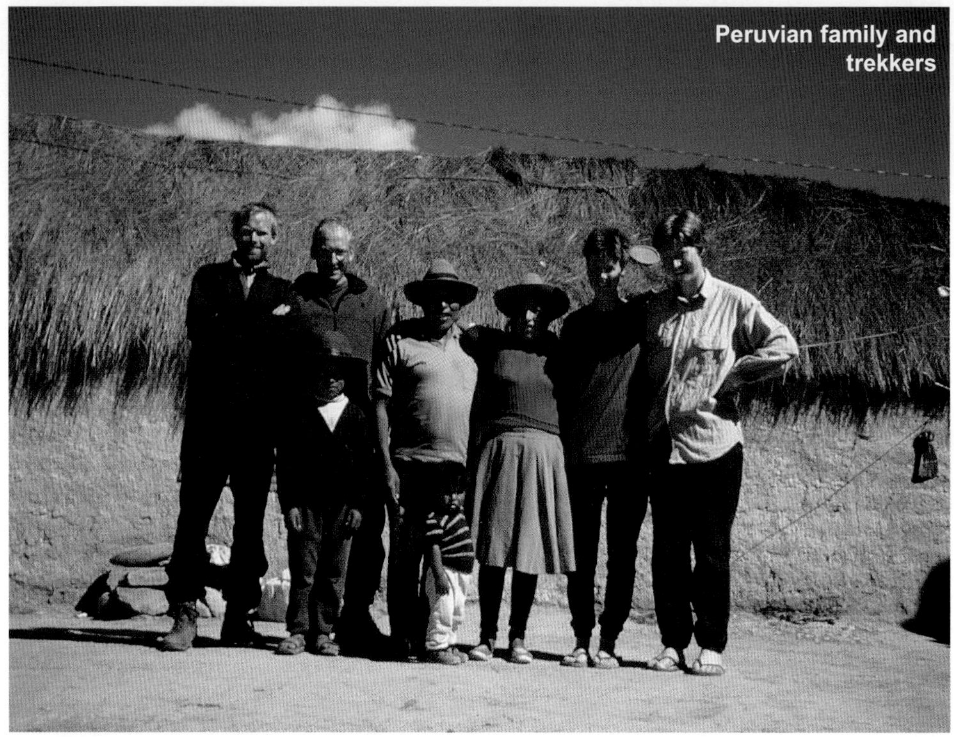
Peruvian family and trekkers

High Places. A larger company offering larger group tours, treks and climbs worldwide, tel. 0114 275 7500. highpl@globalnet.co.uk

Journey Latin America. London based specialist in South America, tel. 020 8747 3108 (Flights) tel. 020 8747 8315 (Tours)

US Tour Operators

In the US the following companies offer mountain travel programmes in the Andes.

Wilderness Travel run hotel based holidays with easy day walks as well as overnight trips, tel. 510 558 2488

Mountain Travel Sobek run hotel based holidays with easy day walks as well as overnight trips, tel. 510 527 8100

The Adventure Climbing and Trekking Company of South America, tel. 719 530 9053 info@adventureco.com

When To Go

Two main factors determine the best seasons to travel to the mountains in South America. South of the Tropic of Capricorn, in Patagonia and most of the rest of Chile and Argentina, the best time for any activities is during the southern hemisphere summer of November to March. In the tropical areas covering the remainder of the continent the best time to go is always in the dry season but this is in June-August for Peru and Bolivia and in December-March for Colombia and Venezuela. There are two transition zones between these major climatic zones with less well defined seasons - Ecuador is wet for most of the year and the Atacama Desert area is totally dry all year.

General Advice for Travel to the Andes

VISAS

At present visas are not needed by most US, Canadian and EU citizens for short stays (up to 60-90 days) in any of the Andean nations. French, Spanish and Portuguese citizens need visas for some countries and Australian, New Zealand and South African citizens will need visas for almost all countries. Other nationalities may need visas for some or all of the countries. The requirements are sure to change so it is best to check with the embassies in your own country.

FLYING TO SOUTH AMERICA

From Europe and the UK there are three main options. **1.** Fly with a European airline via a European capital e.g. Air France via Paris, KLM via Amsterdam, Iberia via Madrid or Lufthansa via Frankfurt. This is often the best option in terms of service and economy, but flights may only be a few days a week. **2.** Fly with either United, Delta, Continental or American Airlines, via the USA. This is often a bit more expensive but the service is very good, you get a larger baggage allowance and there are daily schedules to almost all big South American cities. **3.** Fly with a South American airline, either direct or via some other South American city - these flights are usually cheapest but the service (with the exception of Varig and LAN-Chile) is not very good or reliable. However, you may get a very good deal with a South American airline if you also need an internal flight in the country you are flying to. In Europe, the cities of London, Madrid, Paris, Milan and Frankfurt are well served by LAN-Chile, Aerolineas Argentinas, Varig (of Brazil) and Avianca (of Colombia).

From North America the best option is often to fly via Miami which is served daily by all the major national South American airlines. United, Delta, Continental and American Airlines also have daily services from New York, Miami, Atlanta and Houston to most South American cities. The South American airlines are (as always) cheaper but the US carriers have much better service. There are also some direct flights from Los Angeles and Toronto.

From Australasia there are LAN-Chile (via NZ) and Aerolineas Argentinas (from Sydney) flights direct across the Pacific but these are expensive. It may be cheaper to fly, often on a US airline, via Los Angeles and/or Miami in the United States.

Further details of how to get to each area of the Andes are given in the introduction to each chapter.

BUDGET AND MONEY

South America is not particularly cheap and you should expect to pay prices only a bit less than those in Europe or North America for most services, particularly in the more expensive countries like Chile and Argentina. Patagonia is probably now more expensive than Switzerland. Public transport everywhere is usually cheap. If you need to save money you can use budget hotels and eat from street stalls, but you might not save in the long term if you end up ill or you have equipment stolen.

An average trip staying in clean and secure hotels, eating in reasonable restaurants and using some hired transport and mule services in the mountains will work out at about US$25-30 per person per day, noticeably more for trips to Patagonia where the cost of living is high, slightly less in Colombia, Ecuador and Bolivia. Budgeting carefully and always using public transport you could easily half this figure and still have a great time.

Merida airport, Venezuela

Take your money in a mixture of US$ cash, US$ travellers cheques and ATM and credit cards (particularly VISA and MasterCard). Cash US dollars can be used easily in most countries but it is a risk to carry large quantities. They are often preferred by tour agencies and they can always be used somewhere if you're stuck for the local currency. Travellers cheques made out in US$ can be changed fairly easily in all the main cities. Credit cards are accepted widely by larger businesses in all cities. There are now good networks of ATM's in most of South America, allowing you to withdraw money, in local currency, direct from your credit card or current account. This is very easy to do in Chile and Argentina but can be a bit more difficult in the other countries.

HEALTH AND HYGIENE

Chile and Argentina are quite clean and hygienic but in all the other Andean countries hygiene levels are a bit lower than in the US or Europe. It is a good idea to avoid tap water, ice, unwashed fruit and all seafood.

Vaccinations for tetanus, typhoid, polio and hepatitis are needed for all countries. There is some cholera in Peru and Bolivia so you should consider this vaccination and rabies might be an idea if you will be away from medical help for several days. Malaria and yellow fever precautions are necessary if you plan to visit areas of tropical forest below about 2,500m i.e. Venezuela, Colombia, Ecuador and the Amazon lowlands of Peru and Bolivia. For the vast majority of walks in this guidebook you will not need to take precautions against these mosquito borne diseases.

Biting insects are very common in the tropical lowlands but very rare in the mountains above 2500m, where the majority of our treks are. In a few areas of Peru there are annoying black flies, and mosquitoes (non-malarial) very occasionally come out in Patagonia. Insect repellent is worth having here.

Shepherds dogs can be a nuisance up in the mountains of Ecuador, Peru and Bolivia. They can be very alarming when running at you and barking fiercely. However, most dogs will back off if you throw a stone or even just pretend to throw a stone at them!

If you sleep overnight in poorer houses in the mountains you can be bitten by insects which may carry Chagas disease.

The Lonely Planet book 'Healthy Travel - Central and South America' is a recommended read for health advice while travelling in South America.

A basic medical kit should be carried with plasters, blister kit, needle and thread, spare lip salve, scissors, strong safety pins and some pills for diarrhoea, headaches, coughs, purifying water and perhaps altitude sickness. On more remote trips consider carrying antibiotics (but don't use them for diarrhoea!), antihistamine, strong painkillers, eye drops and an anti-inflammatory. Carry some bits and pieces for general repairs to equipment, e.g. string, wire, strong tape and super glue.

LANGUAGE

Spanish is the main language spoken in most areas of the Andes, while the native languages, Quechua and Aymará, are the first and only languages spoken by many people in more rural areas of Ecuador, Peru and Bolivia. Spanish is an easy language to learn and anyone travelling to South America should learn the basics. The more Spanish you speak the easier your holiday in South America will be.

Only in Cuzco and a few other tourist centres is much English spoken. Out in the mountains there is **no chance** of finding anyone who speaks English, it can occasionally be hard to find some-one who speaks Spanish. If your Spanish is poor you are more likely to be taken advantage of by muleteers, jeep drivers etc. You need to be able to negotiate and make yourself understood to get good prices and good service from the locals.

If you don't speak much Spanish it is definitely better to make any arrangements with a big agency in a town or even book a package holiday from the UK.

HOTELS

Hotel accommodation varies enormously in price and you don't always get what you pay for, particularly when you start paying more. In most areas you'll get a comfortable bed, with private bathroom for about $15-$20 for two sharing. Accommodation down to about $5 per person can still be very reasonable, but budget accommodation tends to be just that - shabby, insecure and with poor service. Note that in Spanish a 'hostal' is often quite a good hotel. Camping is not a practical option in South American cities.

CAMPING AND HUTS

Out in the mountains and on treks you'll mostly be camping. In the Andes it is usually very easy to find a nice pitch with some running water nearby. If camping near a highland village you should ask in the village for permission and be prepared to pay a small fee. Remember you may be disturbing the grazing for these poor people. There are mountain huts in only a couple of areas in South America such as on the volcanoes of Ecuador and in the Catedral range near Bariloche in Argentina. They usually have only basic cooking and toilet facilities and you will need your own sleeping bag.

RESTAURANTS

Restaurants in South America are dependable but not exciting. You can buy chicken and chips in every town in South America and sometimes not a lot else. Pizzas, pasties and hot sandwiches make great lunch snacks. Soups, known as cazuelas, are very common and always good value. Steaks in Argentina and Chile can be superb. Chinese food is also common in many places. Guinea pig and alpaca are local specialities in rural Peru, but it is not to everyone's taste!

TRAVEL AND TRANSPORT IN SOUTH AMERICA

Air travel is quite cheap and may be the best way to get around between cities in South America if you are short of time or travelling a long way. Buses between cities will always be cheaper but distances are huge everywhere and in Peru and Bolivia, long bus journeys can be slow and very tiring. In Chile and Argentina overnight sleeper buses (Salon Cama) are very comfortable and day buses are at least fast and efficient. There are almost no train services left in South America. Specific details of the best transport options to get to each trek or walk are given in the text. Most routes featured in this guidebook can be reached easily using public transport. In rural areas this can be forty year-old buses, gas tankers, minibuses or shared taxis. Particularly good areas to visit if you'll only be using public transport are Ecuador, the Cordillera Blanca and Huayhuash in Peru, the Cordillera Real in Bolivia and the Lake District of Chile. For up to date details of transport connections and prices we would suggest a good general travel guide, but remember things change frequently in South America

In more remote area you may need to hire a taxi or 4x4 jeep from the nearest town to get to the start of your route. This is expensive and good bargaining skills are essential. Expect to pay about $100 for a drop-off 100km away (and another $100 to get picked up). With a brief written contract and a written record of collection dates and times most drivers are very reliable. To find a driver in an unfamiliar town its worth trying either tourist agencies, car hire companies or trekking agencies. For short journeys on good roads just use the local taxi drivers but make sure you agree the price first.

Car hire is usually expensive. It is unlikely to be economical if you are spending long periods away from your vehicle in the mountains but could be very useful if you want to do day walks in many different valleys while based in one town, which is possible in the Chilean or Argentine Lake District.

SAFETY AND SECURITY

South America is safer than its reputation. In ten years of travelling in South America the authors have only had a pair of trainers and a toothbrush stolen but have lost all sorts of things! The overwhelming majority of people in every country in South America are friendly and honest.

You should be careful in Colombia, Venezuela, Peru, Ecuador and Bolivia where pick-pocketing and bag snatching are by far the most common crimes. Violence against people is very rare, probably as unlikely as it is at home. In all areas thieves steal from the easiest targets so stay alert and sober. Don't walk down dark streets at night or through poor suburbs alone and keep valuables such as jewellery and cameras well concealed, or better still in your hotel safe. Be especially alert and very careful in busy public areas such as markets and bus stations and also anywhere there are lots of tourists. Never put a bag down in the street.

Armed robbery and banditry, often linked to the drug trade, do occur occasionally in Colombia, Ecuador, Peru and Bolivia. Colombia has a bad reputation at present (2000) for kidnapping and careful advice should be sought, but the major terrorist problem that plagued Peru in the early 1990's is no longer significant. Banditry is not a problem that should stop anyone going to South America but always seek local advice about the current situation. When visiting these countries there will be areas best to avoid.

A good source for up to date security information is the South American Explorers Club excellent website at www.samexplo.org

Planning a Trek

This section should provide a good background of information for organising your own trek or hike in the Andes.

FEES

There are fees payable for various routes featured in this guidebooks, especially those in national parks or other protected areas such as the Inca Trail to Machu Picchu and the Torres del Paine circuit. The fees are never very high, only $10-$20 per person and the money is sometimes used for the upkeep of these heavily used areas.

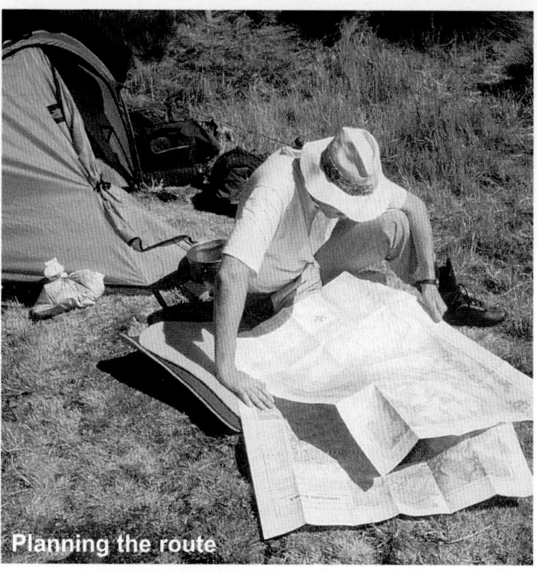
Planning the route

TRAVEL GUIDEBOOKS

Footprint, Rough Guides and Lonely Planet all publish good general travel guides full of information about hotels and travel for each of the countries featured. They will be useful if you are travelling more extensively in the Andean countries.

MAPS

There are very few maps available outside South America. In South America maps can normally only be bought from the Government Mapping Office in the capital city. Maps of remote areas may not have been printed and maps of border areas may be unavailable for military reasons. Maps at 1:50,000 can be obtained in Bolivia, Chile and Ecuador and at 1:100,000 for much of Colombia, Peru and Argentina. Though not as good as the national surveys in Europe and the USA these maps are basically reliable for topographic information - watch out for large contour intervals though! Information about paths, tracks and settlements is often out of date and should never be relied on, and the names used on the maps are often different to those used locally.

Alpenverein of Germany and Austria publish a few excellent sheets for the Cordillera Blanca, Cordillera Huayhuash and Cordillera Real. The best general large scale maps of South America are the ITMB Publishing 1:4,000,000 series. In the UK it's worth trying The

Map Shop (01684 593146) or Stanford's (0207 836 1321) to obtain these and other larger scale maps. Either shop may have a few IGM maps in stock if you're lucky.
In the US try OmniMaps at www.omnimap.com

The addresses for the national IGM's are as follows. Opening hours vary - it is best to go in the morning. Take local currency and your passport.
Venezuela - Edificio Camejo, 1st Floor, Avenida Este 6, (south side)
Colombia - Agustin Codazzi, Carrera 30 # 48-51, Bogota
Ecuador - On the hill, Av. T. Paz y Miño, off Av. Colombia, Quito
Peru - Av. Aramburu 1190, San Isidro, Lima (best to take a taxi)
Bolivia - Edificio Murillo, Calle Murillo, La Paz. The entrance is round the back in a dirty alley off Calle Diagonal.
Chile - Dieciocho 369, Santiago (Metro station Los Heroes)
Argentina - Cabildo 301, Casilla 1426, (Subte D to Ministero Carranza), Buenos Aires

MOUNTAIN RESCUE

There is little organised mountain rescue in South America and on most of the walks featured it will be slow and perhaps difficult to organise a rescue. Trekkers should therefore be self sufficient and able to arrange their own rescue, probably using mules or donkeys they have with them. In a few areas where mountaineering is better developed e.g. in the Cordillera Blanca, Cordillera Real, Ecuador, there is an informal system in place where the local 'guides' will assist anyone in trouble, but this is likely to take several days at least. It is a very good idea to carry a first aid kit with some additional medicines and equipment for use in remote areas.

PACK ANIMALS

Pack animals can be hired to assist with carrying your equipment in many areas. These can be donkeys, mules, horses or even llamas. Donkeys can each carry 40kg, mules and horses up to 60kg, llamas as little as 25kg. Prices are extremely variable but in Peru and Bolivia animals can cost only \$5-\$10 per day. In Chile and Argentina pack animals are much more expensive, costing from \$30-\$50 per day. They can be difficult to find in some areas such as Patagonia. There are sections of terrain on a few routes that horses or donkeys cannot cross, this is particularly true of forests in Patagonia.
Pack animals will always come with an arriero (horseman) to look after them and you'll have to pay his wages. In Peru and Bolivia it is usual for the trekkers to provide their arriero with food and shelter too. You will have to negotiate all fees with your 'arriero'. It is a good idea to get a written contract and pay only 50% in advance.

PORTERS

Porters are available in only a few parts of the Andes, their job normally being done by pack animals. However on the Inca Trail to Machu Picchu they are all that is available because donkeys can't go down the steep steps or through the tunnels. Rates are about \$8-10 per man per day. Do not use children as porters.

GUIDES

There are mountain guides available in a few of the main trekking and mountaineering centres in South America such as Huaraz, La Paz and Cuzco. They can be a lot of help if you want to climb one of the easy

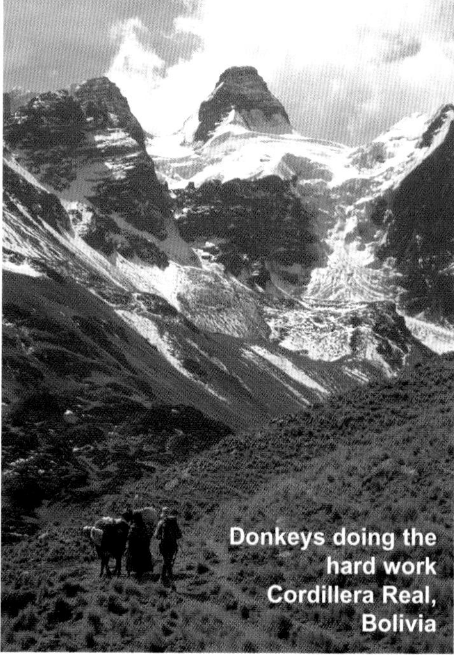
Donkeys doing the hard work Cordillera Real, Bolivia

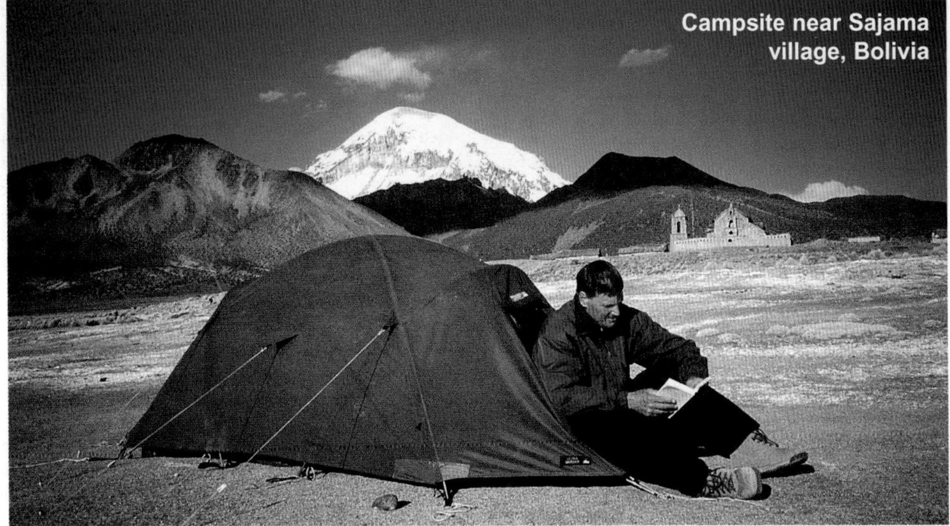
Campsite near Sajama village, Bolivia

peaks on the way round your trek. They can also be well worth hiring if you are unsure about making all the detailed arrangements for your trek yourself. Guides will usually be good at organising arrieros, cooks, porters etc. and they should have very good knowledge of the local mountains and conditions. In Peru and Bolivia a guide will cost about $40 per day for a trek, from $60-$80 for a climb depending on the difficulty of the peak.

COOKS

In some of the more popular areas such as Huaraz, Cuzco and La Paz, cooks can be employed for your trek. They will provide a stove and also buy most of the food, not to mention doing all the cooking and washing up! If you want to relax on holiday they can be well worth hiring.

CAMPING AND TREK FOOD

Most larger towns in South America have a reasonably good supermarket somewhere. The quality and variety of food is very good in Chile and Argentina. Supermarkets are less good in Colombia, Ecuador, Peru and Bolivia, except in the biggest cities. In the small villages used as trailheads it may be difficult to buy anything more than some biscuits, vegetables and pasta so it makes sense to buy your food in a city before leaving for the start of your trek.

Useful camping food which is always available in South America includes :- bread, flour, sugar, dried milk, tea and coffee, packet soups, porridge oats, dried potato mix and pasta. Also available but not cheap are chocolate bars, biscuits, boiled sweets, powdered fruit drinks.

Items which are not easy to find in South America include :- freeze dried food, dehydrated meals, good quality dried fruit and nuts, instant puddings.

Mountain Hazards and Safety

Like any high mountain area the Andes have their fair share of hazards. While the walking routes should all be reasonably safe if walked in season they all involve travel in remote areas far from modern medical facilities. Almost all the routes can suffer from inclement weather, including snowfall. Altitude illness is a potentially fatal problem on many of the treks and getting lost is always a hazard.

The peaks described as optional ascents on many routes will present more serious hazards and it is wise only to attempt these if you have some knowledge and experience of mountaineering hazards and safety precautions or are with a guide or someone who knows about mountain hazards.

ACCLIMATISATION AND ALTITUDE

Anyone travelling to the Andes must make themselves aware of the symptoms of altitude sickness, both mild and severe. Read and absorb a good textbook such as 'Medical Handbook for Mountaineers' by Steele, or better still read one specifically on Altitude Illness such as 'Altitude Illness' by Bezruchka or 'The High Altitude Medicine Handbook' by Pollard and Murdoch.

Generally speaking at least a week should be spent over 3000m before contemplating crossing a pass of over 5000m. A good idea is to first spend three or four nights at 3000m before beginning your trek - many towns are around this height in the Andes so you can acclimatise while enjoying good food and some tourist sightseeing. Once on your trek if anyone in the group shows symptoms of altitude illness at any time stop ascending. If the illness persists for more than 24 hours descend to a lower camp.

Fitness, particularly heart and lung fitness, certainly help with acclimatisation to altitude. However, fit people are just as susceptible to altitude illness because they can do much more. Experience suggests that the best method to avoid altitude illness and acclimatisation problems is to be fit before arrival then do considerably less walking than you would on a trip to the Alps or Rockies. This means some extra time sitting around in camps taking it easy, so bring a good book, a pack of cards, or a pair of binoculars.

FROSTBITE AND HYPOTHERMIA

Hypothermia, a drastic loss of core body heat, is a potentially serious threat on many of the higher treks in this book in Peru and Bolivia and also on treks in Patagonia where there can be long periods of cold and wet weather. Modern fleece clothing which continues to insulate when wet should be carried on all routes and worn when it gets cold. Always have a warm hat and gloves handy. Look out for others in your group. Hypothermia can be quite insidious, an individual may not realise it is happening to them but others may spot changed behaviour.

High treks in Peru and Bolivia in particular may receive fresh snowfall (up to 10-20cm) even in the dry season if unusually cold and stormy conditions prevail and this should be borne in mind when choosing suitable footwear for these trips. Although frostbite is not likely on any route described in this book it is possible on some of these highest treks if poor footwear was worn. Frostbite is a potentially serious hazard on many of the peak ascents described and adequate footwear and clothing should be worn

DEHYDRATION

The climate in most parts of the Andes is very dry and dehydration can occur remarkably rapidly when you are exercising heavily. It is a risk in itself and is also a risk factor in altitude sickness so be sure to drink plenty during the day. In most areas you can pick up sufficient water during the course of your days walk so that only a litre of water need be carried. Always have some form of water purification agent handy so that poor water quality doesn't stop you drinking plenty.

SUNBURN

The sun is much stronger in the Andes than in Europe or the USA. It is higher in the sky, the air is thinner, there are fewer clouds and there is generally more snow cover. A hat with brim and neck flap, sunglasses and high factor sun cream and lip salve are essential for a safe holiday.

SNOW, ICE, GLACIERS AND AVALANCHE

The majority of routes described in this guidebook should be free from any significant snow or ice hazards if walked in the recommended season. Quite a few will have significant snow and ice outside the

Glacier travel, Peru

main season when an ice-axe and crampons and the knowledge of how to use them might be necessary. This is particularly so if you go to Chile, Argentina or Patagonia in the southern winter.

Only one main route described in this guidebook crosses a glacier - the Ice-cap Circuit in Patagonia. Several of the described ascents also cross glaciers. All these will certainly require the use of ice-axe and crampons. The routes in this book are not on the most dangerous of glaciers but they do all have crevasses and precautions against a crevasse fall should usually be taken. See the books recommended in the bibliography on mountaineering techniques for further information on these techniques, or better still only go on these routes if you are with someone who knows what they are doing.

Snow and ice tend to be stable in the Andes in the regular walking and climbing seasons and the ascents described here are largely free from avalanche risk.

River Crossing, Argentina

SCREE AND LOOSE ROCK

Much of the Andes are composed of poor shale type rock, and particularly on the climbs described there are obvious hazards from loose rock or unstable boulder fields. Walk carefully and be aware of those below you. If you are in a large party zigzagging helps to prevent people being in the 'firing line'. If you do accidentally dislodge a rock always shout a clear warning to those below you.

RIVER CROSSINGS

A number of the routes described, particularly in Patagonia have potentially dangerous river crossings. These should be treated with extreme caution and the correct techniques should be used. Cross at the best time, usually early morning for glacial rivers, and allow a river in spate after heavy rain to subside. Always cross facing upstream so that the current can't push you over at your knees. Undo straps on your rucksack so that you can take it off your back quickly. Trekking poles are very useful, both for stability and for probing the river bed ahead of you if the water is murky. Companions can provide a considerably more stable crossing than going on your own. If you do fall over, swim on your back with your feet downstream, don't panic and try to make slowly for the shore.

A rope should only be used for the most extreme crossings when there is no other option, and don't tie into it. Consult a comprehensive textbook for full details of safe river crossing techniques.

Equipment

Suggested equipment lists for the walks in this book appear in the appendix on page 189.

CLOTHING AND PERSONAL EQUIPMENT

In most areas clothing suitable for a summer walking trip to the higher areas of the European Alps or spring and autumn walks in the British hills will be suitable for trekking at up to 4500m. It can feel extremely hot in the valleys in the afternoon sunshine, but overnight in Peru and Bolivia it gets very cold. A modern flexible clothing system should be used. Essential items for all treks are one or two fleece layers and a complete wind and waterproof shell, also a warm hat and gloves.

You'll need a comfortable pair of boots and rucksack. It's far better to take boots and a rucksack that you are already comfortable with rather than suffer uncomfortable new equipment on what might be the holiday of a lifetime, so buy this kit early and test it before you go to South America. Most trails in the high mountains are very dry so a pair of lightweight goretex or leather boots are ideal and gaiters are not normally necessary. In Patagonia it will be a bit wetter underfoot and a more heavy duty and water resistant pair of boots should be used. A pair of gaiters will also be useful.

Very low temperatures (-10ºC) at night mean a 4 season sleeping bag is more or less essential for camps above 4000m in Peru and Bolivia. In Colombia, Ecuador, Venezuela and Patagonia the weather is milder and a 3 season sleeping bag will do for all the routes featured here. You'll obviously want a comfortable lightweight camping mattress too. With long hours of darkness in most of the Andes don't forget to pack a torch and a few good novels.

If you plan to climb one of the easy peaks described in Peru and Bolivia you will need an extra layer of clothing such as a down jacket. In bad weather hypothermia and frostbite are very real dangers so essential items for all peaks are several fleece layers and a complete windproof shell, a warm hat and mountain gloves.

CAMPING EQUIPMENT

Few routes pass through areas where there are mountain huts, so trekking or backpacking in the Andes inevitably involves camping. If you are joining an organised trek this will all be provided, but if you're going on your own the following advice may be useful. Tents need to be lightweight (particularly if you're backpacking) and strong enough to survive the occasional minor storms or snowfalls. There are many such tents available these days from companies such as Mountain Hardwear, Terra Nova and North Face.

Stoves should be light and robust and fuel efficient. There are two main choices for a trip to the Andes. **1.** Multi-fuel stoves such as the MSR which are able to burn almost any petroleum product (but best with white gas or kerosene) are very fuel efficient and the fuel is easy to buy and cheap. These stoves require some skill to maintain them in the field. **2.** Gas stoves are more convenient to use if you know that you can buy the cylinders at your destination. In cities like Huaraz, Cuzco and La Paz gas canisters are readily available, but not particularly cheap. Meths stoves are not recommended in South America.

At higher altitudes a cigarette lighter may be easier to use than matches - flames don't burn well without oxygen! In wet conditions lighters are also very useful as a back up.

RENTING AND BUYING EQUIPMENT IN SOUTH AMERICA

There is some equipment for purchase and rental in major centres like Huaraz, Cuzco and La Paz. The choice is usually very limited and camping equipment

Drying out at camp

is often a bit shabby. If you are planning a trip to South America mainly to trek or walk then hiring is not recommended but if you are only doing a few treks or walks as part of a longer tour of South America then hiring can be a better option than travelling for a long time with a heavy rucksack.

MOUNTAINEERING EQUIPMENT

An ice-axe and crampons are needed for many of the summit ascents described in this guidebook. There is no point in having these with you if you don't know how to use them, so seek instruction and gain some experience before you go to South America. Some of these climbs, as well as the Ice-cap Circuit are also on glaciers and full precautions against a crevasse fall may need to be taken. This will require a rope, harnesses, prussik loops and snow and ice belay equipment - and, of course, the knowledge of how to use this equipment to prevent a serious crevasse fall is also crucial. A chest harness should be used on glaciers when carrying a heavy rucksack.

If you don't have the skills to use this equipment you need to learn. There is nothing better than to go on a week or weekend training course in your own country. You will not get as good instruction from a South American guide. Other ways to learn include going out with more experienced friends, a club or through reading a good textbook and practising the techniques described in safe situations. Recommended books include the 'Handbook of Climbing' by Fyffe and Peter, 'A Manual of Modern Rope Techniques', by Shepherd, and 'NOLS Wilderness Mountaineering' by Powers.

OTHER EQUIPMENT

Trekking poles are a strongly recommended piece of equipment because they save energy on loose ground (like scree), at altitude and when carrying heavy packs. Energy savings of c.20-30% easily make two poles worth the extra weight. Poles are also recommended by sports physiotherapists to prevent long-term damage to your knees. Poles are also useful for navigation markers, river crossings, fending off dogs, making washing lines and walking with bad blisters. If the worst happens they make a great improvised stretcher!

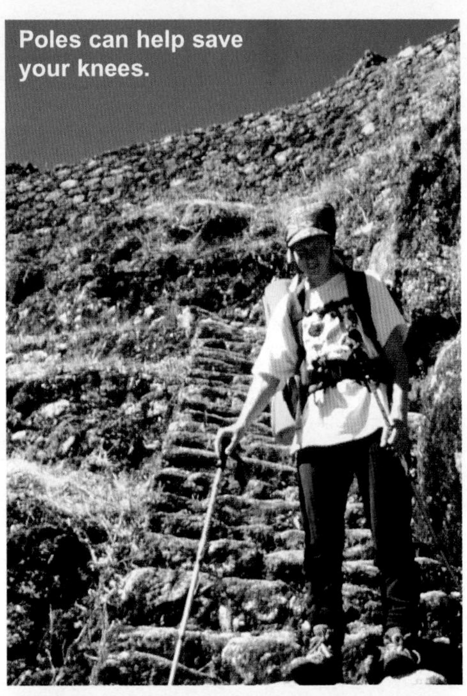

Poles can help save your knees.

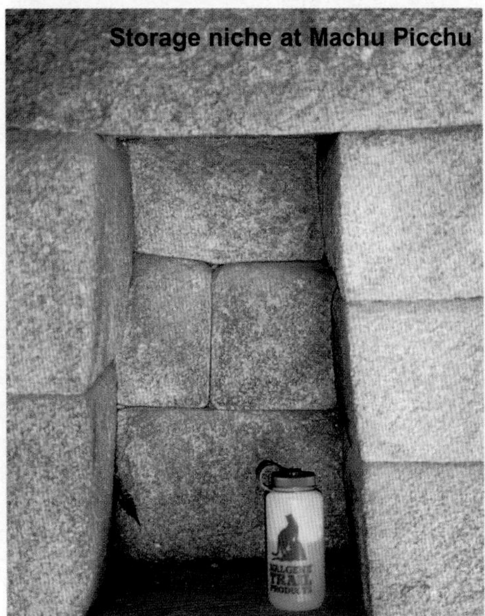

Storage niche at Machu Picchu

Environmental Impact and Responsible Tourism

There is no excuse for the poor attitude of some previous trekkers in the Andes. Always remember people will follow in your footsteps and have to suffer the consequences of your actions. Don't leave rubbish or light fires just because other trekkers are doing so.

We suggest the following code:

1. Travel as a small and lightweight group. This is guaranteed to reduce your impact.
2. Carry as little as possible into the mountains and all your rubbish back out.
3. Be careful where you defecate. In busy areas try to go during the day when away from camp areas if at all possible, or walk a long way (downhill) from your camp and dig a pit toilet. Carry a small trowel so that you can do this. Do not foul water supplies.
4. Do not light any fires anywhere. Use only a camping stove for cooking.
5. Never give unearned gifts. This only encourages begging. If you give a present in return for a favour or good service try to make it a useful or educational item e.g. a pen and paper for a child, a pocket knife for an arriero.
6. Never give kids sweets - they don't have dentists.
7. Respect privacy when taking photos - many people in the Andes do not at all enjoy having their photo taken and may become hostile if you try a quick shot.

Weavings, Bolivia

Chatting with the locals, Cordillera Vilcanota

Ecuador Market

Climbing in the Andes

If you are interested in climbing in the Andes you should purchase The Andes - A Guide for Climbers by John Biggar. Published in 1999 this is the only comprehensive climbing guide to the peaks of the Andes. It includes route descriptions for all 99 of the 6000m peaks, plus 170 lower peaks. There are extensive route diagrams, 35 colour photos, over 80 sketch maps. ISBN 0-9536087-1-9.

In case of difficulty obtaining a copy you can order directly from John Biggar for £19 or US$39, details below.

A French edition, published in 2000 is also available - ISBN 2-9600255-0-4

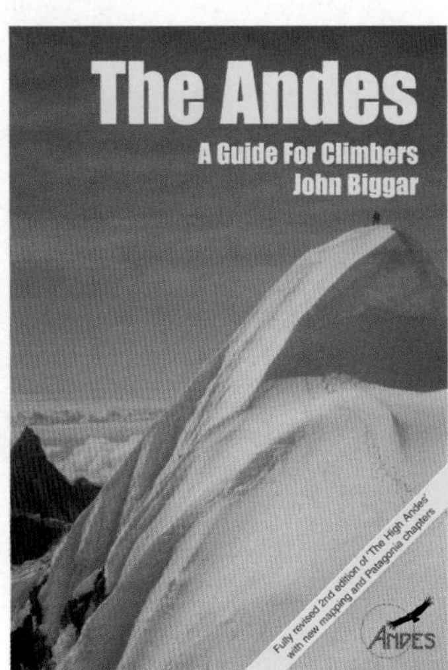

The Authors

This book was written by brother and sister John and Cathy Biggar.

John Biggar has been climbing, skiing and trekking in the Andes regularly for the past ten years. When not in South America he lives in Castle Douglas where he runs 'Andes', a business specialising in trekking, skiing and mountaineering expeditions to South America. For further details of these guided expeditions or for free advice on any mountain activities in the Andes please write, e-mail or fax;

37a St Andrew Street, Castle Douglas,
Kirkcudbrightshire, SCOTLAND, DG7 1EN.
fax 00 44 1556 504633
john@andes.com
andes@btinternet.com

Cathy Biggar has been travelling in South America for over ten years and has trekked in many areas of the Andes. She works regularly as an expedition leader in the Andes guiding groups on treks and on ascents of easy peaks. She lives in Dumfries, working as an outdoor instructor in Scotland and the Lake District.

On La Travesia beneath Pico Humboldt, Sierra Nevada

INTRODUCTION

The Andes of Venezuela are lower than the great ranges further south and the characteristic high Andean plateau is generally absent. The mountains rise directly from the tropical lowlands, and this partly explains the poorer weather which can be encountered in this part of the Andes. The changes in vegetation zones as you walk from the tropical forest to the rocky summits are a fascinating feature of this area. Most of the walks featured travel through a remarkable range of vegetation zones, from thick tropical forest at 1500-2000m, to mist shrouded moorland (known as páramo) at 2000-3000 and above 4000m bare rock and occasionally snow. Particularly attractive are the frailejone plants which grow on the páramo.

There are two main mountain ranges of interest to walkers and both lie very near the city of Merida. The Sierra Nevada de Merida rise dramatically to the south of the city and include the highest peak in Venezuela, Pico Bolivar. There are very accessible day walks from Merida, some of them using the worlds highest cable car which rises straight from the centre of Merida. The **La Travesia** route described here is a two or three day walk through the highest part of the Sierra Nevada. To the north of the city lie the Sierra de la Culata, a lower range of hilly peaks, offering great views to the Sierra Nevada and a short three day trek - **La Culata**.

GETTING THERE

There are flights from London and other major European cities to Caracas, the capital of Venezuela, with Air France, KLM, Iberia and British Airways. From North America there are many daily flights to Caracas from Miami, Houston and New York with American, United and Continental.

To get to Merida a quick internal flight from Caracas is recommended, though the roads and buses are in good condition and the journey overland takes only 12 hours.

CLIMATE AND WEATHER CONDITIONS

The weather is almost uniformly wet and tropical. The driest season and the best time to walk is November to April with January usually the best month. A shorter less pronounced dry spell is also possible in July. However there can be rain and storms at any time in these ranges and snow can fall as low as 4000m and therefore affect some of the routes described. Temperatures fall below freezing at night above about 4000m in the January dry season. The weather generally deteriorates during the day, even in the dry season, and many mountain summits will be in cloud by noon.

CARACAS

Caracas, the capital of Venezuela lies at an altitude of nearly 1000m near the Caribbean coast of Venezuela. There are no particular attractions for the outdoor enthusiast and it may be better to fly directly to Merida if you can. If staying just one night there are more convenient hotels in Macuto and La Guaira on the coast near the airport.

If you are in Caracas it is not an unpleasant city - there are some pleasant parks and soaring modern architecture and the metro is one of the cleanest in the world. To the north of the city the Sierra de Avila have a few interesting walks that can be done in a day or part day. For information about these go to the Direccion de Parques Nacionales at the Parque del Este metro station.

For travel information on Caracas see page 177.

Merida cable car

MERIDA

Merida is a small and pleasant city lying at an altitude of 1600m at the foot of the Sierra Nevada in the west of Venezuela. A cable car (teleferico) connects the city centre with the top of Pico Espejo 4768m. The trip on the teleferico is worth doing even if you are not climbing or hiking in the Sierra Nevada.

The cable car leaves from the centre of town (south end of Calle 24) in the mornings. Booking is recommended at weekends and on holidays if you don't want to queue. Walkers and climbers must register their plans and prove they have adequate equipment at the Inparques office by the teleferico station before going into the mountains (there is a minimal charge for this and it takes only 10 minutes). For travel information about Merida see page 177.

DAY WALK FROM MERIDA - LAGUNA NEGRA AND LAGUNA DE LOS PATOS

About 10km return and 500m ascent, 6 hours return.

At an altitude of 3600m Laguna Mucubaji is a scenic spot set amongst pine forests and fields of frailejone plants (espeletias). A walk from here is an excellent way to acclimatise before attempting a longer trip to the higher mountains. The walk to Laguna Negra and on to Laguna de los Patos is a simple return walk with some really nice scenery. To get to the start of the trail take either a private taxi or a tour bus to Laguna Mucubaji, 1½ hours drive from central Merida.

Start your walk by going round the east side of Laguna Mucubaji. There is a very wide and very easy trail to start with, through groves of espeletia plants. This winds around the hillside to the east then drops a short way before climbing more steeply to the Laguna Negra, about **1-1½ hours**. From here you can continue with more difficulty to the Laguna de Los Patos. Go along the right hand (west) side of Laguna Mucubaji on a narrow path, then climb steeply up thickly forested slopes staying fairly near to the river coming down. The path is not well marked. After about **2-2½ hours** you reach the Laguna de los Patos. There isn't anything in particular to see here but its a nice place. Return by the same route in much less time if you aren't yet used to the altitude.

DAY WALK FROM MERIDA - THE CABLE CAR DESCENT

About 10km, 2400m of descent, 4 hours.

Another excellent day walk from Merida is to take the cable car to one of the intermediate stations and walk back down to the town. The walk is described below from the third station back to Merida, but you could obviously start or end the walk lower if you wanted a shorter day.

From the third station at Loma Redonda (4000m) start by following the obvious trail scar in zigzags down the hill under the wires of the car. The trail is obvious all the way down to the La Aguada station at 3400m, **1 hour**. From here head straight down towards Merida and the forest through frailejone plants. Small trees begin and by the time you reach 3000m thicker forest. At about this altitude the path takes a big bend to the west around the head of a steep valley. La Montana station at 2400m is reached after about **1 hour**.

From this station go down the stairs across from the restaurant and head towards the right hand corner of the flat area; you should pick up the downhill path. This should bring you out after about **1 hour** on a paved road by the Rio Chama, opposite and below the

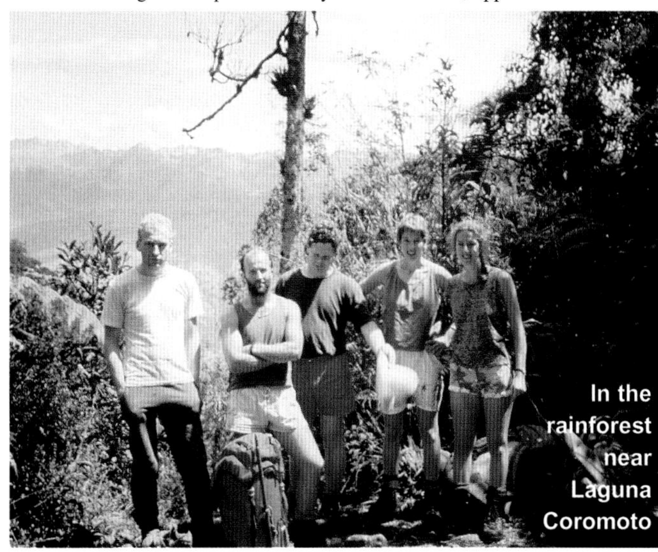

In the rainforest near Laguna Coromoto

bottom of the cable car. Turn left and follow the road a short way until you see a bridge over the river. Cross here and climb up to the city of Merida, **½hour.**

DAY WALK FROM MERIDA - LAGUNA COROMOTO

About 18km return and 1100m ascent, 8 hours return

One other good day walk from Merida is to walk up to Laguna Coromoto from La Mucuy. This is an interesting walk through changing vegetation zones, finishing at a beautiful highland lagoon. For details of this walk see the last day of the La Travesia route in reverse.

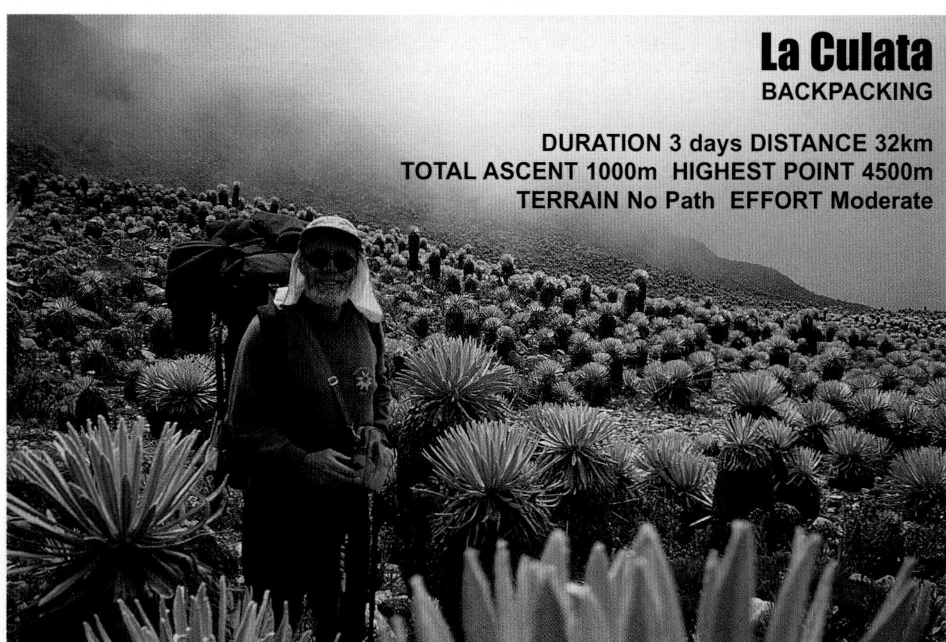

La Culata

BACKPACKING

DURATION 3 days DISTANCE 32km
TOTAL ASCENT 1000m HIGHEST POINT 4500m
TERRAIN No Path EFFORT Moderate

LA CULATA

The walk suggested here is a traverse of the Sierra de la Culata (also known as the Sierra del Norte) from La Toma to La Culata. The walk could be done by a fit and acclimatised party in just two days but the scenery and attractive espeletia groves make this a walk to take your time over. There is an easy hill, **Pan de Azucar 4620m,** which can be climbed by those with even a little hillwalking experience. The walk can be done either way round but there is an altitude advantage of about 200m if you start at La Toma.

ACCESS

To start at La Toma take a taxi or micro (collective minibus) heading up the valley from Merida. Soon after the town of Mucuchies is the small village of La Toma with narrow streets. A narrow road climbs steeply out of town before the river is crossed. The road starts as concrete but deteriorates quickly. However if your driver is adventurous you can drive north for about 6km to a major valley junction. Beyond this it is definitely a 4x4 track only. To start at La Culata take a micro or taxi from Merida to the end of the tarred road at La Culata. There is a simple cafe here but no accommodation.

MAP TO USE

Inparques sheet at about 1:50,000 available from the national park office in Merida

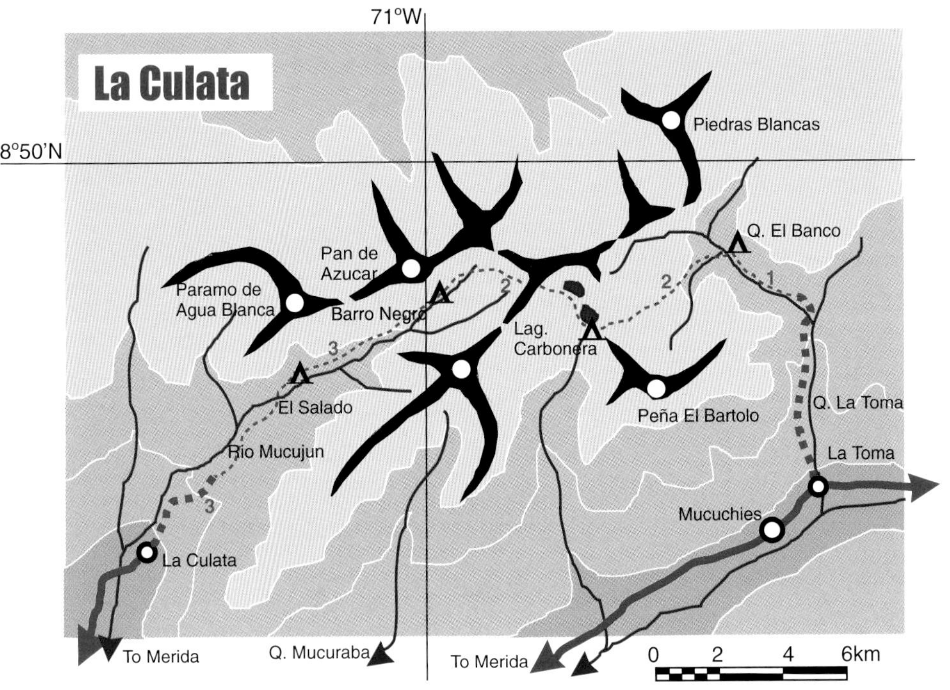

THE ROUTE

1. 4 hours From the valley junction at an altitude of 3500m (which can be reached by walking in about **2 hours** from La Toma if you haven't driven here) take the track up the left fork for about 3km. It climbs steeply then levels out and passes a farm. There are several good campsites beyond the farm by the main river near where the valley splits into three. It is best to stay near your tent if you are camping here. **1½ hours**

2. 5 hours From the camp the route, which is well signposted to start with, takes the valley heading south for a short way then climbs out of this valley by some zigzags on the right hand side. This takes you up to a col at 4200m then drops down to Laguna Carbonera, a nice place to camp, **3 hours.** Go around the left side of the lagoon crossing the outflow stream, and follow a path up to the higher Laguna Escopeta. From here climb a steep but clear path up the ridge to the southwest. Cross a high plateau then drop down to a large round lagoon. Continue due west over paramo thick with espeletia plants to several possible campsites by streams at about 4300m altitude, **2 hours** From this campsite it is quite easy to climb the hill of Pan de Azucar 4620m in a half day.

3. 4 hours. To continue the main walking route from the Barro Negro camp is very simple. Walk down the Rio Mucujun valley staying on the north side of the river till you pass a little hut at El Salado, 3700m. About 1km beyond the hut the path crosses the river and climbs to a col between two low hills. From here follow a grassy path down the valley to a plateau at 3400m (nice campsites) then go down the northwest side of a little valley (Q. los Anillos) to a house on a track at 3200m. Follow the track for 2-2½km to the small cafe at the end of the tarred road. This is La Culata and there are micros every hour or so back to Merida. If doing the walk in reverse and finishing at La Toma you will get a micro back to Merida very quickly from the main road in the middle of the village.

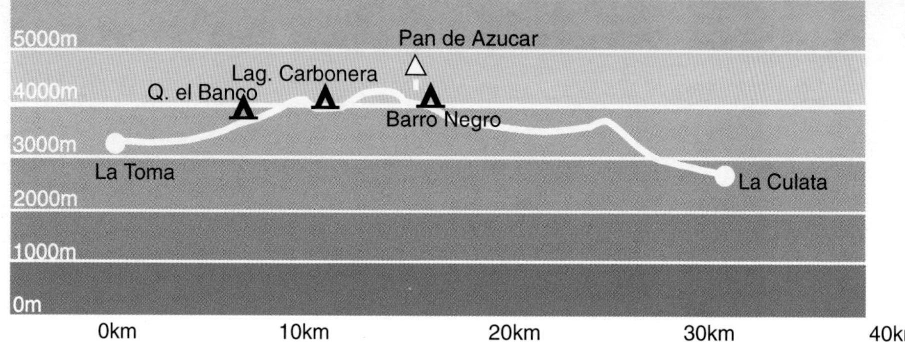

2a. Pan de Azucar 4620m

From the Barro Negro camp area the route should be very obvious, you can climb by either the south or the east ridge, both have some scree. The south ridge has a good trail with some very easy rock steps. The view is great. Allow about **2 hours** for the ascent, as little as **1 hour** for the descent.

Looking towards Piedras Blancas

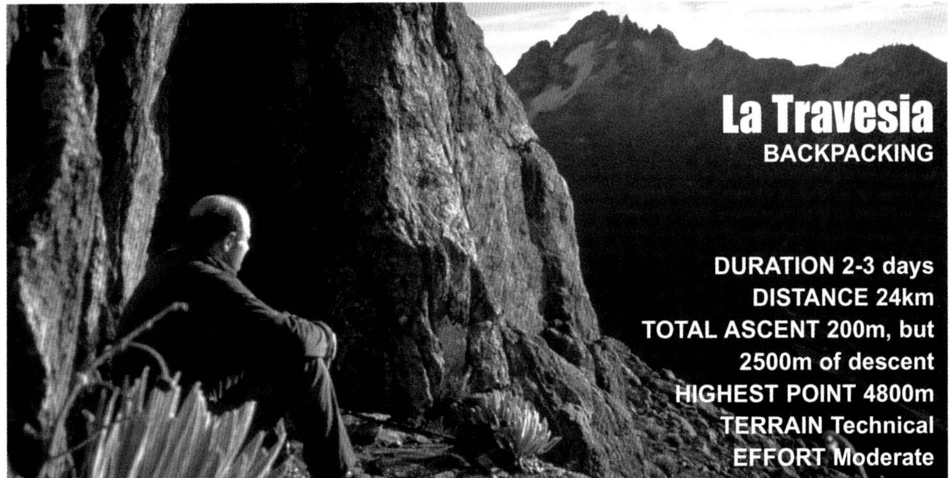

LA TRAVESIA

This is a dramatic and scenic walk along the highest part of the Sierra Nevada. There is quite a lot of scrambling in several different places and route finding can be difficult in the mist, which is quite common.

The walk could in fact be done in one long day of about 10 hours, but this would rather defeat the point of seeing all this spectacular scenery. There are also some beautiful campsites along the way. Quite large numbers of people do this walk in reverse, walking up into the mountains and using the cable car to descend. This must be very hard work. Although you need to be acclimatised before ascending the cable car to start the walk there seems to be no good reason to do the walk the other way round.

WARNING

Because of the very high starting altitude and considerable scrambling difficulties this trip should only be attempted by experienced walkers who have spent some time in the area acclimatising.

ACCESS

A permit is needed to stay out overnight in the National Park. These can be obtained quickly from the little office at the entrance to the cable car in Merida. The park wardens will often ask to see some proof that you are competent, such as membership of a climbing club or guides card, and they may also want to check the equipment you are carrying. The permits cost only a few dollars.

Take the Teleferico from the centre of Merida to the summit of Pico Espejo (about 1 hour, $15). This should only be done if you are already well acclimatised to an altitude of 4000m, but it does save a lot of uphill walking.

MAP TO USE

'Inparques' sheet 1:50,000 of the Sierra Nevada, available from the national park office in Merida.

THE ROUTE

If you are not sure how you will react to the sudden altitude gain involved in going straight to Pico Espejo a good alternative is to get off at the Loma Redonda station. After camping near here for a night or two you can walk up to Pico Espejo (or if you are lazy get the cable car!). It is possible to camp just below this station at the Laguna Anteojos. Equipment should not be left unattended here. There are more secluded campsites at about 4200m on the hills either side of the pass of Alto de la Cruz but there is no water.

1. ½ hour The walk up to the pass of Alto de la Cruz takes **½ hour** and is up a wide and very obvious mule trail. This is the start of the popular trek to Los Nevados and mules can easily be hired at Loma Redonda to carry your equipment to the pass. A very worthwhile side trip from the pass, which can also be done easily in a day from Loma Redonda is the ascent of Pico El Toro, 4758m.

Ascent of Pico El Toro

1a. From the very top of the Alto de la Cruz pass at 4200m turn right (west) over broken ground and make a rising traverse under the south slopes of Toro. There is a faint path and cairns and a possible camp at a small lagoon at 4300m. From here climb more steeply, then traverse screes. Just below the summit block of Toro look for a steep 20m gully which has a large cracked slab for its left wall. Climb this gully with a little rock scrambling, then go left along the exposed rocky ridge to the top. The climbing is not difficult. **3 hours** to the top from Loma Redonda.

2. 5 hours. To reach Pico Espejo on foot from Loma Redonda leave the main mule trail just before reaching the Alto de la Cruz pass and follow a good path which traverses along the north slope of the ridge. After about **½ hour** climb more directly up, make a short traverse then begin ascending a wide gully. At the top of the wide gully (after about **1-1½ hours**) descend about 20m into the valley of the Garganta del Diablo (Devils Throat). Climb up the left hand side of this gully for about **1 hour** over slabs and buttresses (some scrambling) then climb in the gully itself, now very narrow, to reach the south shoulder of Pico Espejo within sight of the cable car station.

3. 1½ hours. From Pico Espejo follow a signpost and paint splashes which lead along a very exposed traverse on the south side of cliffs to reach the Timoncitos screes after **1 hour**. There is some scrambling on this section which is never difficult, but there is a very big drop. Climb the screes for a further **½ hour** to reach Laguna Timoncitos which has several camping spaces and magnificent views of the south face of Pico Bolivar. If you don't like the idea of this exposed traverse, or if there is snow on these rocks, it is possible to descend screes for about 200m from the

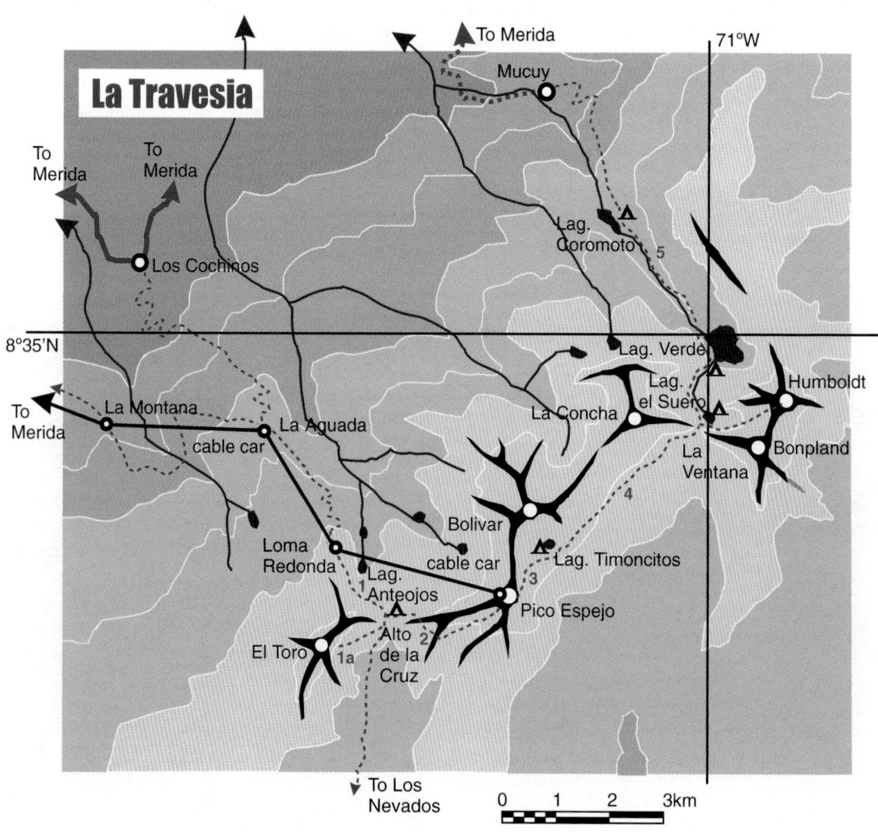

south shoulder of Espejo to go round the base of these cliffs, but this leaves about an extra 200m to climb back up towards Timoncitos, allow about **2½ hours** from Espejo to Timoncitos for this route. Pico Bolivar is an exposed but easy rock climb, at a grade of about V. Diff (UIAA IV, 5.5). A rope and some experience are recommended if you want to tackle this summit.

4. 5 hours From Laguna Timoncitos the route of La Travesia heads east, dropping slightly to 4400m where there are good campsites before climbing again to the col of La Ventana at 4500m. There are actually two cols close together. It is better to go through the southern col, which gives a straight and uncomplicated descent on scree to Laguna El Suero. If you go through the north col you will need to traverse southwards on the other side to reach the same scree descent. Laguna Suero at 4200m below the north slopes of Pico Humboldt is a beautiful place to camp, **4 hours** from Timoncitos. From here walk down the valley through grasslands to reach campsites just before the Laguna Verde, **1 hour**.

5. 7 hours. The trail goes around the left (northwest) side of the lagoon and this involves some more exposed scrambling. Then cross the outflow stream from the lagoon right on the edge of the lagoon and follow the path which descends over some more exposed rock buttresses and giant heather down the right hand side of the valley. At about 3500m is the Puente Quemado an exposed rock step now made much safer with some wooden boards. After **3 hours** you'll arrive at the beautiful Laguna Coromoto, 3300m where there are nice campsites. From Coromoto to the road end at La Mucuy the path through the tropical forest is well constructed with numerous hairpin bends and is very easy to follow, about **4 hours**. Although there are no public buses it is usually quite easy to find transport back to Merida from Mucuy, but if you want to be certain it would be better to arrange for an agency to pick you up.

Scrambling on Bolivar

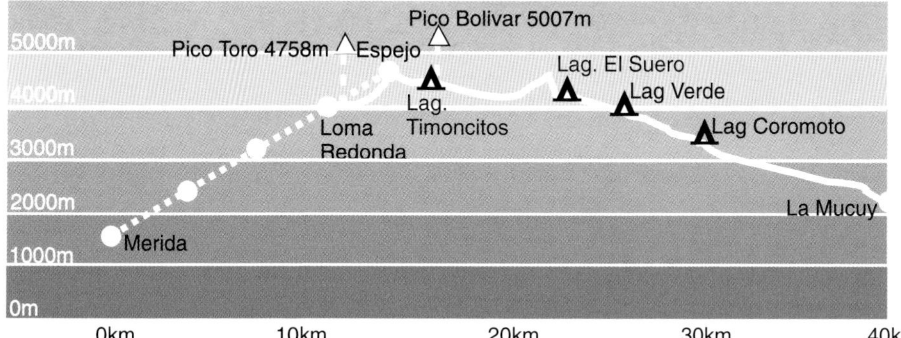

A VERY SHORT OVERNIGHT TREK - LOS NEVADOS

About 15km and 1600m descent, 6 hours

At an altitude of 2500m the secluded village of Los Nevados has become very popular with hikers. It can be reached in just one day from Merida by taking the cable car to Loma Redonda and following the wide mule trail south from there. It is usual to stay overnight and arrange jeep transport back to Merida the next morning. Mules can be hired to carry your equipment from Loma Redonda. The trail is very obvious to follow, it climbs for 200m to reach the pass of Alto de la Cruz, then descends in a long series of zigzags first over the paramo and then through bamboo forest and then tropical forest. After 7km at an altitude of 3200m there is a choice of routes. The left fork is a more direct route to Los Nevaods, the right fork joins a jeep trail but also comes out at Los Nevados. You can use the same Inparques map as for La Travesia for this walk.

Bolivar summit

Laguna Negra

Colombia

Los Nevados national park

INTRODUCTION

The Andes of Colombia are not as high as the great ranges further south and the characteristic high Andean plateau is generally absent. In southern Colombia the Andes divide into three main chains and these ranges are divided by low tropical valleys. Like Venezuela bad weather is prevalent in this part of the Andes.

Treks in three different areas are described below. In the north of the country a long trek into the heart of the **Sierra Nevada de Santa Marta** is described, followed by the classic **Circuit of the Cocuy** range. The descriptions of these two treks are fairly brief as they are in areas not considered to be very safe to travel through at present. Finally in the centre of the country and closer to the capital of Bogota a shorter walk through the **Los Nevados** range is described.

At present (late 2000) many parts of Colombia are not safe to travel through due to guerrilla violence and kidnappings. Only experienced travellers well aware of the risks should consider going to the country until the situation improves. Travel to most of the mountain areas of Colombia is not advisable. The only area considered reasonably safe at present are the Los Nevados range as most other areas have seen recent guerrilla activity. Colombia is nevertheless a very warm and welcoming country and if the situation improves will make a fine trekking destination.

GETTING THERE

There are flights from London and other major European cities to the capital Bogotá with the Colombian carrier Avianca. Air France and Iberia also fly regularly to Bogota at reasonable prices. From North America there are many daily flights to Bogotá from Miami, Houston and New York as well as direct services from Miami to Cali and Barranquilla.

For the Colombian mountain ranges it is probably best to acclimatise in Bogotá for a day or two before flying on to your chosen area. Fly to Bucaramanga for the Sierra Nevada del Cocuy, Manizales for Los Nevados and Valledupar for the Sierra Nevada de Santa Marta. The Los Nevados range are near enough to Bogotá to be reached comfortably by bus but you can also fly to Manizales. For other areas bus is also an option for those on a budget. Roads and buses are generally good in Colombia but crime is a problem, particularly on overnight buses.

CLIMATE AND WEATHER CONDITIONS

The weather is almost uniformly wet and tropical. The driest season and the best time to trek is from November to April with January usually the best month. A shorter less pronounced dry spell is also possible in July. However there can be rain and storms at any time in all these ranges. Temperatures fall below freezing at night above about 4500m in the January dry season. The weather can be poor, even in the dry season and cloud will often rise up from the valleys to obscure the peaks early every day.

BOGOTÁ

The capital of Colombia is a huge city which has a fairly cool climate because it is at an altitude of 2650m. It is a city of both marked prosperity in the northern suburbs and terrible poverty in the southern barrios. Like many South American cities the centre can be roughly divided into old and new districts. Few streets in Bogotá have names; instead numbers are used instead to identify the Calles and Carreras. This is also true of many other Colombian cities.

There are plenty of cultural sights to see - the usual mix of museums, churches and cathedrals surrounding Plaza de Bolivar, of which the gold museum is well worth visiting. **Cerro de Monserrate 3200m** to the east of the city can be ascended by funicular, cable car or on foot for a good view of Bogotá, it is perfectly safe to do this walk on weekends when the walk is busy but don't go at quiet times or at night.

Travel information can be found on page 178.

SANTA MARTA CIRCUIT

The Sierra Nevada de Santa Marta are Colombia's highest mountain range and reputedly one of the most spectacular. The highest peaks are the twin snow capped summits of Colon and Bolivar. The highest peak in the range, and in Colombia, is Pico Bolivar 5775m, although the neighbouring peak of Colon is only a metre or two lower.

Isolated from the main ranges of the Andes the range has an incredible variety of vegetation. Access has however been very difficult for many years. The local Arhuaco Indians are at times hostile - a local guide is usually essential for safe passage.

Reports are that all access to the mountains has been forbidden since 1996.

ACCESS

The start point for access to this trek in the Santa Marta is the small city of Valledupar, (page 178). You can fly here from Bogota or via the city of Barranquilla. From Valledupar you'll need to travel via Pueblo Bello to get to the village of San Sebastian de Rabago (now renamed Nabusimake). There is no regular transport beyond Pueblo Bello, you will probably have to hire transport for the last 25km to San Sebastian (a 4x4 may be needed). This village is only intermittently inhabited by the local Arhuaco indians, though there are also a number of newer houses with very basic supplies and accommodation.

If access is permitted a permit will certainly be necessary from the Casa Indigena just outside Valledupar. From San Sebastian mules can be hired for travel as far as the Lag. Nabobo base camp (4450m) which lies in the heart of the mountains just southeast of the two highest peaks. It is likely to take a day or two to find mules. All food and fuel should be brought from Valledupar.

MAP TO USE

Colombian IGM sheets Magdelana 19, San Juan del Cesar 20, Pueblo Bello 26 and Valledupar 27, all at 1:100 000.

THE ROUTE

1. 7 hours. San Sebastian (Nabusimake) - Durameina. From the bottom of the village walk downstream to a bridge, cross this and carry on down a short way to where a trail climbs on the right. Follow this trail to a pass at 3600m, **5 hours**. From the pass the trail drops down into the Durameina valley going slightly rightwards. Camp in the valley.

2. 6 hours. Durameina - Guiachinacopunameina. The trail climbs to the north and the pass of Bellavista 3900m with great views of the main peaks. Descend to Mamancanaca at 3400m then continue downstream to the Q. Yebosimiena. Climb the low range to the west to reach the Quebrada Guiachinacopunameina

3. 7 hours. Guiachinacopunameina - Nabobo.
Follow this valley upstream for about 3 hours to reach Laguna Usucaca. Go to the left of this lake then the right of the second lake to reach the pass at 4250m. The trail drops towards the lake then turns right and climbs over rocky ground to the large Laguna Nabobo 4450m, with campsites at the east end. From here Pico Colon can be climbed in two days (description below). It is a relatively easy ascent over snow covered glaciers.

4. 7 hours. Nabobo - La Nevadita. 20km. From Nabobo go through the pass to the east, 4500m to reach the headwaters of the Donachui river. From here the walk is entirely downhill and easy to follow. A long day gets you to La Nevadita at 2500m.

5. 4 hours. La Nevadita - Donachui. 12km. Continue easily down the valley to Donachui at 1400m. There is very little transport from Donachui back to Valledupar. You may need to arrange a pick-up before starting the trek, or walk out even further down the valley.

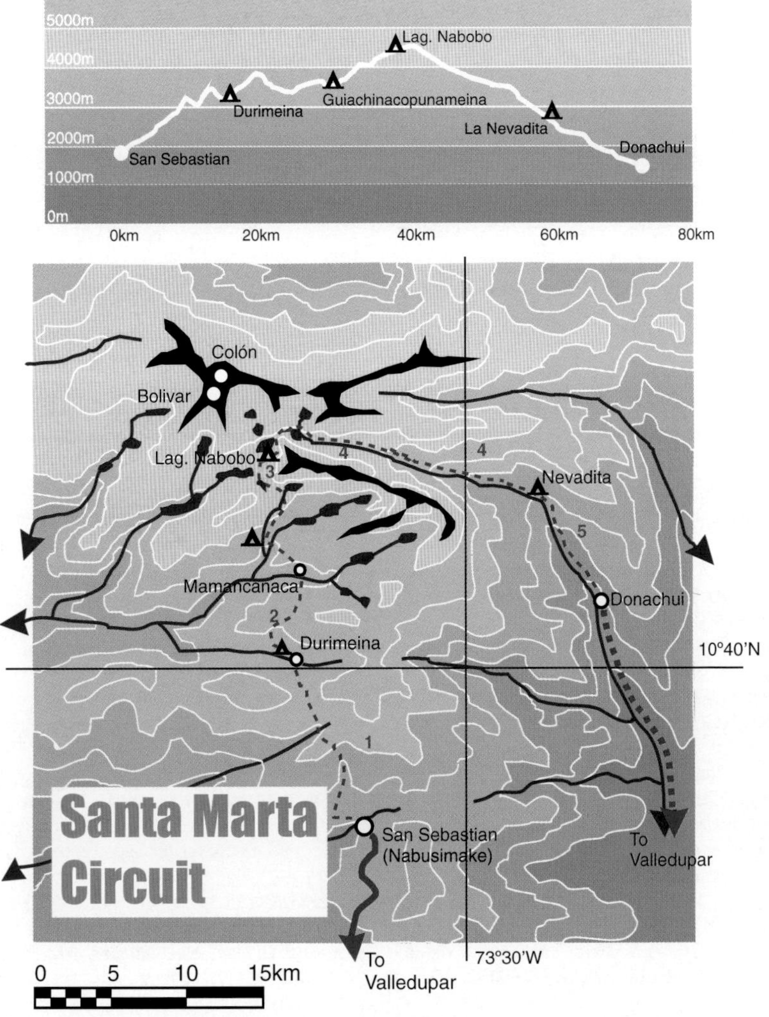

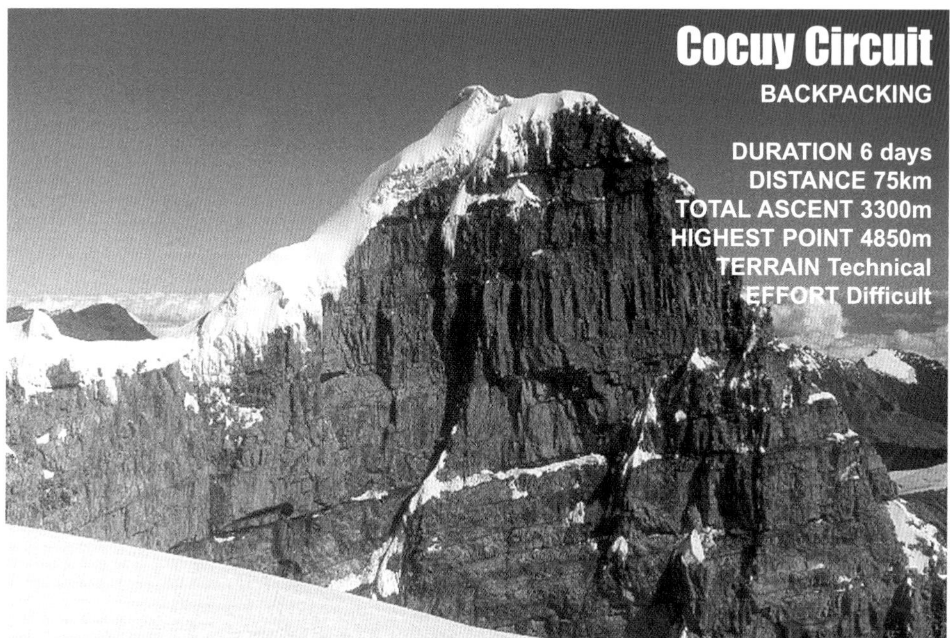

Cocuy Circuit
BACKPACKING
DURATION 6 days
DISTANCE 75km
TOTAL ASCENT 3300m
HIGHEST POINT 4850m
TERRAIN Technical
EFFORT Difficult

COCUY CIRCUIT

The Sierra Nevada del Cocuy are a beautiful mist enshrouded range, with a reputation for bad weather, in the northeast of Colombia. The range consists of two parallel chains running north - south for about 25km. The circuit trek around the Sierra Nevada del Cocuy is a scenically stunning trek which takes 6 or 7 days.

The range is very beautiful with many lagoons, big cliffs and literally thousands of frailejone plants. The walking is generally quite rough, and with the notoriously wet and misty weather this is definitely a range for those with some trekking experience. The Castillo pass is glaciated and depending on conditions may require the use of an ice-axe, crampons and a rope. In addition the far side of the trek is at high altitude from which there is no easy escape to low altitude, so previous experience of trekking at high altitude and some recent acclimatisation to high altitude is recommended.

This walk will be fine in reverse.

ACCESS

Access to this trek is possible from either the town of Guicán at 2900m or the town of Cocuy at 2700m. The towns are about 10km apart on the west side of the range, reached by the same road which branches just past the village of Panqueba.

To reach these towns from Bogotá either fly via the small city of Malaga in the department of Santander or go direct by bus via Capitanejo to Guicán or Cocuy. Both Guicán and Cocuy have a few shops and small hotels but it is best to brig supplies from Bogotá. From Guicán a jeep can be hired to get to Las Cabañas to start the trek.

Pastor Zambrano, who can be contacted through the Hotel de la Sierra in Guicán, can arrange transport to Las Cabañas and mules to take equipment as far as Laguna Grande.

MAPS TO USE

The trek is covered by two IGM sheets at a scale of 1:100,000 - sheet 137 'El Cocuy' and sheet 153 'Chita'. It is best to buy these maps in Bogota though they are reported to be available in the town of Cocuy.

THE ROUTE

The route is described as a circuit from Guicán.

1. 4 hours Guicán - Las Cabañas. This section can be driven in a hired vehicle in about one hour, but it is recommended to walk it for acclimatisation. You can follow the road all the way, or alternatively to avoid the many hairpin bends start by going up Calle 6 in Guicán and then head right as you leave the town. A trail takes you up the hillside to meet the road at about 3200m. Turn right and continue up the road until you see the signposted turn-off to Las Cabañas Kanwara. The cabins are at about 3800m. Accommodation is available in the cabañas or you can camp for a reduced fee. From Las Cabañas you can climb the highest peak in the Cocuy range (Ritacuba Blanco) in a day. For a description see below.

2. 5 hours Las Cabañas - Laguna Grande de los Verdes. From Las Cabañas the path heads northeast over paramo then drops to the Rio Cardenillo. On the other side of the river follow the trail up the right side (southeast side) of a ridge and then over the Boqueron del Carmen pass (4400m). Follow the stream valley down from the pass northeast to the Laguna Grande de los Verdes (4050m) where there are good campsites at the south end of the lake.

3. 6 hours Laguna Grandes de los Verdes - Laguna del Avellanal. Go along the east shore of the lake. From the north end of the lake make a short steep climb up to a pass, then drop just as steeply down the other side towards the Rio de los Frailes, **1 hour**. Descend until the path breaks to the right, then follow this path southwards to reach Laguna de la Isla, then beyond climb up to the Boqueron de la Sierra (4750m), **4 hours**. There are two shrines on the pass. From here it will be less than an hour down screes to the Laguna del Avellanal at 4400m, where you can choose between rocky or boggy campsites.

4. 7 hours. Laguna del Avellanal - Laguna del Pañuelo. This is the most scenic day of the trek and one of the most scenic mountain walks in the Andes. The huge vertical walls of the main range rise for up to 800m on your right above valleys filled with streams, lagoons and frailejone plants. From the Laguna del Avellanal walk down the valley de Los Cojines to the south for about an hour, then look for a way to cut up about 100m on the right to reach a long terrace with many small lakes on it. Follow this rocky terrace southwards, with occasional cairns, past many lakes to reach the larger Laguna Rincon where camping is possible. (It is also possible to take a route along the valley floor below to the east). Continue up over loose rock to the glacier and then up this to the pass of Boqueron del Castillo, 4650m, **4 hours**. From the pass descend the glaciated slopes to the south for about $1^1/_2$ km to reach the spectacularly situated Laguna de los Pañuelos at 4350m where there is a flat area for camping. There are normally no dangerous crevasses on these slopes, but care should be taken and in most conditions a rope, ice-axe and crampons will be necessary.

5. 5-6 hours. Laguna del Pañuelo - Laguna de la Plaza. The route finding on this section is difficult. Follow cairns for half an hour to a cliff. Take a left rising ledge up this cliff. Follow scree and terraces southwards at an altitude of between 4200 and 4300m, with the big rock walls of the main range on your right. It is about **3-4 hours** to the lakes of Laguna Hoja Larga and another hour over a low pass to the very large Laguna de la Plaza beyond. As the next day is long it may be best to go round the east side of the lake and camp by the outflow river.

6. 6-7 hours. Laguna de la Plaza - Alto de la Cueva. Walk southwest from the south end of the lake to pick up a clear well defined trail coming up from the Llanos. Follow this trail westwards over a pass of 4350m, then down slightly to the Q. Calichal before a longer climb to the last pass, Paso Cusiri (4450m). The trail now turns northwest and follows the Rio

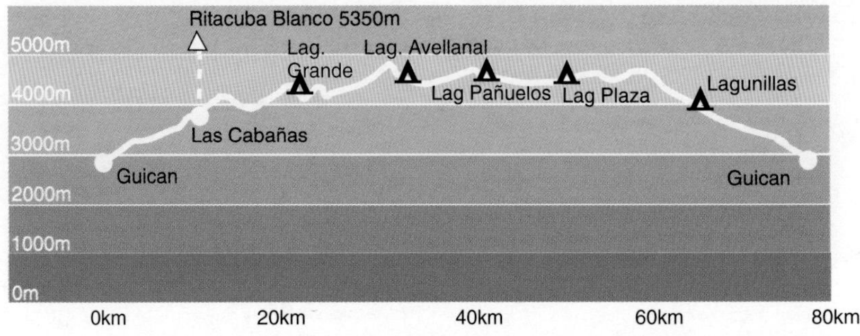

Lagunillas easily to the road at Alto de la Cueva, 3800m. If you need to or want to split this day there are good campsites at Laguna Cuadrada (**4 hours**).
If you can it is best to arrange to have transport meet you here, otherwise either follow the road left for Cocuy (**3 hours**), right for Guican (**5 hours**), or follow paths downhill to Guican (**3 hours**)
6a. A better, but harder finish is through the Paso de Bellavista, which lies west of the lake. This is a glaciated route for which crampons, ice-axe and rope will be needed. The ascent starts from a point on the east shore of the lake at the back of a very wide bay. Climb the valley steeply up to the pass (4800m), **2-3 hours**, which leads to the large glaciated plateau on the west side of the mountains. From the pass head down the glacier, straight towards the left hand side of Laguna Grande (the biggest of the lakes). beyond the lakes the valley leads down to the road at La Esperanza. Total time to the road about **8 hours**.

1a. ASCENT OF RITACUBA BLANCO

8 hours return. From Las Cabañas the peak of Ritacuba Blanco can be ascended in one day. There is a trail up to the snowline via a ridge, **4 hours**. Easy angled snow, with very few crevasses then leads to an exposed ridge to the summit in a further **1-2 hours**.

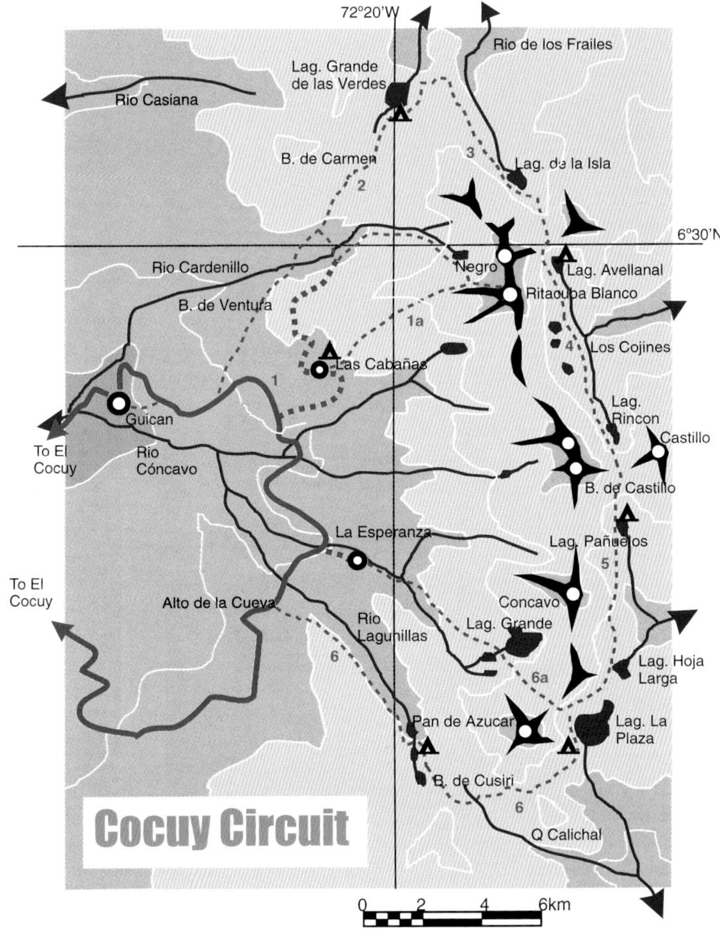

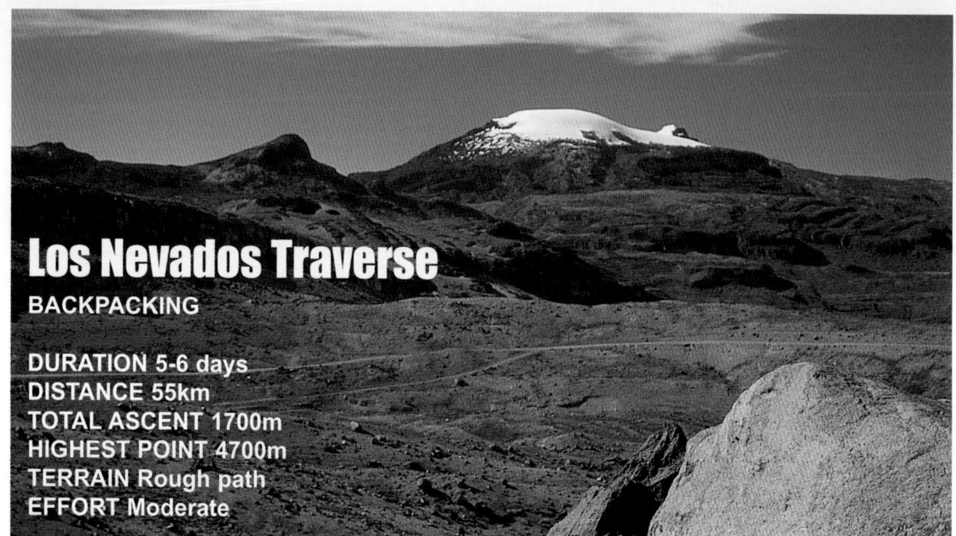

Los Nevados Traverse
BACKPACKING
DURATION 5-6 days
DISTANCE 55km
TOTAL ASCENT 1700m
HIGHEST POINT 4700m
TERRAIN Rough path
EFFORT Moderate

LOS NEVADOS

Los Nevados are a compact range of volcanic peaks in central Colombia and are the nearest and most accessible mountains to Bogotá. The walk described is an interesting combintaion of high altitude lava and volcanic deserts, paramo moorland and montane forest. Nevado El Ruiz, the second highest peak in the range is an active volcano. It erupted in 1985 and a mudslide killed thousands in the town of Armero, over 50km away. There were also minor eruptions in 1996. Most of the walk and the three highest peaks are within a national park.

The route described here is a traverse of the mountains across the high páramo from north to south. The ascent of El Ruiz to the spectacular volcanic crater is also described. The walk could be done in reverse, although this will have a bit more height gain. The 55km and 1700m ascent listed above are for those starting at Chalet Arenales near the northern park entrance - if you drive all the way to Laguna Otun this reduces to about 35km and 600m ascent.

ACCESS

From Bogota travel by air or road to the city of Manizales at an altitude of 2150m. Transport can be arranged in Manizales to the park entrance at 4050m, which lies just south of the Manizales to Murillo road. Check at Inderena office, C 20A, No 21-45 or the tourist office in Manizales about access to the national park. Permits are required but they are easily obtained for $5 at the entrance (2000). Travel information on Manizales can be found on page 178.

The trek is described from Chalet Arenales, a small hut at 4150m on the left side of the road just a few kilometres inside the national park. Meals and drinks can be bought here, there are a few bed spaces ($10) and there is a campground behind the hut. If you don't have previous acclimatisation it might be better to stop at the Hotel Termales del Ruiz, which lies at 3500m just outside the national park, for a night or two, from where some pleasant walks can be made.

MAP TO USE

Colombian IGM sheet 225 'Nevado El Ruiz' 1:100 000

THE ROUTE

1. 7-8 hours. Ascent of Nevado El Ruiz. This peak is a very straightforward glacier walk and can be climbed in one long day from the Chalet Arenales. As a first day this day is quite long and would require some previous acclimatization.

In good conditions it is possible to drive south up the road to within 2km of the summit at a small refugio (4750m). Turn left at the junction at the top of the long series of hairpin bends.If you don't have a vehicle this walk takes **2 hours.** From the higher refugio climb a rib of rock and scree past a flagpole to the skyline ridge. The glacier lies just behind this ridge and is easy to get on to. Climb the glacier to the northeast with almost no crevasses to the highest visible point then over a broad plateau to the highest summit point on the edge of the spectacular Crater Arenas. This takes **3 hours** from the end of the road at the higher hut. The descent will take **2-3 hours**.

2. 4-5 hours. Chalet Arenales - Cisne. If you've kept your transport with you this section can be driven in just one hour. From the Chalet Arenales follow the road south over lava deserts to the series of hairpins. climbing towards the prominent La Olleta cone. At the top of the hairpin bends take the right hand road, which goes over the Olleta pass (4700m). The road then drops down the other side and winds its way along volcanic sands and moorland on the west slopes of Ruiz to reach the hut and camp area at Cisne (4050m). Another interesting side trip from here is the ascent of El Cisne, a very straightforward walk that takes only 3 hours return form the Cisne hut. Go south on the track for just 100m then look for a faint trail heading up the valley to the left. This trail leads eventually to the summit.

3. 4-5 hours Cisne - Laguna Otun. Follow the road southwards along the paramo on the west side of Santa Isabel mountain to the large and scenic Laguna Otun. The road deteriorates beyond Cisne and becomes quite poor. There are nice campsites at the north end of Laguna Otun, 3950m

4. 7-8 hours Laguna Otun - Aguablanca. From Lag. Otun walk south and traverse the hillside to reach the river coming down from Laguna la Leona. Climb up to this lagoon (4050m) and continue up the pass behind, 4300m. This pass leads to the valley of the Q. Aguablanca. Descend the valley until it flattens out and campsites are possible at about 3900m

5. 7-8 hours Aguablanca - El Silencio. This is a long day which might be better split with a camp at Laguna del Encanto. From the campsites in the Q. Aguablanca climb steeply over the pass to south, then up the Rio Totare to the beautiful Laguna del Encanto, 3950m, **3 hours**. Tolima can be climbed from here. To carry on to El Silencio head south to the small pass east of La Piramide, cross a second pass then descend steeply into the Rio Combeina valley. Descend by the river to reach the El Rancho hot spring at 2600m - a beautiful spot with some food and accommodation. The village of El Silencio is **½ hour** further down the valley.

The highest peak in the range, Nevado del Tolima, 5274m can be climbed from El Silencio in two days by the south slopes. This is a tough but quite popular climb - ask for details of the route in El Rancho or El Silencio.

Espeletia Flower

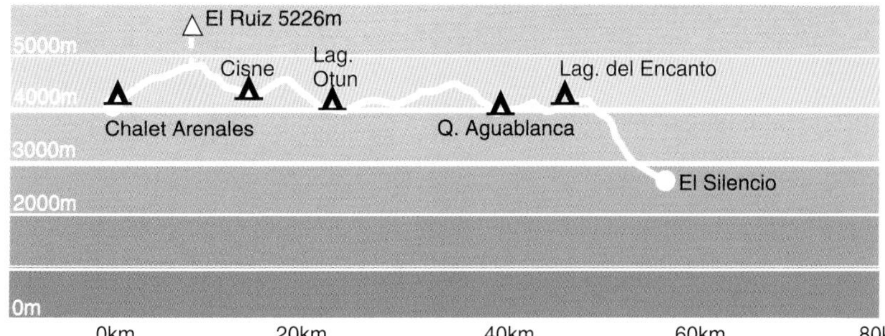

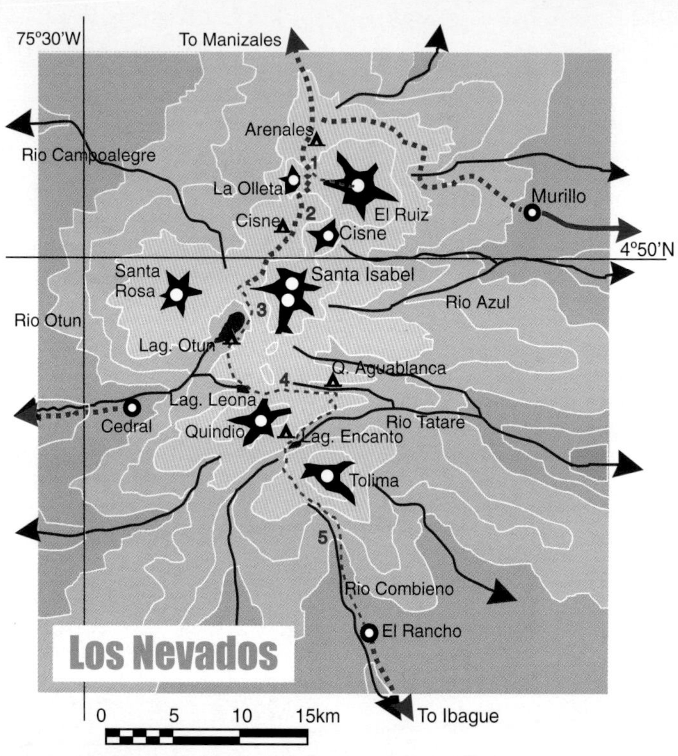
75°30'W
To Manizales
Arenales
Rio Campoalegre
La Olleta
1
El Ruiz
Murillo
2
Cisne
Cisne
4°50'N
Santa Rosa
Santa Isabel
Rio Azul
3
Rio Otun
Lag. Otun
Q. Aguablanca
4
Lag. Leona
Cedral
Quindio
Rio Tatare
Lag. Encanto
Tolima
5
Rio Combieno
El Rancho
Los Nevados
0 5 10 15km
To Ibague

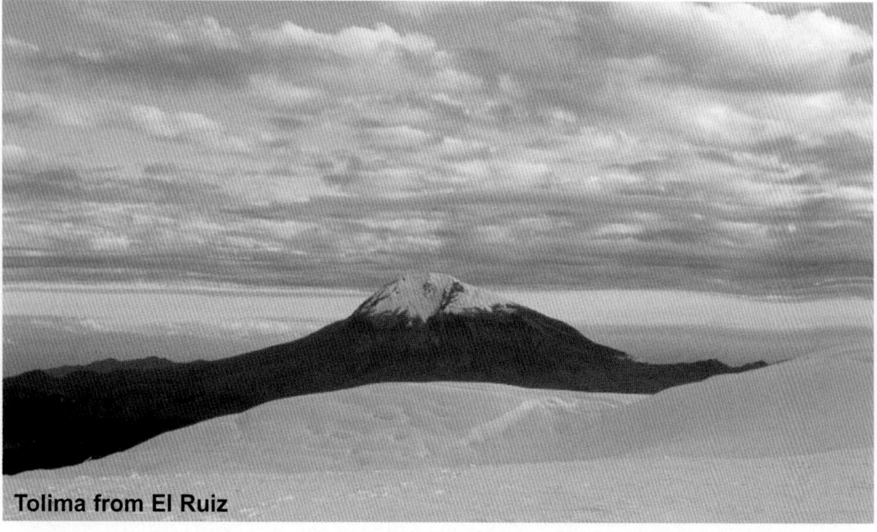
Tolima from El Ruiz

Ecuador

Cotopaxi at sunrise

Antisana to Cotopaxi Trek

TREKKING

DURATION 4-5 days
DISTANCE 50 km
TOTAL ASCENT 1400m
HIGHEST POINT 4400m
GRADE Good path
EFFORT Moderate

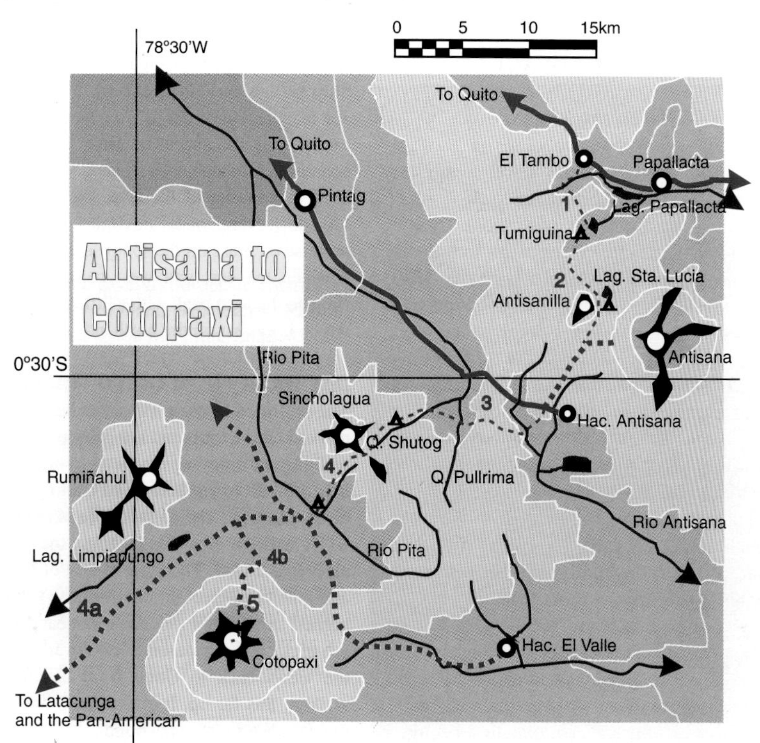

ANTISANA TO COTOPAXI TREK

Described here is the trek from near the town of Papallacta to Cotopaxi volcano. Also known as the Trek del Condor this route passes under two other volcanoes Antisana and Sincholagua on the way. A dramatic way to finish this trek is with an ascent of Cotopaxi, one of the worlds most famous volcanoes. This is a fairly easy ascent by the normal route although an ice-axe, rope and crampons are needed.

The trekking route is largely over wild 'paramo' moorland. The area around Antisana is one of the wettest parts of the Ecuador highlands. Rain is likely even in the dry season and sections of the trek are very muddy. However the trek is very worthwhile even without the ascent, for the magnificent views of the paramo with llamas and wild horses. Unless you are very unlucky you'll also see snow capped volcanoes. This trek would be fine in reverse.

ACCESS

By bus or hired transport from Quito through Baeza and then on the road to Papallacta. The trek starts from El Tambo, about 6km before Papallacta, and at the point where the road makes a sharp bend left to descend towards the Rio Tambo. There a few houses here and a signpost saying 'Paso del Condor' It is best to arrange mules or horses in advance with an agency in Quito if starting here. Bring supplies from Quito if getting off the bus here, otherwise you'll need to go to Papallacta and return by bus or taxi.

MAPS TO USE

Ecuadorian IGM sheet 3992-I 'Papallacta', sheet 3992-II 'Laguna de Mica' and sheet 3992-III 'Sincholagua' all at 1:50,000. For the ascent sheet '3991-IV 'Cotopaxi' is also useful. Another alternative is to buy the 1:100,000 sheet Pintag which covers the whole trek in just one map.

THE ROUTE

1. 3-4 hours. From the signpost go through a locked gate (key available) and walk south above the Rio Tambo on a muddy path. Cross the river after about half an hour on an interesting bridge to get to the left side. There are numerous trails here but head southwest towards the flat topped mountain 'El Tambo'. Just south of this the Rio Tambo valley turns to the west. From here climb southeastwards to reach a low and wide pass 3850m, **1½-2 hours**. Descend southeast to the hidden Laguna Tumiguina (3650m), with campsites on the west and south shores, **1 hour**.

2. 5-6 hours. From Lag. Tumiguina walk up the inflow stream to a triple confluence. Go up the muddy trail between the central and right hand tributaries. This climbs southwards up grassy and wooded hillside then goes eastward around the north end of a small steep hill known as Antisanilla to reach the small Laguna Santa Lucia at 4350m. There are nice campsites here.

3. 6 hours. A very poor vehicle track heads southwest from Lag. Santa Lucia. Follow this for about 6km to reach a gate near where it joins the tarred road (leading to Hac. Antisana), **2 hours**. From here head slightly west of south across an open moor then begin to turn rightwards to the Rio Jatunhuaycu. Cross this river and follow trails west over open paramo, crossing the wide pass of Santanton Chico and then the Q. Pullrima river valley, (nice camps spoiled by new bulldozing) to reach the Quebrada Shutog or Huallanta, **4 hours**.

4. 5-6 hours. Climb up the Q. Shutog, cross the col (4400m) at the top of the valley and follow the muddy

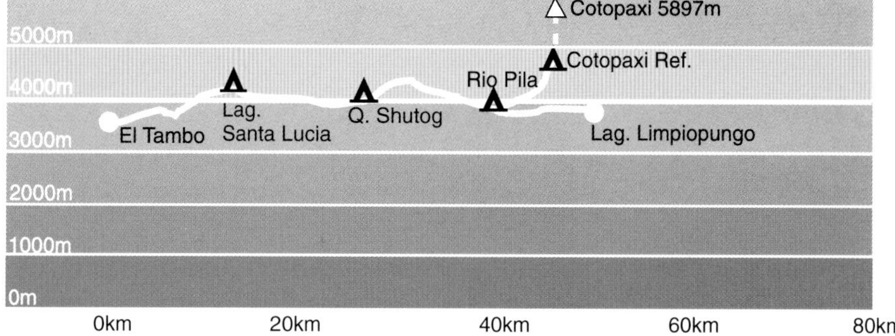

trail across the south side of Sincholagua to a second pass. Descend into the valley beyond (Rio Merced or Tungurahua) with the cone of Cotopaxi directly in front of you. Walk down the valley to join the jeep road at about 3900m near the 'Turco' trig point. From here you can see camping areas down by the larger Rio Pila.

4a. 2-3 hours. For those not climbing Cotopaxi, it is 2-3 hours walk from the Rio Pila camp along the jeep track to the scenic Laguna Limpiopungo, where transport can usually be picked up for a return trip to Quito. An early start will give you a better chance of getting a lift from climbers returning from the Cotopaxi hut.

4b. 5 hours. From the Rio Pila it will take about 5 hours to walk to the Cotopaxi refuge. Head slightly south of east across open terrain, passing south of a low hill (Pamba, 4095m) to reach the track climbing up to the refuge, joined at a height of about 4200m, **2-3 hours**. It will be another **2-3 hours** up to the hut, depending on how much you are carrying, but you may be lucky enough to get a lift.

The hut is about 1/2 hour above the parking area. It has about 50 beds, gas cookers and toilet facilities. It gets very busy on Friday and Saturday nights, so try to time your arrival for mid-week. The climb to the summit takes only a day, but as it is normal to leave at midnight it might be best to have a day of rest at the hut before climbing. From the parking area below the hut it should be easy to pick up transport back to Quito, though you will have to pay.

COTOPAXI ASCENT

Cotopaxi is a spectacular heavily glaciated volcanic cone, seen on the skyline from Quito. The name means 'collar of the moon'. The mountain is often wrongly claimed to be the world's highest active volcano, but several peaks in northern Chile and southern Peru are higher and (at least currently) more active. Cotopaxi was very active from the 1850's to 1870's. The volcano now forms the centrepiece to one of Ecuador's most famous national parks. The normal route is on the north side from the hut at 4800m. The route is normally very well marked and with a clear trail. There is considerable crevasse danger on this route so a rope is absolutely essential. An ice-axe and crampons will also be needed.

CLIMB 5. 7-10 hours return. From the hut climb to the top of the triangular scree slope and then onto the glacier on the right hand side. Move up going around, over and sometimes through large crevasses and passing the huge rock cliff (known as Yanasacha) on the right. Then move back leftwards and up steeper snow slopes to the summit crater. There is sometimes a short snow pitch just before the summit.

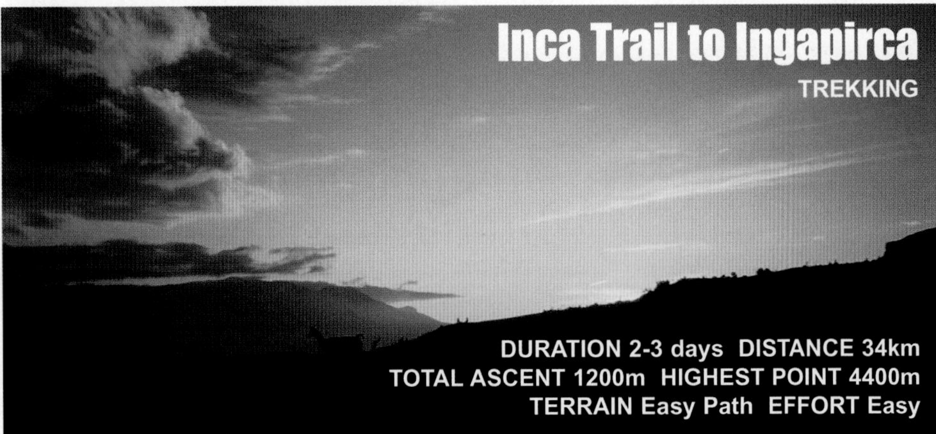

Inca Trail to Ingapirca
TREKKING
DURATION 2-3 days DISTANCE 34km
TOTAL ASCENT 1200m HIGHEST POINT 4400m
TERRAIN Easy Path EFFORT Easy

INCA TRAIL TO INGAPIRCA

Though not as sensational as the 'real' Inca trail in Peru, the Ecuadorian version is nevertheless an interesting walk with some sections of original 'Inca' trail and the best ruins in Ecuador at the end of the trek It is normal to walk the trek from north to south so that you reach the ruins at the end of your trek, but logistically there is no reason not to do the trek the other way round. The walk could quite easily be done in two days, though this would require an early start and late finish. It is more comfortable to do the route in three days, and arrive early enough at Ingapirca for a look at the ruins.

ACCESS

From Quito it is either a long bus journey south to the start of the trail or you can fly quite cheaply to the pretty city of Cuenca (for city information see page 179) and then travel a short way north by bus to the start of the trail. The trail begins in the small village of Achupallas at 3300m. This village is about 1½ hours drive from the nearest town of Alausi which is on the main north-south Panamerican Highway 300km south of Quito. Buses from Quito and Riobamba to Cuenca pass through Alausi, which has basic accommodation and food available. 15km south of Alausi the road to Achupallas turns off from the main road at the small village of La Moya. There is occasional public transport from here to Achupallas. Mules or donkeys can usually be hired in Achupallas on the day you arrive.

MAPS TO USE

Ecuadorian IGM sheets 3887-III 'Alausi', 3886-IV 'Juncal', and sheet 3886-III 'Cañar' all at 1:50,000.

THE ROUTE

1. 5-6 hours. From the plaza in Achupallas walk down to and past the arch and then follow the road south passing the cemetery, with its typical South American high-rise graves. Walk southwards up the narrow valley of the Rio Cadrul, initially on the left side. The track soon crosses to the right. Walk up a zig-zag road to take a path by a powerline back down to the river. After the last house cross the river again and continue to where there is a narrow gap where the trail passes through a short tunnel. After this the valley gradually becomes wider and flatter and there are trails either in the valley bottom or slightly up the west side. You pass ruins at 3900m. There is nice camping at the Laguna las Tres Cruces, 4250m.

2. 3-4 hours. From the Laguna las Tres Cruces climb the pass to the southwest. The best route from the pass is along the narrow ridge of the Cuchilla de Tres Cruces, but it is also possible to walk along the valley to the west (Q. Espindola). For the Cuchilla follow the trail southwest from the pass, eventually rising to 4400m on the crest of the ridge. At the southwest end of the ridge descend steeply into the valley below. You can see the old Inca road in a straight line on the valley floor. The trail, at times marshy, now follows the south side of the Q. Espindola, starting to climb the hillside above Laguna Culebrillas after about 2½km. A short way up this climb are the ruins known as 'Paredones', overlooking the lake. It is possible to camp here.

3. 5 hours. South of Paredones the Inca trail is very clear on stone paving. For the first hour or two it stays high on the moorland. This section can be boggy at times above the houses at Cajon Tambo. As the trail gradually begins to drop into more fertile and farmed country the path becomes harder to distinguish, but stays on the east slopes of the Q. Chaupurcu valley, descending eventually to the Rio Silante which it crosses and joins a road that leads uphill to the ruins of Ingapirca.

Ingapirca ruins are the best Inca remains in Ecuador, displaying many of the features of the classic Inca architecture of the Cuzco region. The complex was built in about 1490-1500. There is an entrance fee to the site and a museum worth visiting. There are a few basic facilities in Ingapirca village. From Ingapirca it is about 8km to El Tambo on the Pan-American highway - there are several buses a day, or you can hire a truck. The nearest town, Cañar is then another 8km to the south of El Tambo.

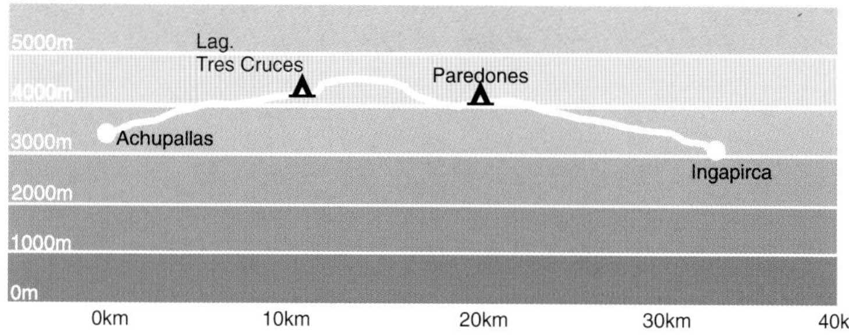

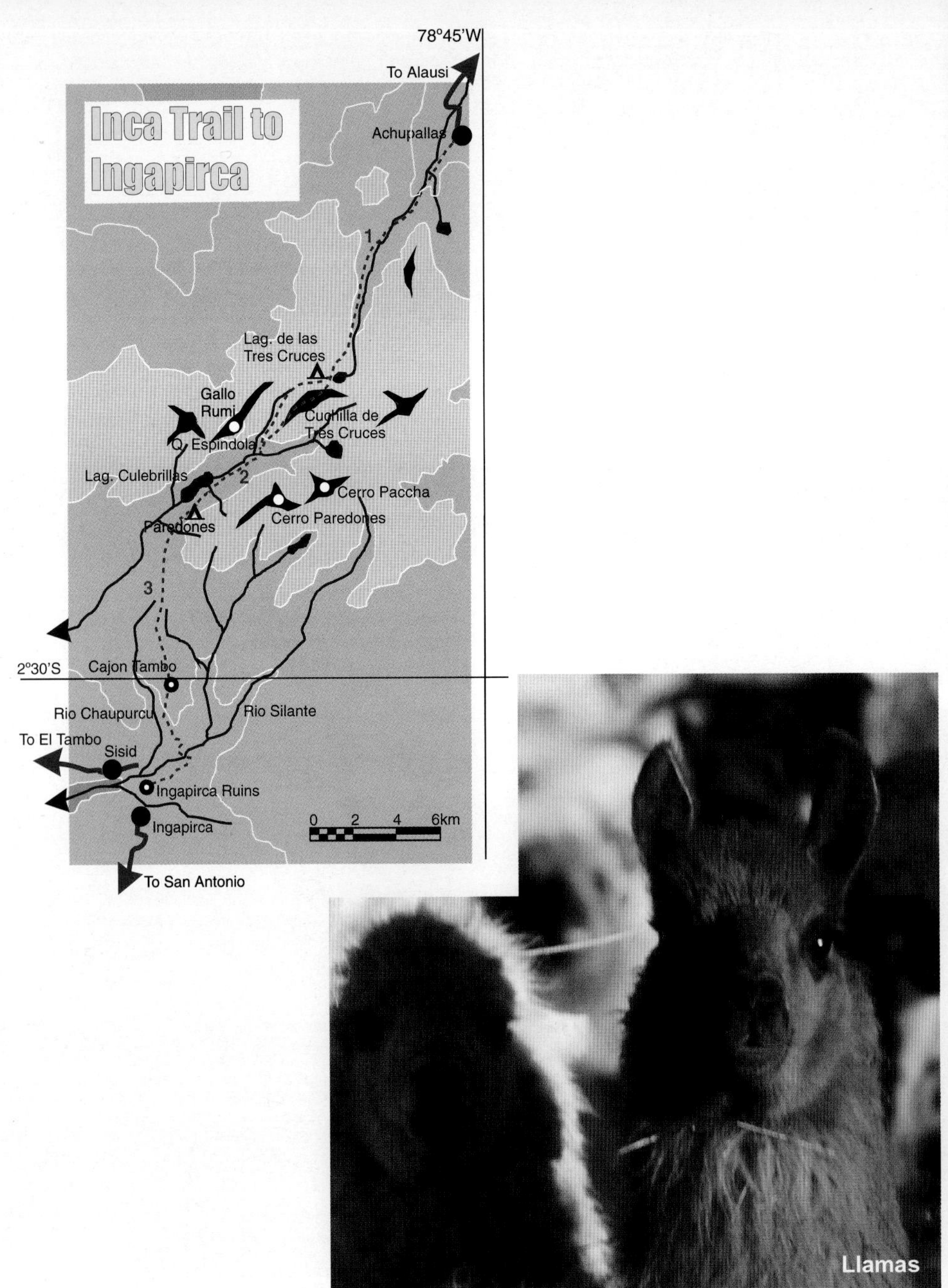
Inca Trail to Ingapirca
78°45'W
To Alausi
Achupallas
1
Lag. de las Tres Cruces
Gallo Rumi
Cuchilla de Tres Cruces
Q. Espindola
Lag. Culebrillas
2
Cerro Paccha
Cerro Paredones
Paredones
3
2°30'S
Cajon Tambo
Rio Chaupurcu
Rio Silante
To El Tambo
Sisid
Ingapirca Ruins
Ingapirca
0 2 4 6km
To San Antonio

Llamas

Siula and Carhuacocha lake, Cordillera Huayhuash

INTRODUCTION

Without a doubt Peru offers the best and most varied trekking in the Andes. The mountains are just as spectacular in Patagonia, but there the cultural experience is far less interesting and you don't have the challenge (or thrill) of being at high altitude. The biggest and most spectacular mountains in Peru lie towards the north of the country and this chapter describes treks in three of these northern ranges - the Cordillera Blanca, the nearby Cordillera Huayhuash and the Cordillera Central which lie very close to Lima.

Several treks in the Cordillera Blanca are included, from the short **Olleros to Chavin** route and the popular **Quebrada Santa Cruz** to the longer and more arduous **Quebrada de los Cedros** route.

These are followed by a description of what is probably South America's grandest and most famous trek, the circuit of the **Cordillera Huayhuash.**

Finally a new and very quiet trek in the Central Cordillera around the impressive mountain **Ticlla** is described.

GETTING THERE

All the areas described in this chapter are easiest to reach by flying to Lima, the capital of Peru. From Europe there are direct flights from Madrid (Iberia), Amsterdam (KLM) and Frankfurt (Lufthansa) to Lima. There are no direct flights at present from London so a change in Europe or a flight via Miami, Bogotá or Caracas will be necessary. From the USA there are many direct flights from Miami to Lima and a few from Atlanta, LA and Houston, with either United, Delta, Continental or American.

For the Cordillera Blanca you'll need to get a bus to Huaraz from Lima. For the Cordillera Huayhuash there are direct buses to the start points at Cajatambo and Chiquian but it may be easier to go via Huaraz, particularly if you have food, mules etc. to sort out and also to gain some acclimatisation before going on the trek.

For the Ticlla circuit in the Central Cordillera the best access will normally involve a bus journey direct from Lima either via the highland city of Huancayo, (which will provide an acclimatisation advantage) or via the coastal town of Cañete.

CLIMATE AND WEATHER CONDITIONS

The trekking season in Northern Peru extends from May to September, with June and July reckoned to be the best months. Though this is the middle of winter, Peru is very near the equator and it is the dry season in the mountains. The weather during the dry season is generally very stable with normally only one or two bad days in a week. Freezing level is about 4500-5000m during the day, but strong sun can make it feel much warmer than this in the valleys. Wind is rarely a problem in the mountains during the dry season. Bad weather comes from the Amazon side of the mountains, from the east or the north.

The central Cordillera (Ticlla circuit) has a noticeably drier climate, being sheltered from the worst of the Amazon weather.

LIMA

Most people dislike the dirty, smoggy sprawl of Lima, Peru's capital city. It does grow on you a little after a few weeks, but it is never a pleasant place. The city must have the world's most bizarre climate; Lima is a desert city with less than 50mm rainfall per year (drier than most of Arabia and Egypt) and a tropical city at sea level. Despite this, during the main trekking season of May - September, Lima is plagued by five months of dreadful cold mist with occasional outbreaks of thin drizzle. It is certainly not tropical (12-15°C) and the damp climate covers everything in grime.

There are some museums and archaeological sites worth seeing in and around the city. Particularly recommended are the Gold Museum and the ruins of Pachacamac to the south of the city. Miraflores, the modern part of the city to the south, has some good beaches if you are here in the Lima summer (November - March).

For details of hotels and other travel information see page 179.

Lima

The Cordillera Blanca

Tocllaraju

INTRODUCTION

The Cordillera Blanca range in northern Peru has an incredible concentration of 6000m peaks, including Peru's highest mountain, the twin peaked Nevado Huascarán 6768m. The mountains run roughly north to south and are easily accessible from the heavily populated Callejon de Huaylas valley which lies to their west. The friendly wee town of Huaraz which lies at an altitude of 3000m and is 500km north of Lima by a good road is by far the best base for treks here. The town has many pleasant hotels and restaurants, plenty of tourist and trekking agencies and spectacular views of the mountains at sunset. Access from Huaraz to the mountains is generally very easy; most trail heads can be reached in only a couple of hours by public transport.

Between the dramatic peaks of the Cordillera Blanca the valleys are dotted with stunning turquoise glacial lakes. Most treks follow these valleys which run mostly west to east through the mountains and will take from 3-5 days but two valleys can often be linked to provide longer excursions. If finishing on the eastern side of the range be aware that it is much more remote and you may have to wait a few days for transport back to Huaraz after your trek.

ACCESS TO THE CORDILLERA BLANCA

Get out of Lima as soon as you can - it can be a damp and depressing city in the trekking season. From Lima the only practical way to Huaraz, the main city of the Cordillera Blanca, is by bus. This is an 8 hour journey. Most buses are reasonably comfortable and the road is now surfaced all the way. Watch out for thieves in Lima bus stations. There are flights from Lima to the airfield north of Huaraz but these are on a small plane with restricted baggage.

MAPS

The names used have mainly been taken from Felipe Diaz's map 'Cordilleras Blanca and Huayhuash' approx. 1:200,000. Considered to be the most accurate, this is a very useful map which is available cheaply in Huaraz. The Alpenvereins maps are fairly good but glaciers and glacier lakes are very out of date. The two sheets covering the Cordillera Blanca were being re-surveyed in 1998 and should be re-issued fairly soon. The Peruvian IGM maps use some unusual names that are not often understood locally. They are however more up to date and show better topographical detail in places than the Alpenvereins maps.

HUARAZ

Huaraz sits at 3090m at the southern end of the Callejon de Huaylas and makes an ideal base for the Cordillera Blanca. It is a cheerful and relatively prosperous town. For trekkers it has as many facilities as you'll get in Peru and most valley road heads can be reached in a couple of hours drive by private transport or less than a day by public transport. The town is a very active trekking and climbing centre in season with lots of gear shops and plenty of cafes along the

main street called Luzuriaga.
The fascinating underground temple complex at Chavin is well worth a visit (take a torch). This involves a 4 hour journey from Huaraz by tour bus, or you can do the 3 day trek described below (see Olleros to Chavin).
For details about Huaraz see page 180.

Huascaran from the main street in Huaraz

DAY WALK FROM HUARAZ - HUILCAHUAIN TO MONTEREY

600m descent, 5km, 2 hours

On the hillside 7km from Huaraz are the ruins of Huilcahuain. The most interesting part of the ruins is on the inside and a torch or candle is necessary. Local boys will act as a guide and also provide candles for a small fee. It's a good idea to take a taxi up to the ruins and walk back down as an acclimatisation day. You can walk down to the hot baths at Monterey and then get a bus back to Huaraz from there. The way is fairly obvious once you get started - ask for directions to get you on the right path.

DAY WALK FROM HUARAZ - LAGUNA CHURUP

600m ascent, 7km, 5-6 hours return

This walk to a scenic high altitude lagoon starts from the small village of Pitec at an altitude of 3850m just above Huaraz. It is best to hire a taxi or other vehicle to get here from Huaraz (1½-2 hours).
Several routes are possible from Pitec. You can start where the road from Huaraz crosses an aqueduct on the way into Pitec. Head for the ridge on the left hand side of the Q. Churup and climb steeply up this. Higher up traverse rightwards into the valley where the gradient eases, but stay left of the little stream that drains the lake. The beautiful turquoise lagoon lies at 4450m with spectacular views of Nevado Churup behind.

Huilcahuain

Quebrada los Cedros
TREKKING
DURATION 7-8 days
DISTANCE 135 km
TOTAL ASCENT 3400m
HIGHEST POINT 4850m
TERRAIN Easy Path
EFFORT Moderate

QUEBRADA LOS CEDROS

This is a popular but quite tough trek over high passes in the north of the Cordillera Blanca. It takes you to the spectacular base camp for Nevado Alpamayo, the unique pyramid shaped mountain, which has famously been declared 'the worlds most beautiful mountain'.

The trek as described will take seven long days from Cashapampa to Vaqueria, indeed many parties may need eight or nine days. A longer finish is to combine this trek with the Q. Santa Cruz trek described below and walk back to Cashapampa, taking a total of nine or ten days. Alternative finishes giving a slightly shorter trek are given, leaving the route for the town of Pomabamba on days 5 or 6. The trek and variations will be fine in reverse.

ACCESS

From Huaraz take a bus to Caraz where there is basic accommodation available, then take a minibus on to Cashapampa village at 2900m. Mules can be arranged in Caraz or Cashapampa if required.

A new route is now possible directly to the ruins at Hualcayan (end of day 1) for those with hired transport. From Caraz drive via Colcas to join the trek here.

MAP TO USE

Peruvian IGM sheet 18-h 'Corongo' and 18-j 'Pomabamba'. Both at 1:100,000

THE ROUTE

1. 2½ hours. This part day can now be avoided by driving to Hualcayan, but it is an interesting walk and provides valuable acclimatisation. From the village of Cashapampa walk on the road north through the village of Conay and on to Baños Huancahuas, with its small but impressive hot springs. Continue on through Cholin (fill up with water) and then follow paths northwards to the ruins of Hualcayan Pampa (3150m) to camp. There are good views of the Cordillera Negra in the evenings from here.

2. 7 hours. From the ruins the path zig-zags steeply up the northeast slopes towards Laguna Cullicocha (Atuncocha) with good views northwards to the Champara massif. The path passes above Yanacocha and the small Laguna Azulcocha. There is a path junction with a refuge hut near by where it is possible to camp at the outlet behind a stone wall. This is the highest camp on the trek at 4600m.

2b. There is an optional **2 hour** walk to Laguna Yuraccocha during the day to Cullicocha. The path starts at a junction at 4400m soon after you first see Yanacocha. At the path junction, turn to the south, then east to traverse the hillside which heads into the wee valley of Laguna Yuracocha with great views to the peaks of Santa Cruz 6259m.

3. 7 hours. From the Lag. Cullicocha camp the trail climbs the north slopes to a small pass called Paso Cullicocha, 4850m. Descend from the pass to a place called Osoruri. From here cross a second small pass, known as Paso Alpamayo or Los Cedros at 4750m, high above the Quebrada Los Cedros. Continue on a trail above the valley which gradually descends to the flat valley floor. There are several camps possible at the head of the valley in a flat area at 4200m. You can also continue upstream to the Laguna Jancarurish at 4350m. There is camping at the far end of the Laguna Jancarurish under the spectacular Nevado Alpamayo.

4. 7 hours. From the valley camps 1km downstream from Laguna Jancarurish ascend the steep grassy slope to the north into a small valley. Keep to the right of the small lakes. The path is not well defined here. The Caracara (or Safuna) pass at 4830m, is at the head of this valley on the northeast side. From the pass head steeply down at first to the more open and flat valley of Q. Mayobamba. When the river turns north you climb the slopes to the southeast to cross Paso Mesapampa 4500m (or Paso Contadera), into the Q. Tayapampa valley. Cross the flat swampy valley moving southwards now to rise gently to Laguna Sufana (Sajuna) 4250m. Nice campsites. An alternative place to spend this night (or a possible side trip) is to continue up the Q. Tayapampa to the Laguna Pucacocha at 4500m. This will take at least another hour.

5. 7 hours. Return down the Q. Tayapampa and follow the track into the village of Huillca. Climb up a steep narrow valley to the southeast and the pass of Huillca, 4600m, then descend the other side to Laguna Sactaycocha with beautiful queñoa groves. Continue easily down the valley to the settlement at Pishcopampa (Pisgospampa) at 3600m, where you can camp. You can reach Pomabamba in 4-5 hours walk down the valley from here.

5b. 8-10 hours. An alternative finish from Huillca which gets you to Pomabamba in one long day. Climb steeply north out of the village to the Laguna Shuitococha and then traverse high valleys eastwards to cross the Paso Collata 4350m. From here make a long descent down the Q. Yanacollpa through the village of Yanacollpa to the town of Pomabamba, a major regional centre on the east side of the cordillera at 2950m. There are regular buses back to Huaraz from Pomabamba.

6. 7 hours. From the village of Pishcopampa climb up the Q. Tacllush to reach the Paso de Yaino at 4150m. Then trek along a high ridge running eastwards to the ruins at Yaino. From Yaino retrace your steps along the ridge for 2km then drop down southwards into the Quebrada Ingenio. Climb up this valley keeping to the right hand side, to reach the small village of Quisuar. You can camp near the village here or continue up the side valley for ½hour to beautiful campsites by Laguna Huecrucocha.

6b. 5 hours. Alternatively you can shorten the trek by going directly from Pishcopampa to Quisuar. Go almost due south from Pishcopampa climbing up the narrow Q. Ñañayoc to reach Quisuar over the pass of Tupatupa, 4400m in about 4 to 5 hours

7. 8-9 hours to Vaqueria. From the Huecrucocha camp climb the valley to the steep pass of Alto de Pucaraju 4650m, **3-4 hours**. On the other side make a steep zig-zag descent to the Quebrada Huarapampa. From here you can finish either downstream and southeast to Vaqueria in a further **4-5 hours** (described under day 4 of the Santa Cruz trek) or return west through the heart of the mountains over the Punta Union 4750m and back out by the Q. Santa Cruz to reach Cashapampa (described under days 1, 2 and 3 of the Santa Cruz trek)

Cordillera Blanca Campsite

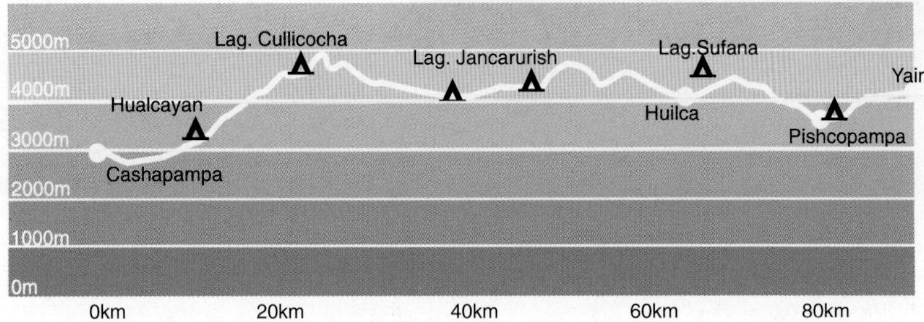

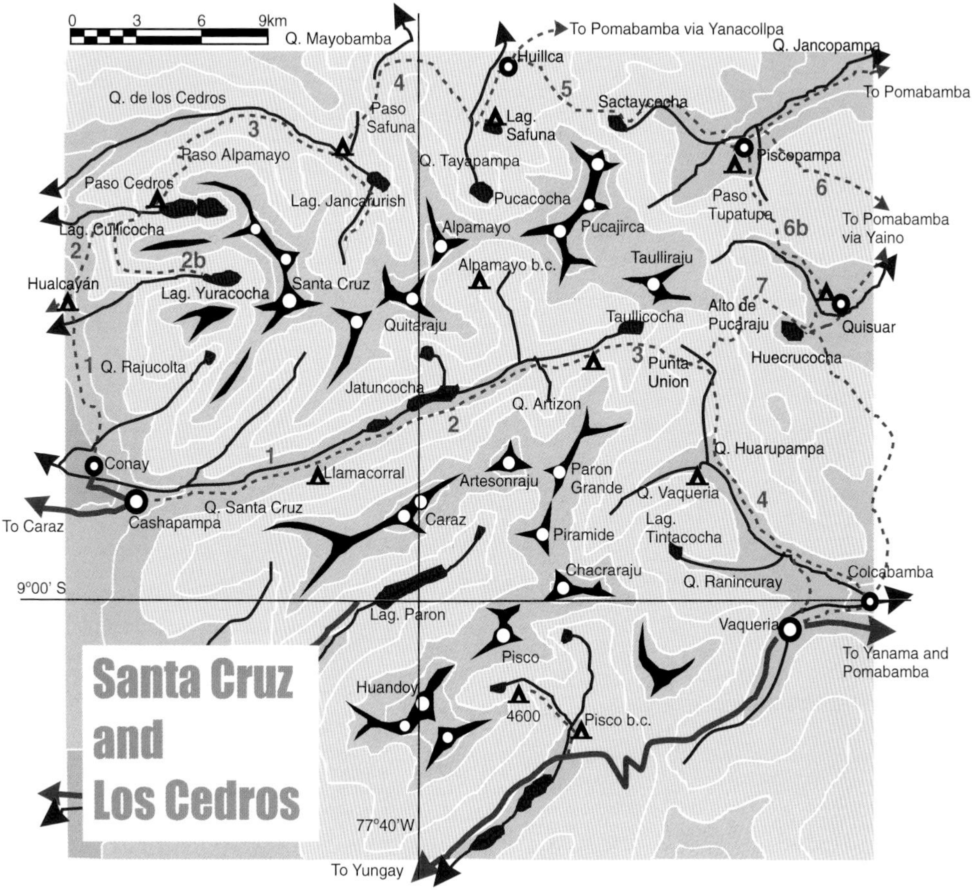

Santa Cruz and Los Cedros

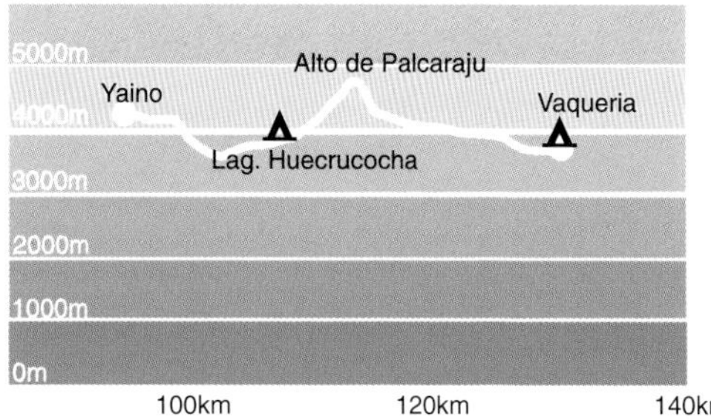

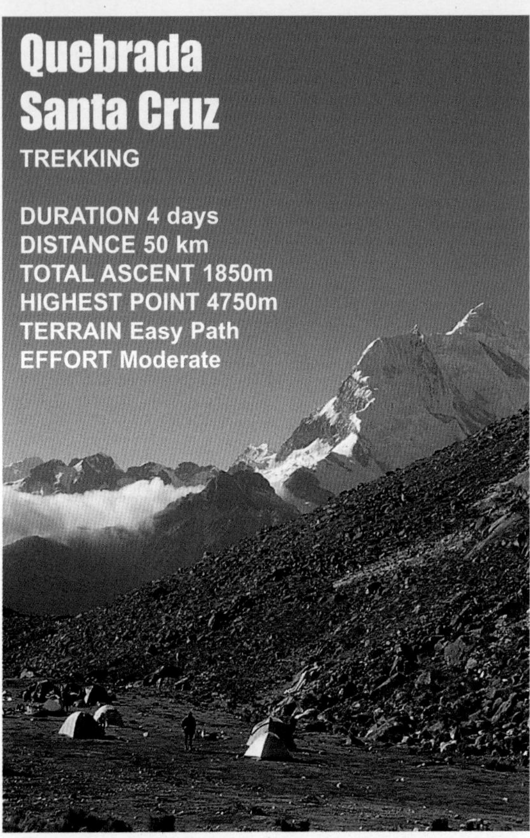

Quebrada Santa Cruz

TREKKING

DURATION 4 days
DISTANCE 50 km
TOTAL ASCENT 1850m
HIGHEST POINT 4750m
TERRAIN Easy Path
EFFORT Moderate

QUEBRADA SANTA CRUZ

The Cordillera Blancas most famous trek from Santa Cruz to Llanganuco is now a bit shorter due to the opening of a new road over the mountains, but what is left is still very worthwhile. The trek described is from Cashapampa north of Huaraz to Vaqueria on the eastern side of the range, via the 4750m high Punta Union pass. There are superb views of some of the Cordillera Blanca's most spectacular mountains such as Chacraraju, Alpamayo and Artesonraju. There are typical Andean flora in the beautiful meadows of the Quebrada Santa Cruz. The route can be busy in season and is well marked and easy to follow. There are now pit toilets at all the campsites. There are fees of a few dollars per person to use these sites. There are some small black biting flies in this valley.

This trek will be fine in reverse, starting at Vaqueria.

You'll still see the beautiful glacier green Llanganuco lakes on the drive from Vaqueria to Huaraz and its worth at least a short stop to admire them.

ACCESS

From Huaraz take a bus to Caraz, where basic accommodation and supplies are available, then another minibus on to Cashapampa village at 2900m. The total journey will take 2½ or 3 hours. Mules can easily be arranged in Caraz or Cashapampa if required.

MAPS TO USE

Peruvian IGM sheets 19-h 'Carhuaz ' and 18-h 'Corongo', both at 1:100,000.

THE ROUTE

1. 4 hours. From Cashapampa walk up the zigzagging path into the Quebrada Santa Cruz valley to the north east. Keeping on the right hand side of the river the gradient lessens after **1½-2 hours**. It is a further **2 hours** along the valley to camp in a meadow area called Llamacorral at an altitude of 3600m.

2. 7 hours. Continue up the wide valley on the path passing Laguna Ichacocha and Laguna Jatuncocha (also known as Chica and Grande) after which the trail can sometimes be a bit boggy. At Q Artizon you pass a big landslide scar. Camping is possible at Q. Arhuaycocha or Q Artizon. Each of these side valleys can also be explored for half a day. Alpamayo base camp is at the head of Q. Arhuaycocha's magnificent cirque. To continue on the main trail head up the Q. Santa Cruz, following the valley generally eastwards, for a further hour or so to camp at Taullipampa camp area, 4250m.

3. 7 hours. From the Santa Cruz valley ascend on the right hand side up to the Punta Union pass at 4750, with spectacular views of the surrounding peaks and down to the Laguna Taullicohca below. Descend, steeply at first, from the pass into the Huaripampa valley passing through more meadows of liga-liga and rima-rima and other typical Andean flowers. It is possible to camp at the small lakes just below the pass. Or you can continue on to pleasant camping at Cachinapampa, 3850m at the mouth of Q. Vaqueria (also known as Paria), **3-4 hours** from the pass.

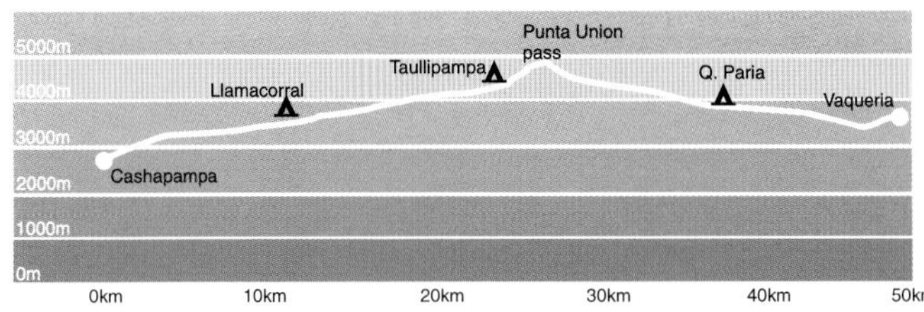

This side valley also offers a spectacular side trip as it leads up below the east face of Chacraraju, the steepest and most difficult 6000m peak in the Andes.

4. 2½ hours. Continue down the main valley passing through the village of Huaripampa. From here you can explore another spectacular side valley to Laguna Tintacocha. Park rangers are sometimes encountered in this area. To get to Vaqueria take the path which cuts off, crossing the bridge just south of Q. Ranincuray and then rising slightly. Ask locals for the directions. If you miss this path you end up down in Colcapampa which also has basic accommodation and supplies. It is then an uphill climb back to Vaqueria for transport out. Vaqueria has basic accommodation, cafes and supplies From Vaqueria take a bus back to Yungay on the main road from where it is easy to travel to Huaraz or Caraz.

ASCENT OF PISCO

The ascent of Pisco Oeste, 5752m is one of the easiest and most frequently done climbs in the Cordillera Blanca. The views from the summit to the neighbouring peaks of Chacraraju, Huandoy and Huascaran are superb. There are however some potentially serious crevasse crossings on the southwest ridge. A rope ice-axe and crampons will be needed. Many people do this climb after completing the trek from Cashapampa to Vaqueria. Pisco is named after the Peruvian liquor, large quantities of which were drunk after the first ascent in 1951. The mountain is called Matarrojo on the IGM map.

ACCESS From the Llanganuco lakes go uphill to a bend where the road turns to the south about 2km beyond the second lake. Buses run from Yungay to Vaqueria and Pomabamba run along this route. Descend a short way to the main valley and the meadow known as 'Pisco base camp' at the entrance to the Q. Demanda, **10min**. Donkeys can usually be hired here but it is better to arrange in advance from Huaraz to be sure. Cross to the north side of the river and follow signposts to gain a path rising steeply up the hill left of the stream coming down between Huandoy and Pisco. The path is easy to follow. It goes over a flatter area, up a moraine crest, moves right, climbs two substantial rises, passing left of a rock outcrop on the second, to a camp at 4600m beneath a huge moraine (100m high), **4 hours.** There are now toilets and a private hut at this camp.

Pisco can be climbed from here in one long day but most parties camp higher. Climb the huge moraine and descend the very loose inside wall. Cross a boulder covered glacier heading generally left and pass above one circular lagoon (marked on IGM map) to camp at a higher, smaller lagoon (4900m - not seen until there), **4 hours** from the 4600m camp.

The summit of Pisco

CLIMB From the 4900m camp climb over rock slabs then directly up the glacier to the col (5350m).

Turn right at the col and climb the north side of the broad southwest ridge. There are usually one or two large crevasses and sometimes a final short steep section of 50° snow. **6-8 hours return**

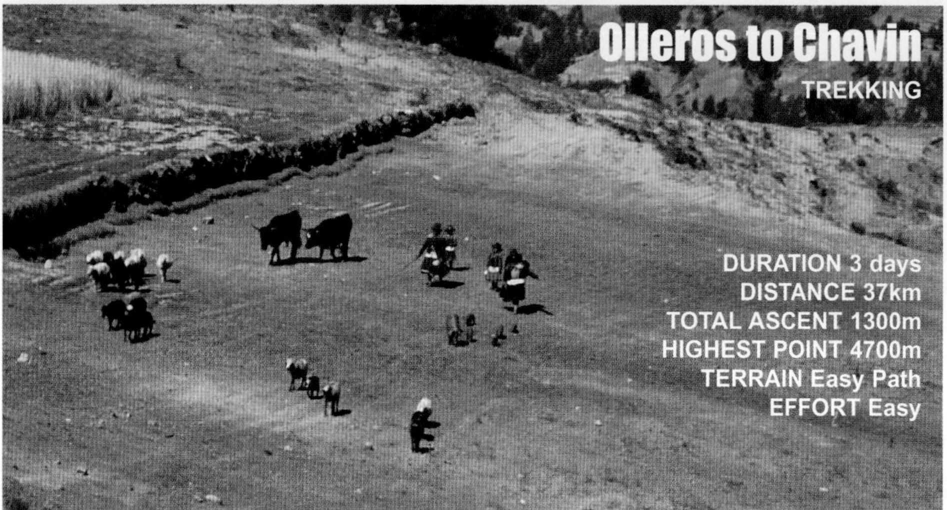

Olleros to Chavin
TREKKING
DURATION 3 days
DISTANCE 37km
TOTAL ASCENT 1300m
HIGHEST POINT 4700m
TERRAIN Easy Path
EFFORT Easy

OLLEROS TO CHAVIN TREK

In the southern part of the range another well known trek is the three day trip from Olleros to Chavin via the 4700m Punta Yanashallash pass. This trek can be done in reverse.

The trek ends at the village of Chavin where there are the extensive pre-Inca ruins of Chavin de Huantar founded in 900 BC. The ruins are an unusual underground labyrinth containing the El Lanzon and Raimondi stones. There are also many carved heads adorning the high walls of the New Temple which was completed in 200 BC. Be sure to bring a torch because there is a lot to see underground.

ACCESS

From Huaraz take one of the regular minibuses leaving from near the town centre to the village of Olleros higher up the Callejon de Huaylas valley at a height of 3400m. It takes 40 minutes. There are a few basic shops, cafes and hotels in Olleros and donkeys can be hired here if required. Locals in Olleros will show you the start of the trail to Chavin.

MAP TO USE

Peruvian IGM Sheet 20-i 'Recuay', 1:100,000

THE ROUTE

1. 5 hours. Walk through Olleros to the east and follow the track crossing the Rio Negro river to its right hand bank outside of the village. The first part of the trek follows this track above the valley in an easterly direction. The track rises away from the river with increasingly good views of the rocky hills and the snow capped peaks of the southern Cordillera Blanca as you turn a corner. Eventually the track becomes a path on the right of the flat bottomed valley. Camping is possible at the place known as Sacracancha (4100m) near Laguna Collotaccocha. Just beyond the camp the

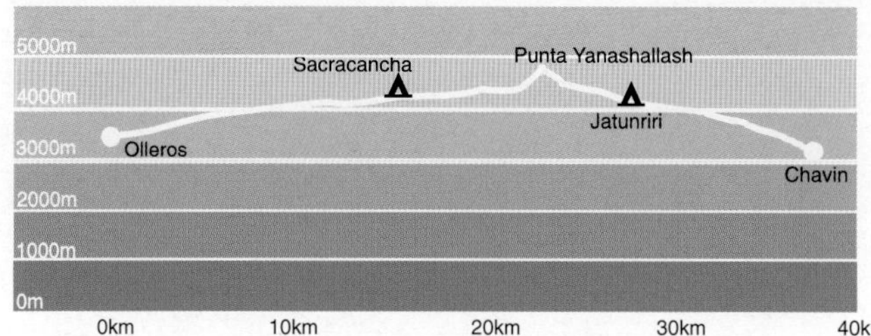

Chavin

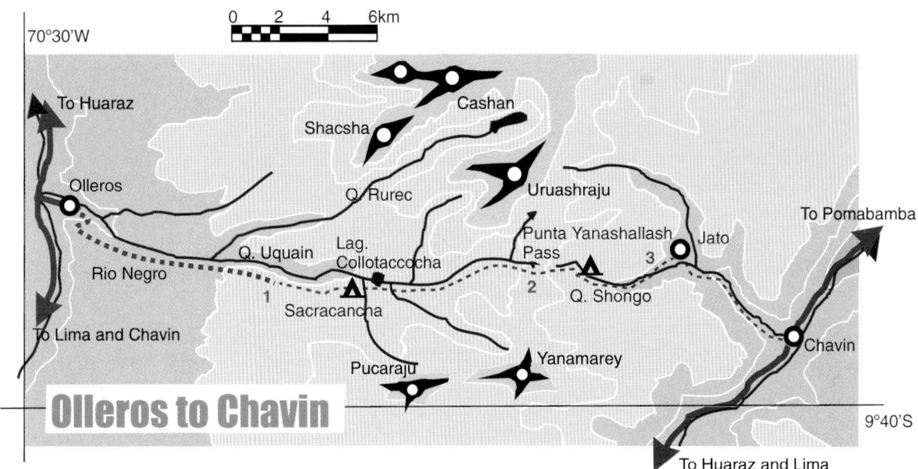

path begins to rise up through moraines.

2. 4-5 hours. From the camp continue upwards, now in a north-easterly direction through rocky moraines on a good path. Passing several small lakes as you near the pass of Punta Yanashallash at 4700m, **3 hours**. There are excellent views from here. Descend into the Q Shongo valley on the steep paved zigzagging track, passing thatched huts. Camp above the tree-line, before the habitation becomes too concentrated.

3. 3 hours. The path continues to descend the valley, crossing the river to the village of Jato at 3850m. Continue down below Jato to join the main valley and eventually the road to the town and ruins of Chavin.

The ruins are fenced and patrolled by armed guards. It is possible to leave bags at the entrance and it is easy to find a local 'guide' to show you around the ruins. There are accommodation and supplies in the village of Chavin. Many buses leave every day for the 4 -5 hour journey back to Huaraz via the Cahuish Tunnel.

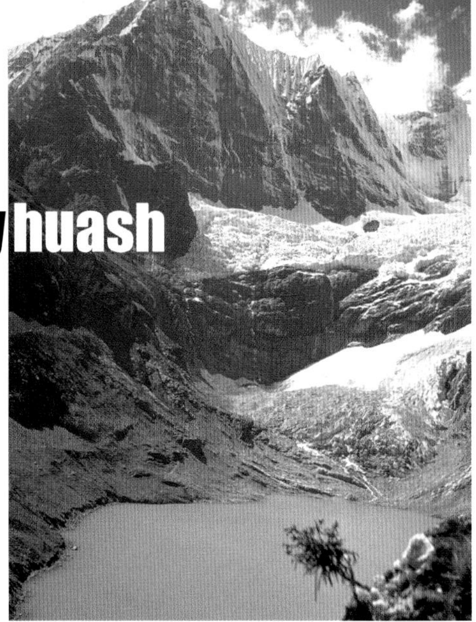

The Cordillera Huayhuash

INTRODUCTION

The Cordillera Huayhuash are a compact but spectacular group of mountains. They lie south of the Cordillera Blanca and are normally reached from Huaraz via the village of Chiquian. The scenery is without equal in the Andes for drama, with soaring peaks, beautiful lakes and stunning glaciers. The biggest peaks of the Huayhuash are all extremely difficult ascents - Yerupajá 6634m the highest of these is one of the highest and most difficult peaks in Peru. Described here is the famous circuit trek around the whole massif along with the easy ascent of Suerococha 5350m which makes a fine viewpoint on the trek.

Huayhuash Circuit

TREKKING

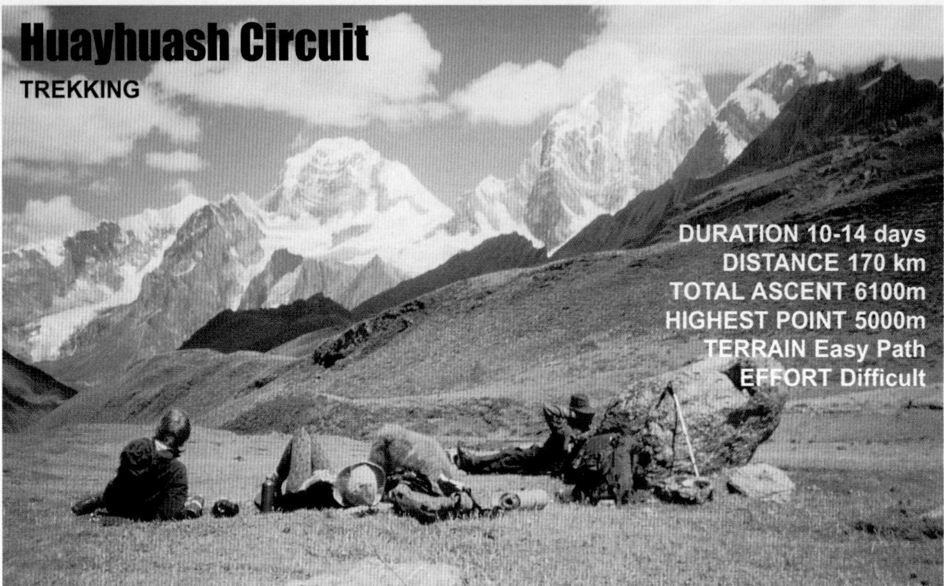

DURATION 10-14 days
DISTANCE 170 km
TOTAL ASCENT 6100m
HIGHEST POINT 5000m
TERRAIN Easy Path
EFFORT Difficult

THE HUAYHUASH CIRCUIT

The circuit trek of the Cordillera Huayhuash is well known as one of the world's greatest treks. With ever changing views of the Cordillera Huayhuash, this trek takes most people about two weeks, camping most nights above 4000m, crossing high passes and traversing beautiful high altitude meadows. The full circuit crosses six passes over 4500m high and covers a total of 170km. From all the passes there are spectacular views of the highest mountains, many of them over 6000m, and in the lower valleys that you trek through there are many small lakes and beautiful campsites. The local Quechua Indians who still live and work in these valleys are always keen to catch fresh trout to sell to trekkers The trek also passes through a number of their remote villages and you can even (occasionally) buy a beer !

ACCESS

The Huayhuash trek is usually started from Chiquian to the northwest, but can also be started from the village of Cajatambo to the southwest side of the range. It is also possible to do a through trek from Chiquian to Cajatambo in eight days. There are direct buses from Lima to both of these villages. It is about 7 hours travel direct from Lima to Chiquian.

If starting from Chiquian it is easier to go via the town of Huaraz (at 3100m) to buy supplies and perhaps to book pack animals with an agency there. Huaraz is a good place to base yourself for a few days of acclimatisation before starting your trek. There are several buses a day from Huaraz to Chiquian, taking about 2 hours.

For Cajatambo you can take a direct bus from Lima or go via the coastal town of Pativilca. Travelling from Huaraz to Cajatambo is not simple.

The trek could easily be walked in the reverse direction to that described here.

CHIQUIAN

The small town of Chiquian has become famous as the main entry point to the Cordillera Huayhuash. Facilities in Chiquian are a bit limited, but there are simple hotels and restaurants and it is easy to obtain pack animals for the circuit trek, within a day or so. For more information on Chiquian see page 180.

CAJATAMBO

The Huayhuash circuit can also be started from the small town of Cajatambo. There are few facilities for tourists here beyond some spartan accommodation and basic food.

NOTE
There is continuing road construction in the north end of the Cordillera Huayhuash and this will affect the trek over the years to come. A new road is being built to link Chiquian and Llamac. It will soon be possible to start and finish the trek in Llamac, taking two days off the itinerary described. There is also road construction and new mines in the upper Llamac valley just below Cacanampunta pass.
Due to these new roads and mines the classic circuit is becoming less appealing. A circuit from Cajatambo may give a more enjoyable high mountain trek, though the logistics of organising the trek will be more difficult.

MAP TO USE
Peruvian IGM Sheet 21-j 'Yanahuanca' 1:100,000

THE ROUTE
The classic circuit is described below in eleven sections. If one section is done daily this would be a fairly quick trip around the mountains, probably only possible if well acclimatised. Most parties take 14 or 16 days which can include a couple of side walks up valleys or time to take a couple of rest days.

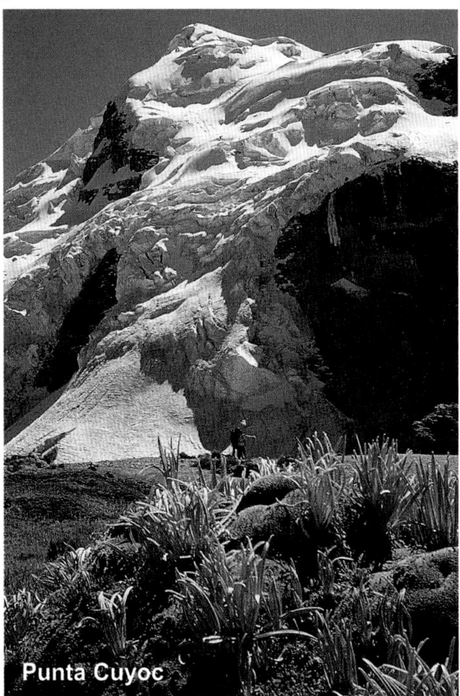
Punta Cuyoc

1. 7 hours. From Chiquian head through the streets east, then south-east to pick up the path to Llamac, or ask the villagers for directions. The dusty track to Llamac is easy to follow and is well used by locals. It joins the Rio Pativilca (or Achin on some maps) after **1 hour** of gradual descent. Follow the river downstream for another **2½ hours**, crossing once to the left hand side, and crossing the side tributary of Rio Quero on a good bridge. At the next river junction it is possible to camp. The path now ascends up the Rio Llamac (above the river at first) to the east keeping on the left hand side until nearer Llamac. Cross to the right hand side before the village, which is **3½ hours** away. Basic supplies can be bought in Llamac. Camping is permitted in the football field for a small fee. Public toilets are at the east end of the village. It is also possible to camp further along on the trek between Llamac and Pocpa.
2. 5-6 hours. Continue up the Llamac valley through the village of Pocpa, **1½ hours**, then through the village of Pallca **1½-2 hours** after which the valley widens and there is a new road. Continue along until you reach the Quedabra Rondoy dropping into the main valley from the right (south). Good camping can be found at various spots up this side valley. Ascend into the valley on steep grassy slopes until you reach the first camp area at a corral.
3. 6 hours. A footpath traverses out from the Rondoy valley on the east slopes to join the main trail in the valley. Head up this for about 4 km until you spot a clear trail heading upwards on the open slopes above you to the east, **1 hour**. Work your way up a rounded ridge, followed by a zigzagging path which then traverses rightwards under a rocky bluff, descending slightly before the last dusty rise to the summit. The pass of Cacanampunta (4650m) is reached after **2 hours** of steep ascent. The more gentle descent on the other side contours round on the grassy southeast slopes of the wide Q. Caliente valley, **1 hour**, before turning south for the last **½ hour** into Janca. It is possible to camp here on the right hand side of the river below the houses but you are asked to pay for tents and use of grazing if you have donkeys. Alternatively walk further up the Rio Janca to camp at the Laguna Mitococha, less than **1 hour**.
4. 4-5 hours. From Janca cross the river to head up the narrow valley southeast on steep slopes which become more gentle and cross two grazing pastures. Follow

this valley for **2 hours** to a grey scree pass (Carhuac, 4600m) then descend for just over **1 hour** until you come out, high above Laguna Carhuaccocha, into a spectacular valley with great views of the east faces of Yerupaja and Siula. The usual camp is down at the east end of this lake but it is also possible to camp at the west end.

5. 6-7 hours. Cross the large outlet stream of Laguna Carhuaccocha It is usually possible to jump between boulders not far from the lake shore. Continue down the valley on a good path for 2 km to a house by the opening of the Q. Carnicero valley to the south. Cross this stream then on the left hand side follow a path steeply at first up into the valley. The path crosses the river, then continues easily through a narrow defile, then begins to descend, passing in between two long thin lakes. Finally there is a short steep descent to the village of Huayhuash. Camping is easy in the small settlement of Huayhuash.

6. 5-6 hours. The path continues in a southerly direction from Huayhuash, rising gently on the left hand side of the valley. There is a short steep climb to a pass of 4750m. From here the path descends to the west side of Laguna Viconga. Camping is possible at the north end of the lake, **5 hours**. Or continue along the western side of the lake shore to the dam. Where the path goes over a rise bear right (northwest) into the next valley and camp after a further **½hour** or so. There are hot springs nearby. To find them head down the main valley, crossing the main outflow river from Viconga safely and easily in the steep, narrow sided gap where the water disappears under a huge boulder. Go on for **20 minutes** towards a large circular white salt pan. The springs are situated on the western side of the main valley. Ask your arriero or a local to show you the way. Be careful of your belongings at the springs and do not leave your tent unattended.

From Laguna Viconga the town of Catajambo can be reached in about a day and a half, by descending 22km down the Rio Pumarinri valley, then crossing a low col of 4150m on the south side of the valley.

7. 5-6 hours. Continue up the left hand side of the valley from the camp until moraine is visible. The path deteriorates but continue up past big boulders, cutting right then left into a basin. The path now makes it way up to the pass of Punta Cuyoc in a north-westerly direction, passing a small lake on its left, to the top of the pass at nearly 4950 meters, **2½ hours** from the camp. The descent is very steep at first through boulder scree then more gentle following the left hand side of the valley and crossing over three lateral moraines. On the third moraine cross the river easily on stepping stones to the right side of the valley and continue down for **2 or 3 hours** on an easy flat path to various possible camp areas in the flat bottom of the Guanacpatay valley before it narrows and turns northwards.

8. 8-9 hours. Walk further down the Rio Guanacpatay valley on the right hand side of the river to where it narrows. The path levels and slightly rises as the river starts plunging below. Follow this easier path to descend to the Huayllapa valley. It is also possible to cross the river at this point and descend carefully on steep loose ground on the left hand side by a long waterfall. These paths converge on the valley floor and continue on the left hand side of the Rio Huayllapa to cross the river on a bridge before the village of Huayllapa at 3600m, **3-4 hours**. Basic supplies and accommodation can be found here. It is also possible to reach Cajatambo from here in about two days.

To continue the circuit trek head back out of the village for **10 minutes** the way you came in. Cross the bridge over the side stream and rise steeply to the level again. Go through the broken wall beside the path. The path heads up into a narrow gorge and steadily rises for **2 hours,** crossing the river once. The gradient

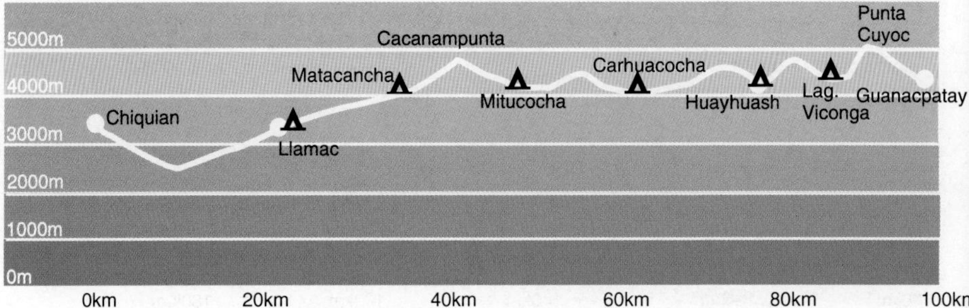

decreases and after crossing a side stream it is possible to camp. It is another **2 hours** of steady uphill northwards to two dry lakes, then **1 hour** of easier gradient to the top of the pass of Punta Tapush, 4750m. Camping is possible just over the far side of this pass by the Laguna Susococha at 4750m. Or you can continue lower to the wide valley floor where there is a corral to camp in known locally as Gasapampa.

From either of these campsites it is possible to climb Suerococha, 5350m, see description below.

9. 4-5 hours. From the Gasapampa camp contour around the right hand side of the valley into the next valley to the east. The path goes gently down through queñoa trees to the river Angocancha. Once across the river it is possible to camp.

The path now crosses a col to the east. You can see in the valley on your right an orange coloured stream. Rise up between the first rocky bands on a grassy slope. Follow this slope to the end and up scree or alternatively rise up through the rock to the next grassy ledge with a small lake. The scree path now slants up on the left hand side to the pass (Yaucha, 4800m). From the pass the path descends through pasture and turns northward keeping on the left hand side of the valley as it opens into the spectacular main valley of Laguna Jahuacocha. The path goes left and zigzags steeply down to the valley floor. Walk east to camp at the busy area on the west end of the lake. A day can easily be spent strolling around the two large lakes in the valley here, with great views of Yerupaja and Jirishanca.

10. 6 hours. To return to Llamac from Jahuacocha head down the valley past the small settlement of Jahuacocha to where the valley narrows after **1 hour**. The path splits at a small area of white scree. Cross over the aqueduct and follow the rough path on the right over this scree. The path improves and now rises to contour at a higher level through trees and crossing gullies until you reach the open shoulder marked with a cairn. Take in your last spectacular views of the mountains as you then head down to Llamac from here. The path, a little vague, heads down passing a small vegetated rise on its right and then more steeply descends into Llamac below. An alternative longer but less steep route to Llamac would be to follow the aqueduct (dry and unused) around the hillside.

11. 6-7 hours. Repeat the first long day in reverse (but now a wee bit more acclimatised!) to return to Chiquian.

CHIQUIAN TO CAJATAMBO TREK

To trek from Chiquian to Catajambo follow days 1 to 6 as described to Laguna Viconga then walk out in two days down the Rio Pumarinri to Cajatambo.

CIRCUIT TREK FROM CAJATAMBO

To start and finish the trek in Cajatambo the following itinerary is suggested.

Day 1. Cajatambo to Uramaza. Cross the pass of 4150m to the north of Cajatambo and descend into the Rio Pumarinri. Follow the valley northeast and downstream to the settlement of Uramaza, on a high plateau above the confluence of the Pumarinri and Huayllapa villages.

Day 2. Uramaza to Gasapampa. Follow the right hand side of the valley to the village of Huayllapa then day 8 above.

Day 3. follow day 9 above to Jahuacocha.

Day 4. From Jahuacocha walk along the north shore of the lake and then start to rise above the north shore of Solteracocha. The path climbs steeply over the Sambunya pass at 4750m with magnificent views, to reach the Quebrada Rondoy.

Days 5. to 8. follow days 3 to 6 as described above.

Days 9. and 10. Walk out from Viconga down the Rio Pumarinri in two days.

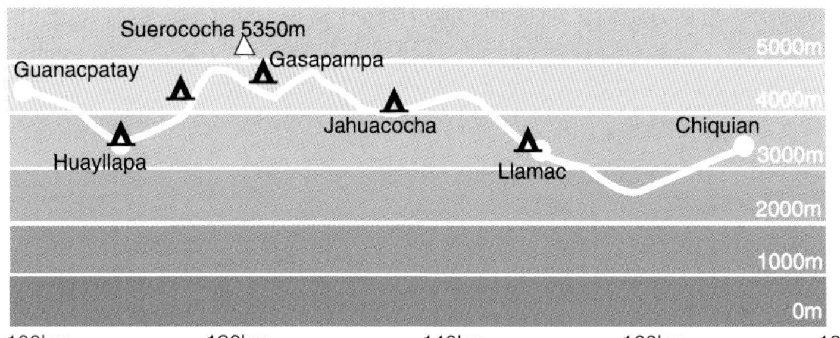

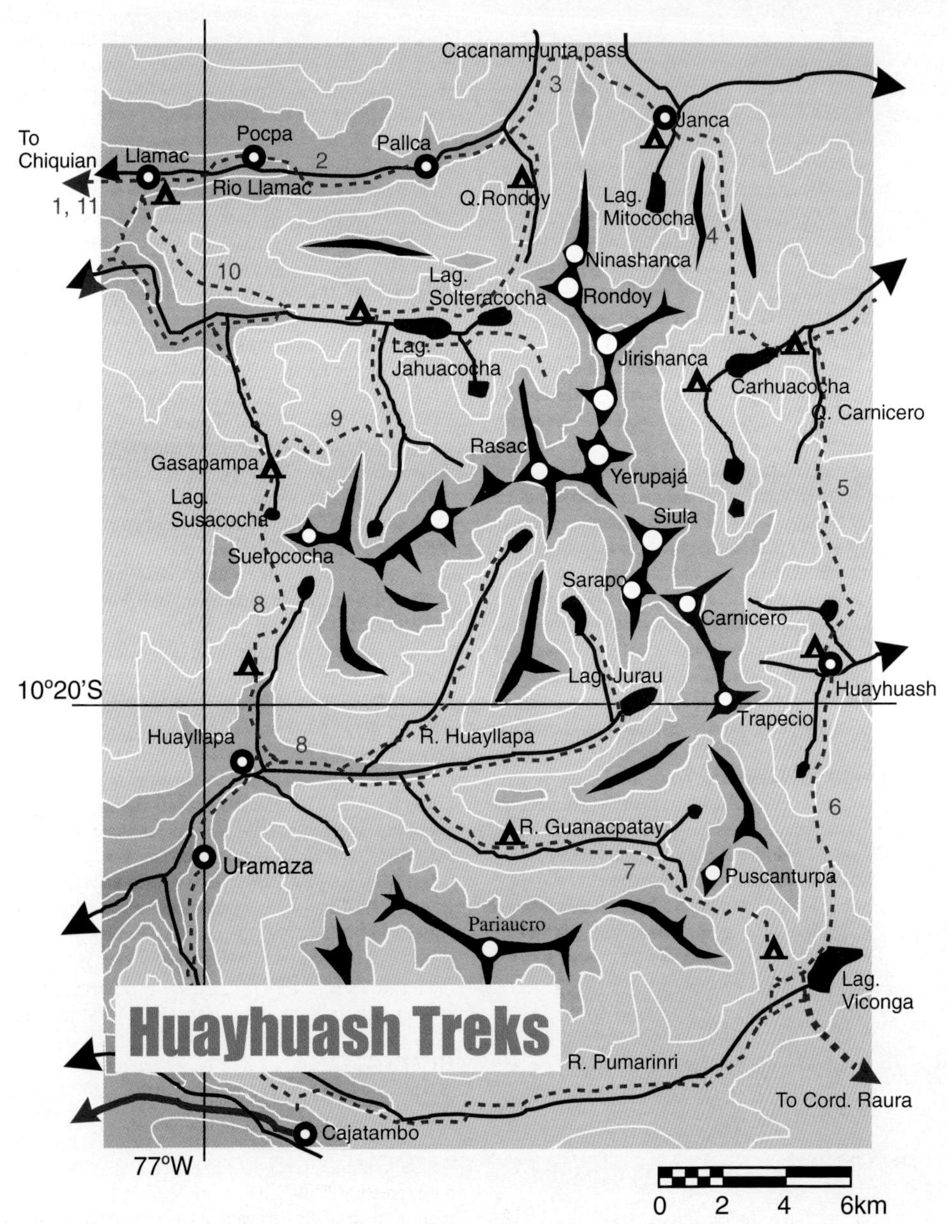
Cacanampunta pass
3
Janca
To
Chiquian
1, 11
Llamac
Pocpa
2
Pallca
Rio Llamac
Q.Rondoy
Lag.
Mitococha
4
Ninashanca
Rondoy
10
Lag.
Solteracocha
Lag.
Jahuacocha
Jirishanca
Carhuacocha
Q. Carnicero
9
Rasac
Gasapampa
Yerupajá
5
Lag.
Susacocha
Siula
Suerococha
Sarapo
Carnicero
8
Lag. Jurau
Huayhuash
10°20'S
Trapecio
Huayllapa
8
R. Huayllapa
6
R. Guanacpatay
Uramaza
7
Puscanturpa
Pariaucro
Lag.
Viconga
Huayhuash Treks
R. Pumarinri
To Cord. Raura
Cajatambo
77°W
0 2 4 6km

Climbing Suerococha

ASCENT OF SUEROCOCHA

Perhaps the easiest snow peak to climb in the Huayhuash is the 5350m mountain known as Suerococha. Also known as Diable Mudo the peak is a good viewpoint and is often climbed as part of the Huayhuash circuit. An ice-axe, rope and crampons will be needed to make the ascent safely.

CLIMB

From the Gasapampa or Laguna Susocochaa camp go up the valley passing the left hand side of Lag. Susococha. Climb onto the glacier tongue and follow an easy ramp line left to a couple of rock outcrops above the shoulder in the northwest ridge. Before reaching these outcrops traverse up and right (steeper) to a shallow col, then follow the ridge to the summit. In descent the lower slopes of the glacier can be avoided by following the northwest ridge over the rock outcrops (II).

The Cordillera Central

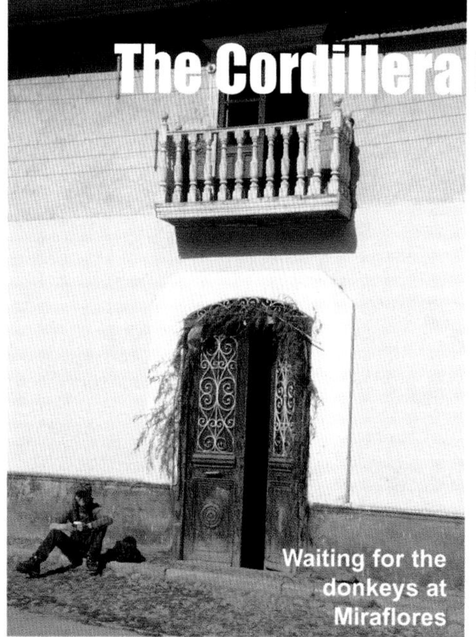
Waiting for the donkeys at Miraflores

THE CORDILLERA CENTRAL

This range of mountains lie directly inland from Lima and offer many interesting treks and walks though they have very rarely been explored by westerners. The scenery is very beautiful, with numerous small lakes and high pastures. There are far fewer trekkers and the weather is also noticeably better than it is in the Cordillera Blanca or Cordillera Huayhuash. A circuit of the highest peak, Ticlla, is described here, starting and finishing in the wee village of Miraflores.

HUANCAYO

Huancayo is a big inland city in the fertile Mantaro valley. This city, which is well and truly off the tourist trail, makes a good base for treks in the Cordillera Central and the nearby Cordillera Huaytapallana. It is an interesting 8 hour bus journey from Lima via the mining town of La Oroya and over the 4800m Ticlio pass. See page 181 for further details.

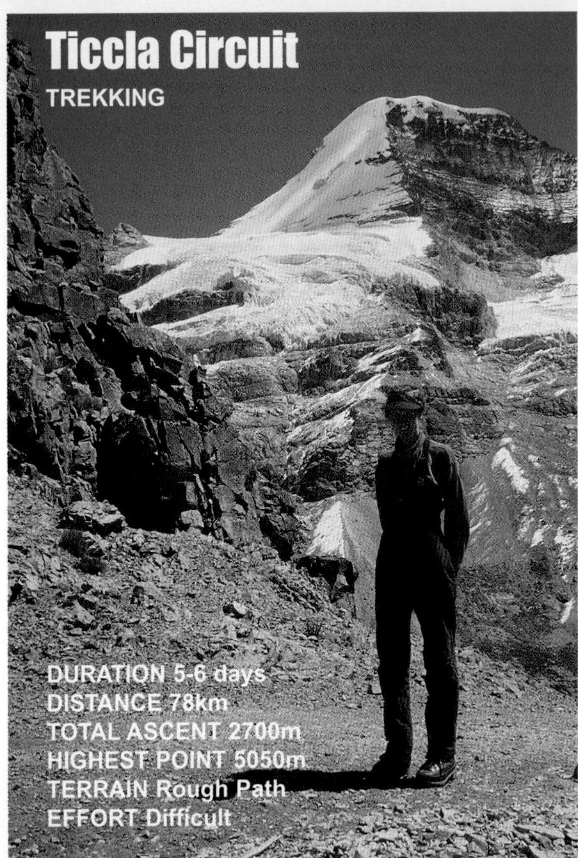

Ticcla Circuit
TREKKING
DURATION 5-6 days
DISTANCE 78km
TOTAL ASCENT 2700m
HIGHEST POINT 5050m
TERRAIN Rough Path
EFFORT Difficult

THE TICLLA CIRCUIT

The Cordillera Central offer some excellent trekking and the focus of the range is this circuit trek around the highest peak, Ticlla 5897m. There are some exceptionally beautiful high altitude lagoons, interesting wildlife and very friendly local people. The range is much, much quieter than the popular treks in the Cordillera Blanca and Huayhuash to the north, and the weather is better too. The dry season runs from May to September.

The easiest place to start this trek is from the village of Miraflores to the southeast, but a similar itinerary could also be followed from Ayaviri to the west or Tanta to the north west. A brief description is also given of a longer variation to the basic circuit. Being a circular trek it would be quite feasible to do this walk in reverse.

ACCESS

There are two main ways of approaching Miraflores. These are either from the inland city of Huancayo or from the coast at Cañete.

Approaching from Huancayo has a big advantage for acclimatisation because of the altitude of this city. From Huancayo travel via Angasmayo and San Jose de Quero to reach Miraflores; there was reported to be a bus on Sundays only, otherwise you will have to arrange private transport - it's a 5 hour drive on a reasonable road. From Cañete travel via the town of Yauyos, from where you may need to hire a private vehicle.

MIRAFLORES

The village of Miraflores is a friendly wee place at an altitude of 3650m. There are only a few very small and basic shops. Accommodation, donkeys and any other basic tourist facilities can usually be found here. For all of these try asking at the mayor's office on the southwest corner of the square or just sit and wait in the square and ask the locals who come past.

MAPS TO USE

Peruvian IGM sheets 25-k 'Huarochiri' and 25-l 'Yauyos' at 1:100,000

THE ROUTE

1. 6 hours. From Miraflores walk up lanes in the Quebrada Tomapampa valley which leads west to a high pass of 4750m. There are lots of nice flowers and cacti in this valley. It is possible to camp in high pastures at Ancacucho just before the pass, **3-4 hours**. There are good views of the dramatic southeast face of Ticlla from near here. From Ancacucho climb over the pass and descend to the long Laguna Huasacocha (4250m) under the south slopes of Ticlla. There are good campsites at the near (northeast) end of this scenic lake, **2 hours**.

2. 4 hours Walk down the south side of the lake to the far end. Then cross the outflow stream and begin gradually ascending the hillside on the north side of the valley. This leads into the Quebrada Suero and a short walk up this valley to the scenic Laguna Suerococha, where camping is possible, **3-4 hours**.

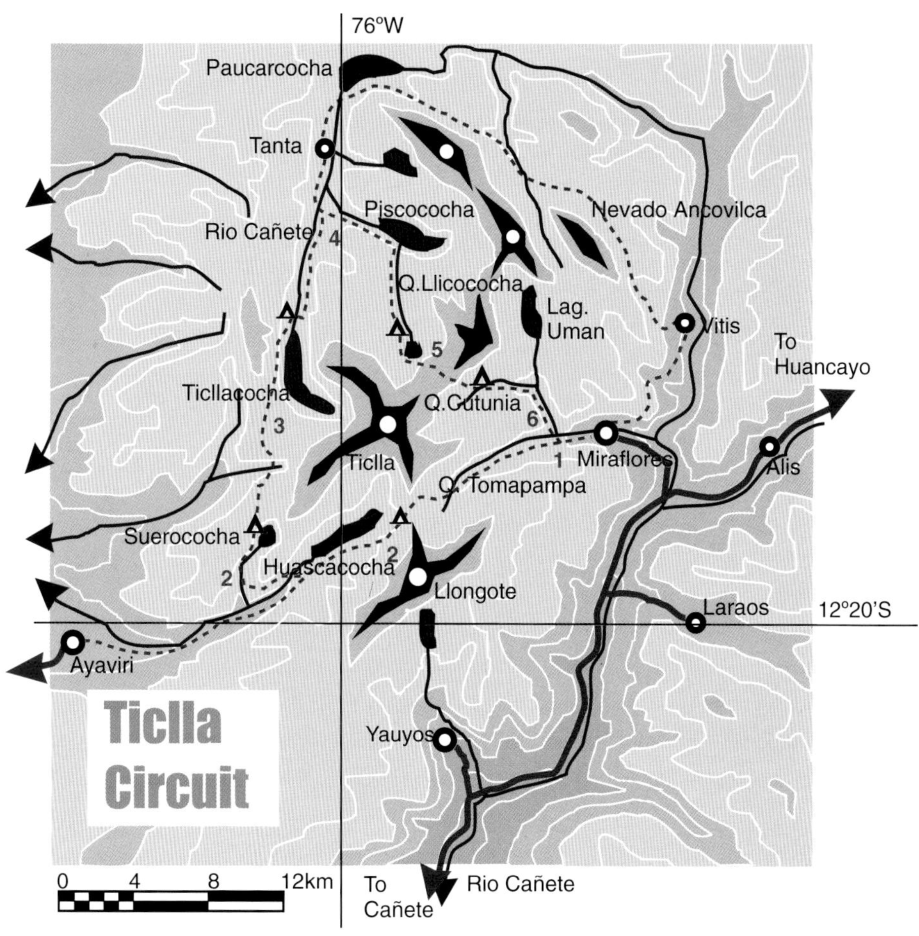

3. 4 hours From Laguna Suerococha climb grassy slopes to the northwest and a pass at 4800m. Go down the valley on the other side till it begins to steepen and then traverse right on animal tracks to the head of the Quebrada Pichahuacra. **2 hours**. Climb a steep side valley to the north and a pass of 4750m with views of the beautiful curving Laguna Ticllacocha. It is a steep descent to the north to reach campsites at the outflow stream of this lake, **2 hours**. A worthwhile side trip from here if you have time is to walk up to the end of the valley on the north side of the lakes to the spectacular mountain cirque under the northwest side of Ticlla

4. 3 hours Walk down the headwaters of the Rio Cañete to the north for about 7km (2 hours) until another wide valley joins form the right, turn into this valley and follow the stream up to Laguna Piscococha. There are nice campsites at several points on the south shores, **3 hours**. From the junction of the major valleys the small settlement of Tanta is just an hour to the north. It is possible to start or leave the trek here, though it might be difficult to arrange transport. (There is reported to be a once a week colectivo to Jauja) In Tanta you can also purchase some basic supplies, such as Inca Kola.

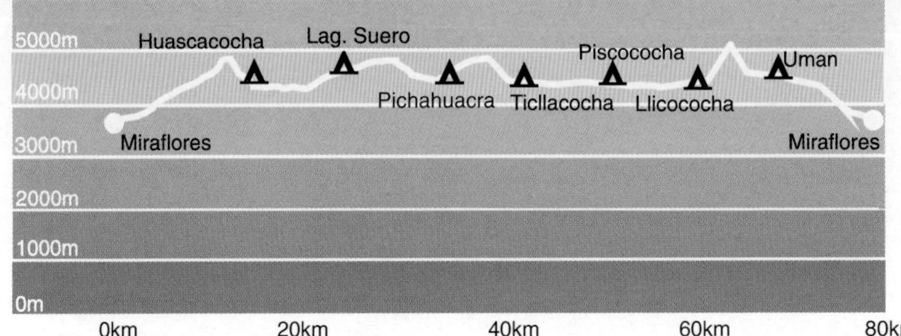

5. 5-6 hours From Piscococha walk up the swampy Quebrada Llicococha to the south, there is a good path on the right hand side, to the blue green waters of the scenic Laguna Llicococha, **2-3 hours**. Just beyond this lagoon the path climbs steeply up and over the highest pass of the circuit, at 5050m, then descends steeply to the Quebrada Cutunia at 4600m. **2-3 hours**.

6. 4-5 hours. Walk out down the Quebrada Cutunia passing the settlement of Uman at the valley junction. From here there is a worthwhile side trip to the impressive Lagunas Uman to the north, (2 hours return). Then descend the steep and narrow Q. Huayllacancha by a rocky path on the right hand (west) bank. You rejoin the original route out of Miraflores for the last hour. **4-5 hours** from Cutunia to Miraflores.

A LONGER ALTERNATIVE RETURN FROM TANTA TO MIRAFLORES

From the village of Tanta follow the Rio Cañete north for to Laguna Paucarcocha and climb southeast into a hanging valley. A track leads southeast from here crossing three high passes of up to 4800m and going round the north side of Nevado Ancovilca to reach the village of Vitis**, 3 days** from Tanta. From Vitis it will take another day through fields and pastures to return to Miraflores.

Campsite at Ancacucho

Southern Peru

Loading mules after a snowstorm, Ausangate circuit

INTRODUCTION

Southern Peru, particularly the area around Cuzco, offers an unbeatable combination of trekking and cultural experience in the Andes. The mountains are spectacular and there are world famous ruins in and around the city of Cuzco, including the legendary 'lost city' of Machu Picchu. The biggest and most spectacular mountains in southern Peru are the Cordillera Vilcanota which lie a few hundred kilometres southeast of Cuzco.

The long **Ausangate circuit** trek around the Cordillera Vilcanota is described, as well as the famous four day trek along the **Inca Trail to Machu Picchu** and the two day extension to this from Mollepata.

In southwest Peru the very different scenery of the **Colca Canyon** is the setting for a long trek. Also included is a description for the shorter circuit trek and ascent of **Misti** volcano.

GETTING THERE

The two base cities for these treks, Cuzco and Arequipa are both easiest to reach by flying to Lima, the capital of Peru then taking an internal flight. From Europe there are direct flights from Madrid (Iberia), Amsterdam (KLM) and Frankfurt (Lufthansa) to Lima. From the USA there are many direct flights from Miami to Lima and a few from LA and Houston, with either United, Delta, Continental or American.

From Lima several Peruvian carriers have services to Arequipa and Cuzco. In the last few years many of these have gone out of business to be replaced by new carriers.

It is also possible to go by bus from Lima to Cuzco but this is a very long (33 hours) and difficult journey. The bus journey to Arequipa takes over 16 hours along good roads.

For details of services in Lima see page 179.

CLIMATE AND WEATHER CONDITIONS

The trekking season in Southern Peru extends from April to September, with June and July reckoned to be the best months. Though this is the middle of winter, Peru is very near the equator so temperatures are not too much colder. More importantly this is the dry season in the mountains. The weather is generally quite stable with normally only one or two bad days in a week. Freezing level is about 4500-5000m during the day, but strong sun can make it feel much warmer than this in the valleys. Wind is rarely a problem in the mountains during the dry season. Bad weather comes from the Amazon side of the mountains to the east.

The Colca Canyon and Misti have a much drier climate and trekking is possible here all year round, but will still be best from about April to October.

Huayruro Punco, on the Ausangate circuit

Cuzco Street

CUZCO

The city of Cuzco sits in a high basin at 3310m on a plateau between the rivers Urubamba and Apurimac. For walkers the city makes an ideal base for acclimatisation. It is wise to spend a couple of days in Cuzco when you first arrive from sea level, getting used to the altitude - an ideal opportunity to explore some of South America's most spectacular tourist sites while acclimatising.

Cuzco (or Qosqo) was the ancient capital of the Inca Empire and in and around the city are many traces of the fabulous architecture they left behind. No-one should come to this part of South America without spending some of their time exploring the fascinating archaeology. Many ruins from the days before the Spanish conquest of Peru are still visible in the city and surrounding foothills. There are countless examples of the Incas incredible skill as stonemasons. Huge granite blocks fit so well that a knife blade cannot be inserted between them. The most famous ruins are those at Machu Picchu described in detail below. There are so many other ruins around Cuzco that no guide could list all those worth seeing but Sacsayhuaman, an incredible toothed fortress which sits on the hillside immediately north of Cuzco is probably the most spectacular. There are also good views of the Vilcanota mountains from here. In the city ruins worth visiting include the Temple of the Sun and the streets around Callejon Loreto and Calle Hatun Rumiyoc for their skilful stonework. There are also some beautiful buildings in the city built by the early Spanish colonists, such as the cathedral on the Plaza de Armas. Also worth visiting out of town are the ruins at Ollantaytambo and Pisac in the 'sacred' valley of the Rio Urubamba.

For further information on hotels and facilities in Cuzco see page 181.

Precise Inca Stonework

Sacsayhuaman

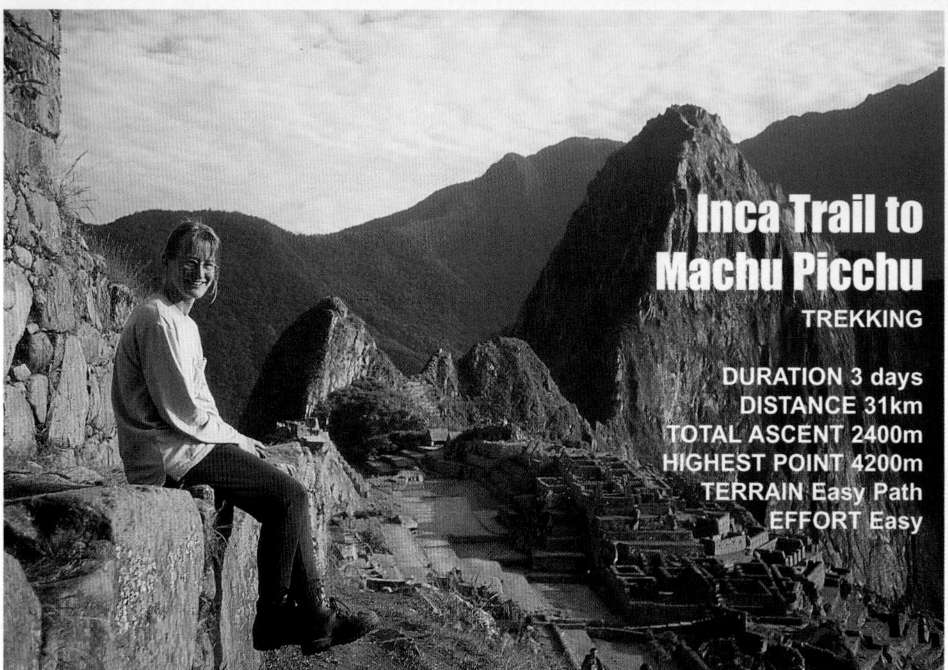

INCA TRAIL TO MACHU PICCHU

A few hours from Cuzco by train are the famous ruins of Machu Picchu, rediscovered by Hiram Bingham, an American explorer, early last century. He was looking for a fabled 'lost' Inca city in the deep valleys around Cuzco. Machu Picchu is the most famous ruin in South America and not without reason. It sits on a mountain ridge, high above the deep gorge of the Urubamba river and surrounded by dense forests. The ruins themselves are extensive with many houses, temples and fortifications.

The most spectacular way to arrive at Machu Picchu is undoubtedly the way the Incas designed the city to be approached. The classic Inca Trail to Machu Picchu described here is a three or four day walk along beautifully engineered Inca 'roads' crossing several high passes up to 4200m above sea level. The Inca 'roads' include long flights of steps, traverses above deep ravines and tunnels cut through solid rock. On the way to Machu Picchu the scenery becomes increasingly spectacular with views to Salcantay and other snow capped peaks. You also pass many smaller ruins from the time of the Incas, some still half hidden in the thick forest and all worth exploring. On the very last day you get your first view of Machu Picchu from the pass known as Intipuncu - the Gateway of the Sun. It is well worth buying the book 'Exploring Cusco' by Peter Frost if you are going to hike the Inca trail and are interested in the archaeology. It has excellent information about the ruins you'll see along the way. You are not permitted to walk the Inca Trail in reverse.

ACCESS

There is a fee of about $15 to do the Inca Trail, which includes your entrance to Machu Picchu, though this is likely to go up to $50 in 2001. You can hike it yourself with a lightweight backpack or go on an organised tour with porters to carry your belongings, easily arranged in Cuzco. To get to the start of the trail at a station known simply as km88 you need to take the train from Cuzco. This is the same train that runs to the Machu Picchu ruins themselves and is an entertaining journey with several switchbacks and great views of the Urubamba river and mountains. The journey to km88 from Cuzco takes about three hours. You can't go by road to km88, but you can reach as far as km82 by road.

The ruins of Huiñay Huayna

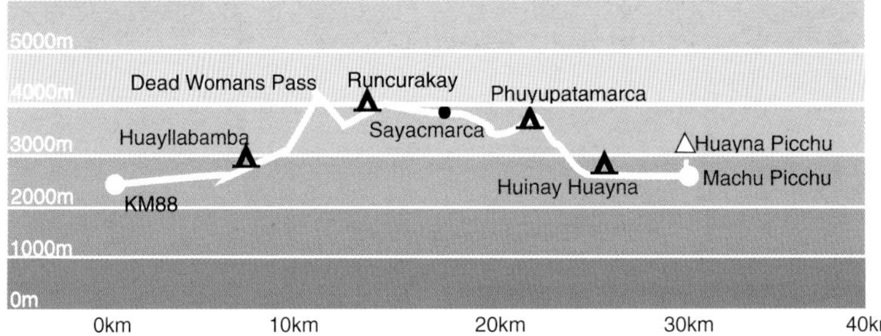

MAP TO USE

The Inca trail sketch map available in Cusco is all that is needed as the path is very obvious. For the extension Peruvian IGM sheets 27-q, 'Machu Picchu' and 27-r 'Urubamba' 1:100 000 are useful.

THE ROUTE

1. 4-5 hours. There are two common starts to the Inca Trail which meet up at the first ruins of Patallacta. The shorter start from km88 is described first.

A. From the railway station at km 88 a path cuts down to the Rio Urubamba and a bridge. Just before the bridge is a little booth marking the entrance to the park where you will have to pay your entry fee (and the fees for your porters too). Across the bridge the trail cuts sharply left and follows the river bank on a good path through eucalyptus trees to the first ruins of Patallacta, possible to camp here, **½ hour**.

B. From the station at km 82 the path descends to the river where you pay. Cross and follow the good path downstream for **1½ hours.** After crossing a small gully and rounding a bluff you will soon see the first ruins of Patallacta.

Both **A.** and **B.** From Patallacta the path then turns up the side valley by the ruins. Follow the clear trail on the left hand side. After about one hour cross the river on a bridge. It is possible to buy cold drinks on this section of the trail from various houses. **2 hours** after

Patallacta you reach the small village of Huayllabamba. There is a signpost indicating the start of the route ascending the valley on the right. The path climbs and soon the first camping area, on grassy terraces on the right, is reached. The next camping is **1 hours** up where the path crosses the stream again at an area known as the "Forks". This camp area is very messy and has unhygienic water supplies. If time permits it is better to walk on a further 2 hours to Llulluchayoc.

2. 6 hours. From the Forks the path crosses the stream and cuts round to the valley on the right, then rises for **2 hours** to reach the pleasant camping area at Llulluchayoc. This is the last camping until after the first pass. Another **1½ hours** of steady uphill on an obvious trail will get you to the "Dead Womans Pass", Huarmi Huañuska, at 4200 meters. Ahead you can see the next camping area in the valley floor and the rise up to the next ruins on the other side of the valley. The steep descent on a modern paved section of path takes **1 hour** to reach the camping at the Rio Pacaymayo. Continue up the other side of the valley for **1 hour** to reach the ruins of Runcurakay, with its distinctive round building. It is possible to camp either here or **20 minutes** further up in an area with two stagnant looking lakes either side of the path.

3. 4-5 hours. From the small lakes it is a steep **½ hour** to the second pass at 4000 meters. This pass, sometimes known as Abra de Runcurakay, has views ahead towards the snow clad Pumasillo group of mountains. Descend on what is now some of the original Inca Highway to the next ruins of Sayacmarca, reached after **1 hour**. These ruins are very near the main trail and well worth a visit - follow the short steep steps which rise leftwards on a bend off the main trail. Continuing on the main trail descend for a short way, passing through another camping area and small ruin before the long gentle rise to the last "pass". This section has great views ahead to Pumasillo and leftwards to the giant Salcantay (6264m) so is worth doing early in the morning before clouds obscure the views. The trail is on some fine Inca pathway and also goes through a small Inca tunnel. From the last pass, which is just a broad saddle in the ridge, there are some great views of the Urubamba valley. There is camping here and the ruins of Phuyupatamarca are just 100 meters below, **2 hours**. The path continues through the ruins and down a long set of Inca steps. If it is clear you will see the path heading towards the electricity pylon line and down to the red roofs of the last camping area. You may also see the ruins of Huiñay Huayna below. This section is a long downhill, with nearly 1,000 steps, and takes **1 hour**. The camping terraces and restaurant at Huiñay Huayna are busy and the crowds can be unpleasant. There is no choice but to camp here if you want to arrive at Machu Picchu early in the day.

The ruins of Huiñay Huayna are well worth a visit and are reached in 10 minutes along a nearly level sign posted path from behind the restaurant.

4. 1½ hours. The path to Machu Picchu begins down at the bottom and far left (looking down) of the camp area. Within 10 minutes of leaving the restaurant building you pass through the entrance gate. This is locked overnight and opens at 5 am. It is worth leaving as early as possible to get to Machu Picchu before the day visitors arrive from Cuzco at mid morning.

The path traverses the hillside through rain forest vegetation, rises up a first steep set of steps and continues on to the second steps and the Gateway of the Sun, Intipuncu. From here you'll see the first views of Machu Picchu. If you are lucky you will be here at sunrise on a clear day and have a magnificent view of the ruins. Follow the path down into the ruins and down to the entrance gate. You will need to show your Inca trail pass to enter the ruins without paying again. There is a left luggage, restaurant and cafe facilities at the entrance.

MACHU PICCHU

Set on a spectacular neck of rock almost 1000m above the deep gorge of the Urubamba river, Machu Picchu is a sight that should not be missed. You get a great view of the ruins and can escape some of the crowds by ascending the steep peak which forms the classic backdrop to Machu Picchu. **Huayna Picchu, 2660m.** There is an easily followed path to the top, but several steep staircases almost merit a rock climbing grade. The path round the left hand side of Huayna Picchu to the Temple of the Moon is an even more spectacular walk, but there is less to see and you are left with a long uphill walk back to the main ruins.

INCA TRAIL EXTENSION

It is common to walk this two or three day extension from Mollepata to join the Inca Trail (as described above) at Huayllabamba. There is some spectacular mountain scenery as the trail passes right under the magnificent peak of Salcantay. The extra distance is approximately 42 km, with about 2000m of extra height gain.

ACCESS
From Cuzco it is a 3 hour bus journey to the village of Mollepata at 2800m. Buy your supplies in Cuzco although basic supplies can be bought in this pleasant village. If mules are going to be used for the first section an overnight stay in the village may be required to arrange this.

MAPS TO USE
Peruvian IGM sheets 27-q, 'Machu Picchu' and 27-r 'Urubamba' 1:100 000.

THE ROUTE
1. 6-7 hours From the top of the Mollepata village find the trail heading up the left hand side of the river following an irrigation channel towards a ridge crest. Ask locals for the start of the trail. Go up the ridge crest to the right, still rising steeply, then slant down and across the valley to the northeast. The trail becomes a bit vague here but traverses for about **40 minutes** to join the main path in the Rio Blanco valley. Follow this trail up the valley with views ahead of the glaciated mountain peak, Humantay 5910m (labelled Tucarhuay on the IGM map). Continue up the valley as the gradient eases to Soray near an obvious fork in the valley, with magnificent views of the huge south face of Salcantay. Camping is possible at Soraypampa just after a big wash out area, or continue further up the valley towards Salcantay to camp.

2. 6-7 hours. Continue up the valley northeast towards the south face of Salcantay for **2-3 hours**. From here the path begins the long climb to the Incachillasca pass. Start up the right hand side of a large moraine then continue upwards following faint paths and cairns over a number of meadows and some short steeper sections until the final zigzagging climb over screes to the pass at 4800m, reached after **2 hours**. There are excellent views from here. It is another **1½ hours** down steeply on the right hand side of the valley to a pleasant camp on grass by the stream.

3. 5-6 hours. Continue down the valley on obvious trails for **3-4 hours** to a big river junction (Rio Quesja or Quesea). The Inca ruins of Paucarcancha are up on the right.

To join the Inca Trail cross to the left hand side of the river here and walk downstream for a further **½hour** to Huayllabamba where the mules will have to stop. It is possible to hire a porter here for the Inca Trail proper. You will see the sign post and path for the standard Inca trail leading up the valley on the left. The first campsites are at the forks about **1hour** up this valley.

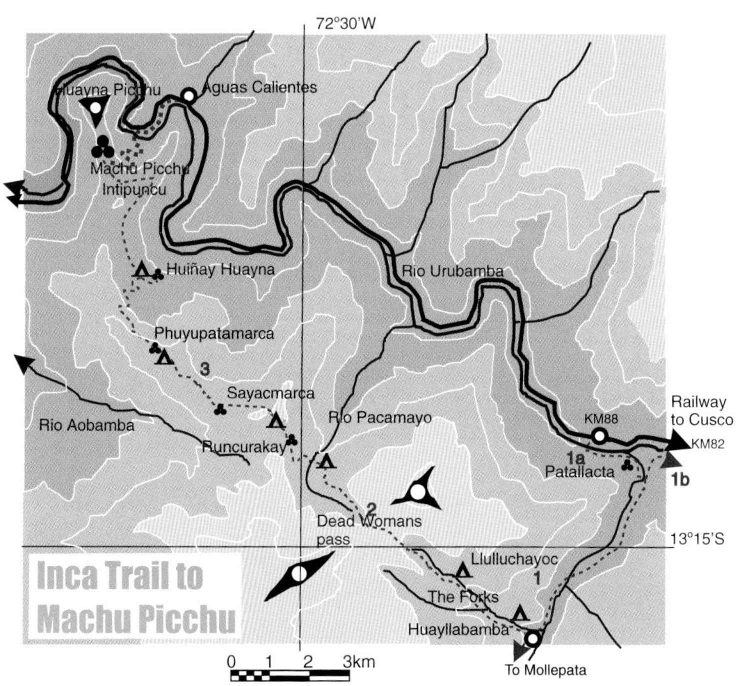

Ausangate Circuit
TREKKING
DURATION 5 days
DISTANCE 80km
TOTAL ASCENT 2500m
HIGHEST POINT 5050m
TERRAIN Easy Path
EFFORT Moderate

AUSANGATE CIRCUIT

One of the best high mountain treks in Southern Peru is the circuit trek of Ausangate in the Cordillera Vilcanota. The Cordillera Vilcanota are a large mountain range south east of Cuzco. They are some of the most rugged and most remote mountains in Peru. The range contains several peaks over 6000m and the highest of these is Ausangate, 6372m. You get spectacular views of many of these peaks from different sides if you do the circuit trek round Ausangate.

This is a relatively hard and wild trek, the highest regularly done in the Andes, with many camps above 4600m and two passes of over 5100m. There are some idyllic campsites in the valleys, several beside natural hot springs. Most of these valleys are still used as pastures by the Quechua speaking Indians and this is the best place in Peru to see llamas and alpacas grazing. It is also a good area to see some of the exotic wildlife of the Andes including vicuñas, vizcachas, humming birds and the wonderful condor. The basic trek takes from five to seven days but if you have time there are numerous longer possibilities in the very remote southern section of the Vilcanota mountains.

This trek can easily be done in reverse.

ACCESS

The normal start and finish of the trek is in the small village of Tinqui (see page 181) on the northern edge of the Vilcanota mountains at 3800m. Horses can be arranged here and there are two very basic bunkhouses and now a new cafe serving great chips. Mules or horses are easy to arrange in Tinqui within one day, just ask at the two hostals.

Tinqui is a long and gruelling 8 hour bus journey from Cuzco via Urcos. This is made even worse because there is no bus - you have to stand or squat in the back of a truck! This is one journey that it might be worth hiring private transport for, a private minibus will take 5 hours drive from Cuzco and cost about $200. Ask in the Cuzco agencies for someone who knows the road.

MAP TO USE

Peruvian IGM sheet 28-t 'Ocongate' at 1:100, 000

THE ROUTE

1. 5 hours. In Tinqui take a road on the right just east of the large plaza, go down and across a bridge and follow this track through houses. Continue on the track for 200-300m, with another river on your right. Cross this at the bridge and follow the track gently upwards until you reach the first tiny downhill section to a wee stream crossing on a sharp corner. Rise up 20 metres then take the path off left. Continue in a southeast direction along a path. From here there are several paths, all leading towards Upis, which is reached after **5 hours** of gradual uphill walking. Camping is possible on the valley floor at 4400m about 1 km beyond Upis near the hot springs. The hot springs are quite small but a concrete tub has been built. Please take care to leave them in a clean state for those who will follow.

2. 5-6 hours. From the camp at the springs make your way up the valley and find somewhere to cross the main stream. Then follow the path on the west side of the valley. Continue over rocky terrain, rising up through a boggy grassy area, then pass a solitary house and corral to its right. An orange coloured hill is seen. The path to the pass rises up behind this hill. The pass is marked with a cairn, reached after **2½ hours**. From here a more distinct path traverses high on the left hand side of the valley to reach a knoll with views round into the next valley to the southeast. From the knoll follow the path down, gently at first then more steeply to a flat area with signs of camping. Then rise gently to meet the outflow of the first big lake, Laguna Uchuy Pucacocha. Cross the outlet stream then rise up and around a large rocky bluff on the south side of the lake, losing sight of the lake. When the lake comes back into view the path descends to a grassy open area with a house. Cross this area and rise again on the far side to the right of the large rocky hill. Still walking southeast you come out from behind the hill and get a view of Laguna Jatun Pucacocha and the camping flats at the south end of this lake in a wide open valley. The camping area is reached in around **2 ½ hours** from the pass. There are dramatic views of the ice-fall at the west end of Ausangate mountain from here.

3. 5 hours. From the camp at Pucacocha continue up the valley on the south side. After about **1½ hours** of steady uphill the first pass, of 4850m is reached. From here you can see the beautiful Laguna Auzangatecocha below and the next 5000 meter pass ahead of you. The path descends steeply to the valley floor and the moraine at the outflow of this laguna, **20 minutes.** It is possible to camp here on a flat grassy area. To continue follow the trail on the east side of the lateral moraine up a small grassy gully northeast until after **15 minutes** you reach a spur in front of you with a trail rising steeply up it. Follow this path, cross one flat grass area then continue rising around the right hand side of a rocky outcrop to the next dusty flat area. The last section to the pass is now in view as a rising traverse on scree from right to left to the top, which is a little over 5000 meters, **1½ hours**. Take time to enjoy the well earned views of Ausangate and the mountains to the southwest. Following the descent path for the

Campa Pass

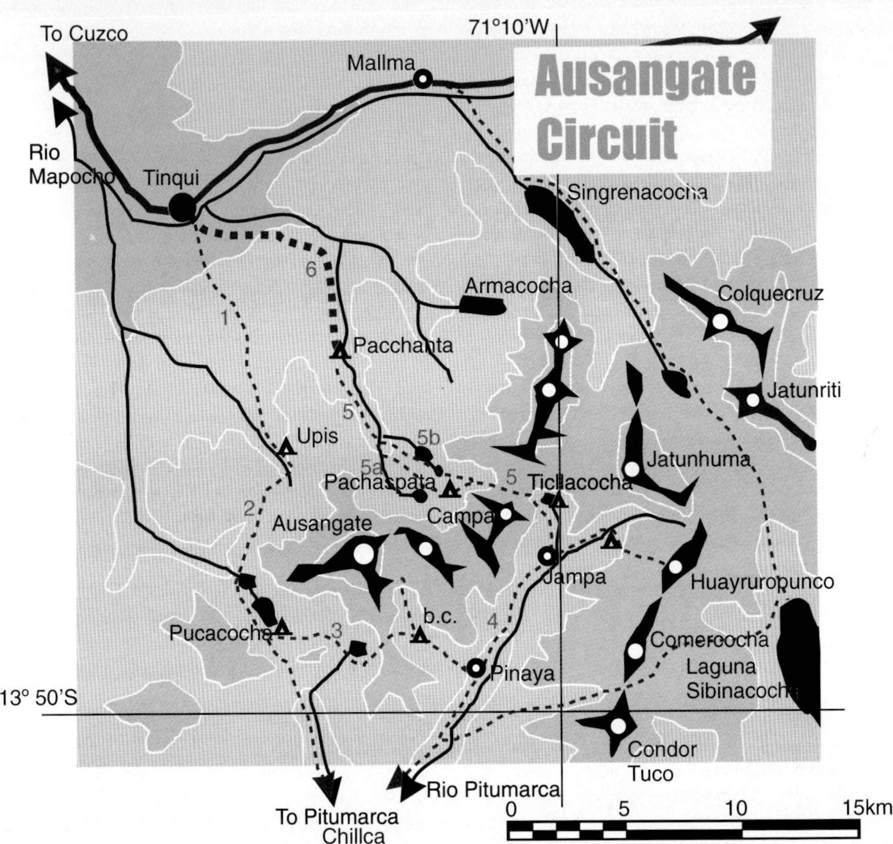

first **10 minutes** you can choose a gentle descent on the path to the valley floor or to descend more steeply straight down to the top of the valley. At the top of the valley you can camp by the glacier moraine beside a stream on a tiny grassy meadow. Known as Ausangate base camp this is where climbers leave to climb this challenging 6372m peak. From here there is also a short side walk to a small lake above the camp and at the foot of the glacier to the northwest, **½ hour.**

Otherwise continue down the valley to the southeast following the stream. The small rodents known as viscachas are commonly seen amongst the boulders here. You can camp at any point along the flat valley floor.

4. 5 hours. Continue down this side valley on the right hand side of the stream to join the main valley of the Pitumarca river at Finaya (Pinaya). Turn left, northeast, and staying on the left side of the valley floor walk through the settlement and gently rise to avoid the very boggy valley floor. The valley then narrows and you ascend more steeply beside the river, which is tumbling down in a small gully below. Once up this rise the valley again widens and the path continues on the wide flat valley floor to the settlement of Jampa, **3-4 hours** from Ausangate base camp. If you want to do the side-trip to climb Huayruro Punco rise up into the valley northeast of Jampa to a camp in the area known as Yanamayo, almost at the head of this valley, **1 hour** or more from Jampa.

The main circuit continues up the main valley. It is possible to camp in various places from 1/2 **hour** beyond Jampa to the small lagoon at the very head of the valley **1 1/2 hours** away.

5. 7 hours. As you get higher stay on the left side of the valley, which turns through northwards to westwards the path begins a rising traverse on grassy slopes followed by red screes. There are views down onto the glacier below which actually fills the lowest point of the pass. The top of the path, known as Campa pass, 5050m, is marked by a multitude of small cairns left to ward away evil spirits. It is about **3 hours** walk from Jampa Ahead the distinct path traverses high on the south slopes of the pass, crossing one steep patch of loose scree and then gently descends down through the lateral moraine boulders to the first grass meadow, **1 hour**. From here for the next 5km or so there are two possible routes, around either side of a long rocky hill.

a. Before you walk down to the flat grass area take the path on the level towards the east and descend into the valley to a spring at an area known by the locals as Pachaspata. It is possible to camp here and this is the best place to camp if you want to climb Campa. To carry on the trek follow the valley down to reach Pacchanta in another **3 hours.**

b. Alternatively continue down the northern valley passing the three large lakes (Uturungococha, Caycocha and Comercocha) on the left hand side. There are great views back to the mountains from these lakes. Turn east past the houses at Quecmojo and continue down to join the larger Pacchanta valley and follow this to Pacchanta village, **3 hours**.

Camping at Pacchanta is on the flat grassy area the other side of the river from the village. There are two hot spring sites. Very basic supplies are available. Watch your belongings at this camp.

6. 3 hours. From the camp at Pacchanta follow the road leading northwest over a rise and then down across open ground through a scattering of houses to Tinqui.

There are two mountains that can be easily climbed on your way around the Vilcanota circuit for even better views of the mountain range.

ASCENT OF HUAYRURO PUNCO, 5550m

4-6 hours return. There are excellent views of the huge Laguna Sibinacocha and the remote southern Cordillera Vilcanota from this easily climbed peak. Camping in the valley floor at Yanamayo (near the base of Pampa Puta Puta) climb straight up the steep grassy slopes to the southeast to a flat boggy area from where Huayruro Punco's glaciated summit can be seen. Ascend by the north or northeast ridge. A path also follows a rising traverse up the scree slopes between these two ridges. The actual summit is free from glaciation. In normal years this peak is climbed easily on rock and scree and an ice-axe and crampons are not required.

ASCENT OF CAMPA, 5500m

4-6 hours return. From the camp at Pachaspata make an early start back up the path toward the Campa pass. Just short of the pass summit you will see the glacier tongue from Campa's northeast slopes up on your right. Head up through the loose moraine and onto this glacier tongue. Climb the easy snow slopes above to the summit, which is the left hand of the two high points. An ice-axe, crampons and rope are essential to travel on this glacier, though there is no difficult climbing.

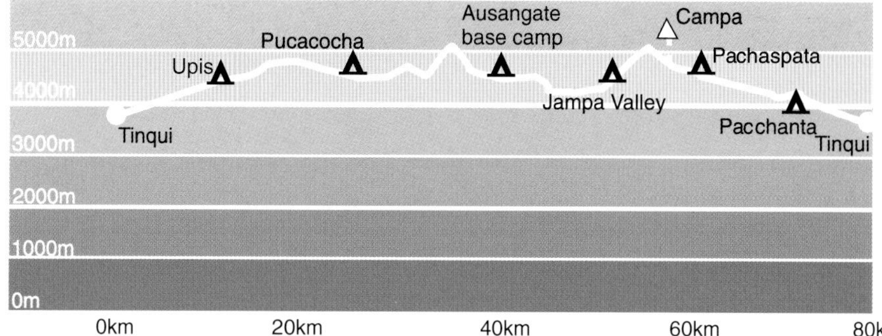

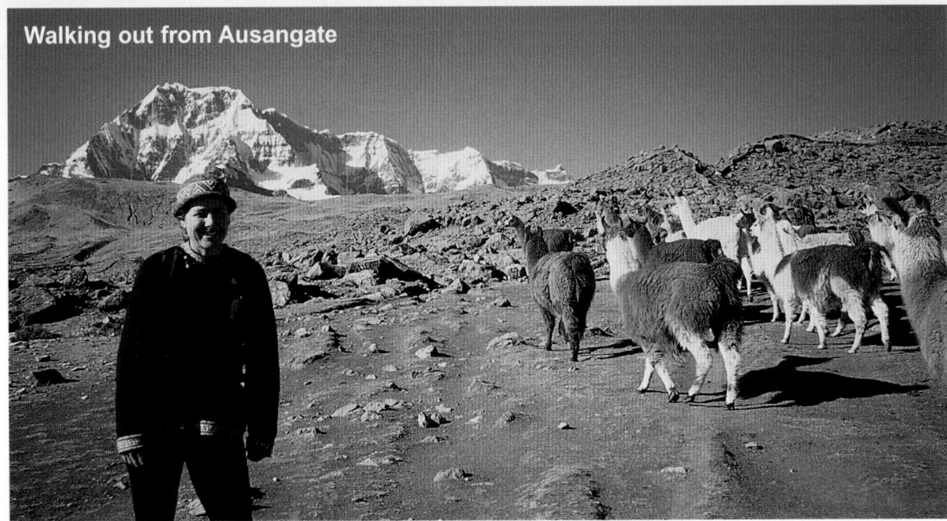
Walking out from Ausangate

The Cordillera Occidental

The impressive Colca Canyon

THE CORDILLERA OCCIDENTAL

In south west Peru the volcanic Cordillera Occidental rise around the city of Arequipa and are notable for easy ascents including the volcanoes El Misti and Chachani. Also near the city are a number of huge canyons, including Cotahuasi and the spectacular Colca canyon, famous as the worlds deepest canyon. This part of Peru is very dry, (indeed it has not rained in Arequipa for many years) so trekking and walking is possible all year.

The canyon is well worth seeing even if you are not trekking here - the drive from Arequipa to Chivay is a beautiful drive reaching heights of 4800m and the canyon is one of the best places in the Andes to see condors. The canyon can also be descended in raft or kayak but this is a serious trip which needs to be well researched. There are organised tours from Arequipa to visit this vast canyon and see the highlights.

AREQUIPA

Arequipa is a pleasant and relatively prosperous city in southern Peru. It sits in an oasis at 2325m at the foot of the volcano El Misti. There is a particularly beautiful Plaza de Armas, with the snow-capped peak of El Misti forming a stunning backdrop. For travel information on Arequipa see page 181.

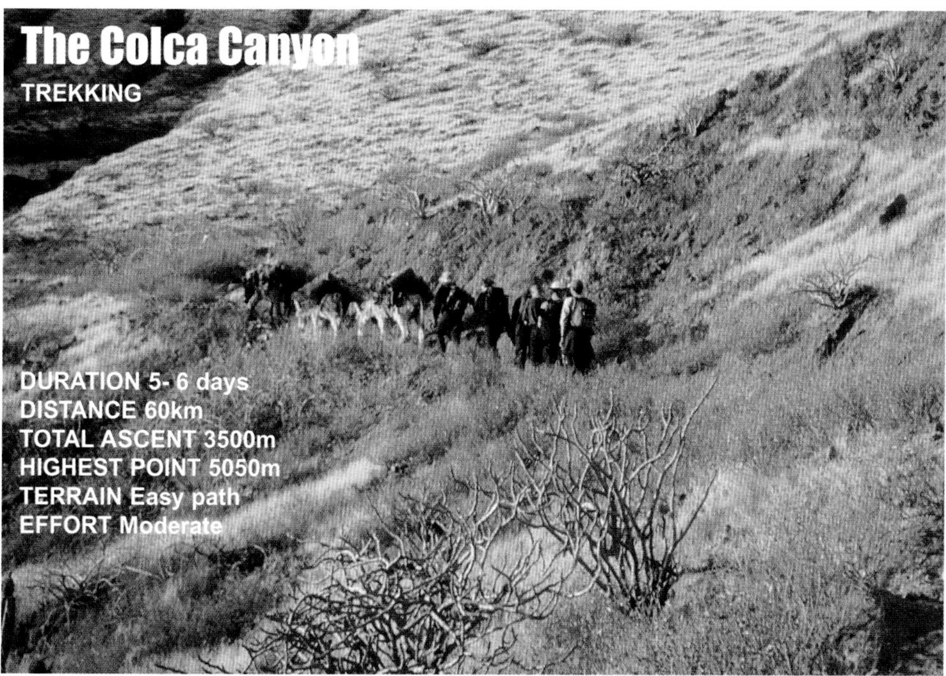

COLCA CANYON TREK

The most sensational walk in the area is undoubtedly this trek through the Colca Canyon. The canyon is the deepest canyon in the world. Just west of Choco the canyon drops from 5100m to 1500m in just 8km, then rises again to 4200m in another 8km. It is both narrower and much deeper than the Grand Canyon in Arizona.

The standard trek from Cabanaconde to Andahua is described below. It should not to be underestimated as it has large altitude losses and gains. It is extremely important to carry lots of water during the day, up to 4 litres, as the area is particularly dry and streams are very scarce. In places you also need to carry water to the camp areas. Make very early starts to avoid the heat of the day. If using thermarests (air filled sleeping mattress) be sure to have a repair kit as cactus spines are very common.

The trek starts in the friendly wee mountain village of Cabanaconde at 3300m where the women wear beautiful embroidered clothes. Condors are easily seen in this area, especially at dusk and dawn. If you have spare time in Cabanaconde the two hour walk to the Cruz del Condor lookout (or take the truck leaving from the Plaza around 6am) is worthwhile offering great views and a quiet spot for viewing condors. This lookout gets busy around 10am with day visitors.

In reverse the trek would be harder work but still possible.

ACCESS

From Lima either fly or take a bus south to the city of Arequipa. From Arequipa take a long and dusty 8 hour bus journey to the town of Chivay by the Rio Colca at 3600m. This town is a pleasant place to stop and to visit the thermals at Yanque or you can continue by bus (2-3 hours) on to Cabanaconde, from where the trail begins. It is best to buy food and fuel supplies in Arequipa although you could top up with basic supplies in Chivay. It is possible to hire mules once you have arrived in Cabanaconde, but this village has only very basic stores, restaurant and accommodation (no hot water).

MAPS TO USE

Peruvian IGM sheets 32-r 'Huambo' and 32-s 'Chivay' at a scale of 1:100 000

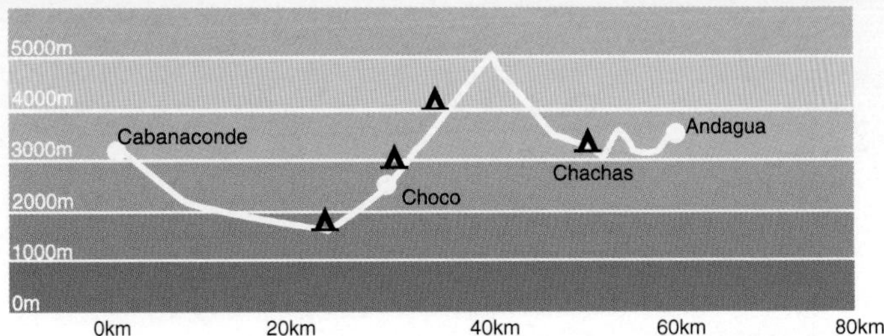

THE ROUTE

1. 6 hours. Soon after you leave Cabanaconde you begin the long steep and dusty descent down into the Colca canyon. Head northwest out of the village on a good stone path, ask the locals for directions to Choco as the way can be confusing until you are on the canyon path. The path is dusty and descends gradually into a river valley, staying right then crossing the dry river then climbing slightly to join a road after about **2 hours**. Follow the road for about **½hour** to where the path to Choco turns off left. This path descends further into the canyon and reaches the valley floor and the bridge over the Rio Colca at 1800m. There are some very small camping spots across the river here. There is no water on this section until you reach the bridge.

2. 7-8 hours. From the bridge ascend steeply for **1 hour**. Continue now contouring gently upwards to the village of Choco at 2500m, reached after a further **2 hours**. To avoid the intense heat make an early start and have full water bottles as the first water supply is not until Choco. Choco is a beautiful, quiet village nestled in rich cultivated farmland. There are no facilities and there is only intermittent electricity and telephone connections. Camping is possible near the village.

Fill up with water in Choco and ask for directions to Chachas. Follow the river northwest out of the village on a steep but good path. After about **1 hour** you follow the well marked path which leaves the river to ascend the steep slopes up the Achacota valley. The first stream encountered is another **3-4 hours** from here, with some good camp areas.

3. 4-5 hours. From the camp at the first streams encountered above Choco it is another seven or more hours to the top of the pass at over 5000m so it is much better to camp again before the pass. Simply follow the valley with spectacular views back to the canyon along the way. Camp higher up the valley where there are some good, but cold, camping areas closer to the pass after **4 or 5 hours**. Remember to carry up your water because higher up the valley above the cultivation there is no water source.

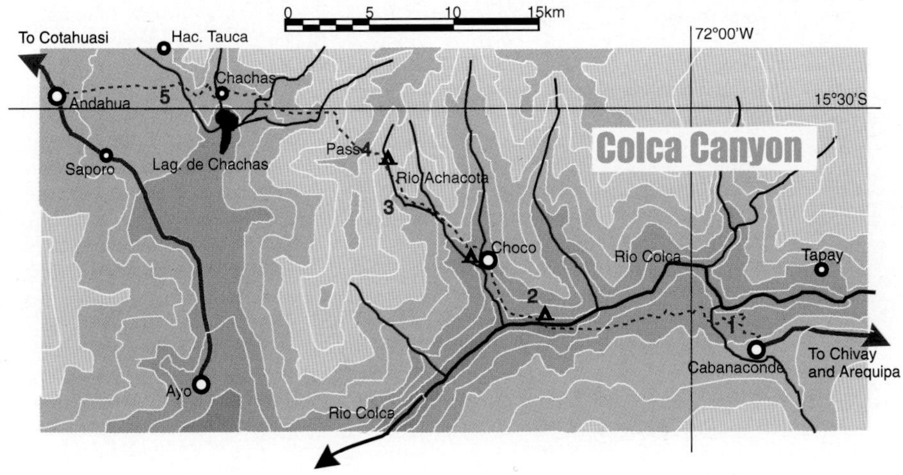

4. 7-8 hours. The final steep ascent to the pass at just over 5000m awards you with spectacular views. From the pass descend the valley, rich in vegetation, on the left side, steeply at first, for **2 hours** to a wee waterfall. Continue on the trail for a further **3 hours** to reach the village of Chachas, 3100m on the edge of the mountain range just above a lake. Ask the locals where to camp, water is available.
5. 6 hours. The road from Chachas to Andahua has occasional trucks travelling along it. However if you are walking ascend the pass using the short cut footpaths to reach the pass after **1 hour** with good views over the valley of volcanoes. Follow the road down to the river and take another shortcut, leaving the road, direct up the hill to reach Andahua, 3600m and **4-5 hours** from the pass. Andahua has basic supplies and accommodation if needed. A longer alternative is to walk out by the Hacienda Tauca in the next valley to the north, 9 hours from the pass to Andahua.
Buses and trucks leave daily for Arequipa taking around 12 hours.

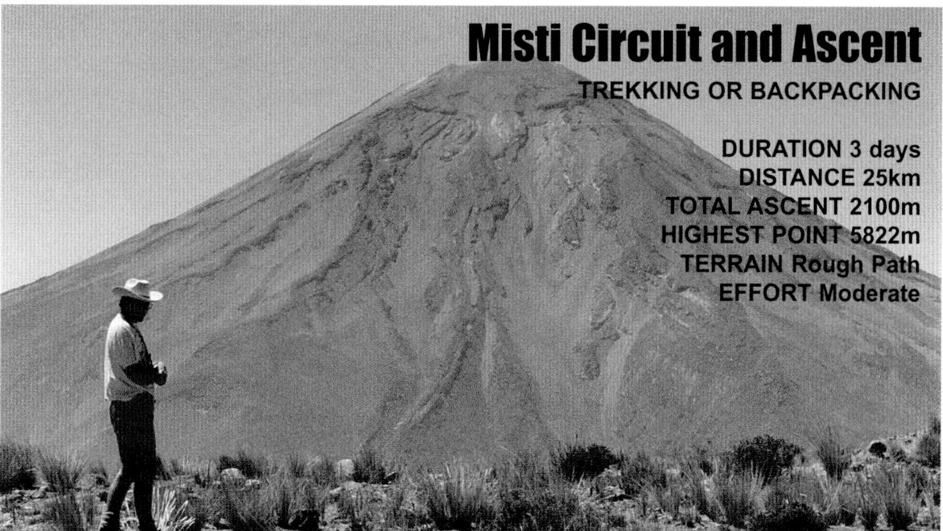

Misti Circuit and Ascent
TREKKING OR BACKPACKING
DURATION 3 days
DISTANCE 25km
TOTAL ASCENT 2100m
HIGHEST POINT 5822m
TERRAIN Rough Path
EFFORT Moderate

VOLCAN MISTI
The perfect cone of El Misti, 5822m towers over the main square of Arequipa. Sometimes there is a little snow on the summit, but it can also be completely dry. Hundreds of people make the tiring ascent to the summit every year and the mountain is very suitable for people with no mountaineering experience. You won't need any special mountaineering equipment just a good pair of boots and warm clothes. There is no water on the mountain except at the Aguada Blanca reservoir. The mountain was climbed several hundred years ago by the Incas.
The trek described here will take you from the reservoir at Aguada Blanca around the back of Misti, from where you can climb easily to the summit, and then out to the road at Chihuata.
Misti is also commonly climbed directly up from Arequipa in 2-3 days and a description of this route is also given.

ACCESS
It is a 3 hour drive from Arequipa to Aguada Blanca along the old Cuzco road, which winds steeply up the west bank of the Rio Chilli canyon, with excellent views of Misti. There is no public transport on this route. If you need mules or donkeys it would be much easier to arrange them in advance in Arequipa or start the trek in Chihuata.

MAP TO USE
Peruvian IGM sheet 33-t, 'Characato', 1:100,000

THE ROUTE
1. 5 hours. The route begins from the reservoir of Aguada Blanca (3700m) on the northeast side of the mountain. It is possible to camp by the reservoir. You need to fill up with water here too because the reservoir is the last source of water on this side of the mountain. For acclimatisation it may be useful to spend an extra day and another night here, perhaps carrying some water up towards the next camp. From the bridge over the outflow stream head directly across country for the prominent northeast rib of Misti (or follow the road for a short way before it hairpins back to the north). There is no clear path. There are a few tent sites behind walls at 4600m just before the rib steepens, **5 hours**.
2. 6-8 hours return. From the camp at 4600m follow the path which makes a rising traverse up the unstable north slopes of Misti to the summit. There is bad scree in places and trekking poles are recommended. On the top is a small crater with a little snowfield inside and a summit marked by an iron cross. Return the same way you came.
3. 6-8 hours. From the camps at 4600m walk out to the village of Chihuata to the south. Head first to a very broad pass east of Misti (4020m) then walk south to pick up a dry river valley. After about 6 or 7 km this joins the river Huasamayo. Contine down this valley before making a final short climb up to the village of Chihuata, **6-8 hours**. From Chihuata there are regular buses back to Arequipa, taking less than an hour.

DIRECT ASCENT OF MISTI FROM AREQUIPA
A longer climb on Misti but with quicker and easier access is from the shanty town of Apurimac San Luis on the northern side of Arequipa. The shanty town is not safe to walk through due to robberies, so use arranged transport to get to the start and check before you go that it is still safe to use this route on Misti. The route is brutally direct! First head uphill for an area known as Tres Cruces (3000m) then continue up under the electric pylons to an area known as Los Pastores at 3300m. From here follow the path uphill on a rib to a camp at 4200m, **6-8 hours**. The next day continue upwards to the summit on paths up steep screes, and then descend the same way, **8-10 hours** return.

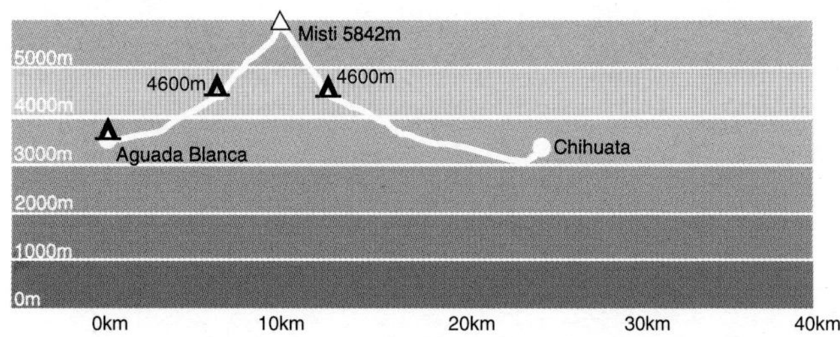

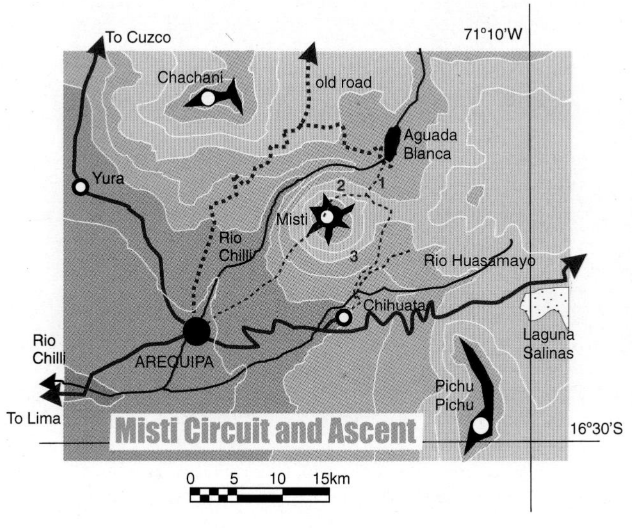

Illimani seen from above La Paz

INTRODUCTION

Bolivia normally has the most stable weather in the Andes during its winter dry season from May to August. Trekking here can be a wonderful experience because in several weeks you may see almost no clouds.

Bolivia is the poorest country in South America and also the country with the highest percentage of native Indians in the population. This is not entirely a coincidence and the large social and economic divisions can be quite disturbing. However the majority of the people are very easy going and the mountain scenery and cultural experience is superb.

The country is also divided geographically between the high and dry altiplano in the western areas around La Paz and the low lying forests of the Amazon basin. Two of the treks included in this chapter make a fascinating descent from the mountains of the Cordillera Real to the hot and humid foothills that are known as the Yungas. These are the **Taquesi Trail** which takes only a few days following a well preserved ancient paved highway and the **Choro Trail** a four day trekking route almost entirely downhill to the jungle town of Coroico at 1500m.

A third trek in the northern Cordillera Real is the **Illampu circuit**, a week long trek around the most spectacular mountain massif in Bolivia.

Two treks in more remote areas of the country are also described. A trek through the remote southern **Cordillera Apolobamba** near the Peruvian border and the high altitude **Pomerape circuit** in the western deserts near the Chilean border.

GETTING THERE

No direct flights are available to La Paz, the capital of Bolivia, from anywhere in Europe, although both Lufthansa and KLM fly with a change of plane at Lima. Other options for getting to Bolivia from Europe are with American Airlines via Miami, or with Varig via Sao Paulo in Brazil or Aerolineas Argentinas via Buenos Aires. From the USA there are daily flights from Miami with American Airlines and the Bolivian airline LAB.

CLIMATE AND WEATHER CONDITIONS

Trekking in all areas is at its best from May to August. This is winter so temperatures are very low, but it is the dry season and rain and clouds are at a minimum. Bolivia has very stable weather at this time with typically only three or four bad days in a month. Trekking in the Cordillera Real and Apolobamba can still be done in reasonable weather in September and October, with noticeably warmer temperatures but more afternoon cloud and a chance of rain. The trek around Pomerape in the Cordillera Occidental is dry enough to be possible all year round.

Village band in western Bolivia

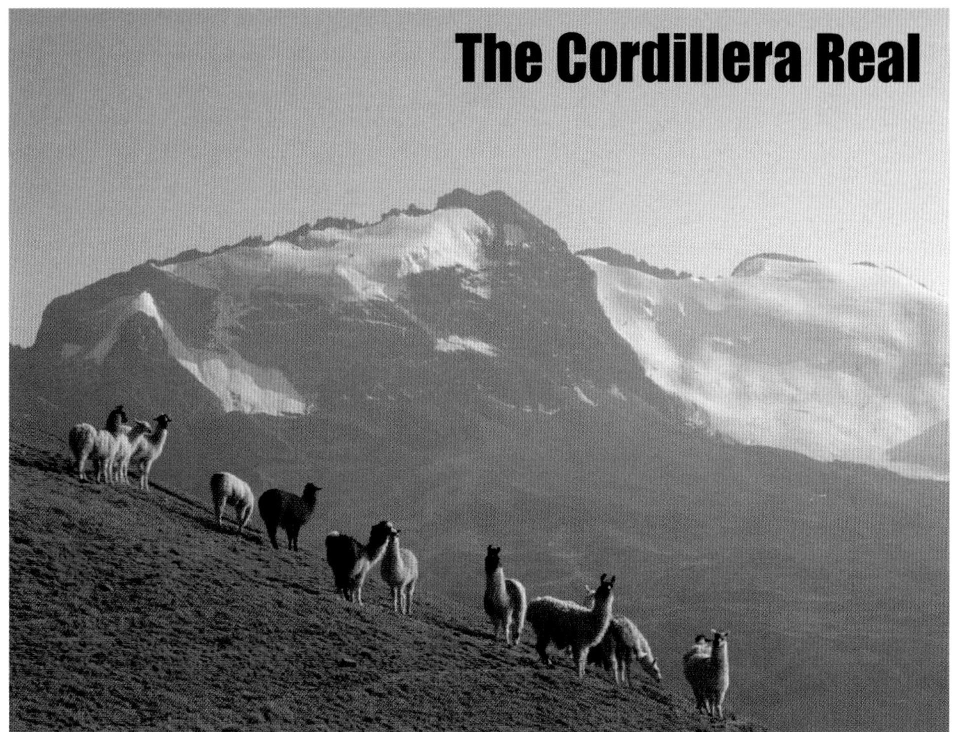

The Cordillera Real

THE CORDILLERA REAL

Bolivia's highest and most extensive mountain range, the Cordillera Real, are also one of the most accessible mountain chains in the Andes. They lie immediately above La Paz and you get a great view of the mountains as you come in to land at the international airport.

There are several peaks over 6000m high in the Cordillera Real, including Ancohuma 6427m and Illampu 6368m at the north end of the range and Illimani 6438m at the south end. The latter is a distinctive long snow-capped ridge with three summits which is a clear landmark from all over La Paz.

LA PAZ

La Paz has a spectacular setting in a deep canyon on the edge of the high plateau known as the 'Altiplano' with magnificent views to the huge mountain Illimani. At an altitude of 3700m it is the worlds highest capital city. The international airport is up on the Altiplano at almost 4100m, so you will feel the altitude as soon as you land and you might even need to use the oxygen they have waiting at baggage reclaim! A number of people feel poorly for a few days after arriving in La Paz and everyone will need at least a day or two to get used to the altitude. However there are several interesting tourists trips possible from the city while acclimatising and once you get over the initial problems the high altitude of La Paz makes the city a great base for trekking in the Cordillera Real. There are good hotels, restaurants and supermarkets and the mountains are only a short drive away. Many treks can be reached quickly on public transport.

For further information on the city of La Paz see page 182.

Tourist trips to the pre-Inca ruins at Tiahuanaco and the islands of the legendary Lake Titicaca can be recommended while acclimatising. A trip to Chacaltaya mountain (detailed below) is also worthwhile. In the city the traditional market area uphill from Calle Sagarnaga is well worth looking around.

DAY TRIP FROM LA PAZ - CHACALTAYA MOUNTAIN, 5395m

One of the more unusual attractions of the Cordillera Real is the world's highest ski resort. This is on a mountain called Chacaltaya on the outskirts of La Paz and skiing is possible all year round at about 5100m. The piste gets a bit icy in the dry season and the wet season from November to March is better for skiing. The views are great and the excursion, which can be easily arranged in La Paz from many agencies, is recommended even for non-skiers. The journey time from La Paz is about 2 hours.

You get great views from the top of Chacaltaya after an easy, if breathless, walk of about **½hour**. Don't come half way round the world for a skiing holiday though. There's only one tow which you have to hang on to until the point of exhaustion, and it may not be running anyway!

It is also possible to walk north along the ridge of Chacaltaya mountain to the northeast before descending leftwards (north) to the main road at Zongo pass. This is an easy walk with a number of possible routes, **4-5 hours**.

Monolithic statue, Tiahuanaco

DAY TRIP FROM LA PAZ - MUELA DEL DIABLO

Walk - 4 hours return

An interesting walk up to the base of this rocky outcrop with splendid views back to La Paz and the Cordillera. From La Paz take public transport, colectivo number 213 from Plaza Murillo or Prado, to its journeys end. The trail is easy to follow, since the Muela itself, which is distinctive, is in sight for much of the way. Ask locals for directions. The walk is mostly uphill rising through a canyon to a large grassy area, **2 hours**. Continue for a further **½hour** to reach the base.

You can scramble up the rock a short way however the top is precipitous and you would need climbing equipment to climb to the summit.

Plaza San Francisco, La Paz

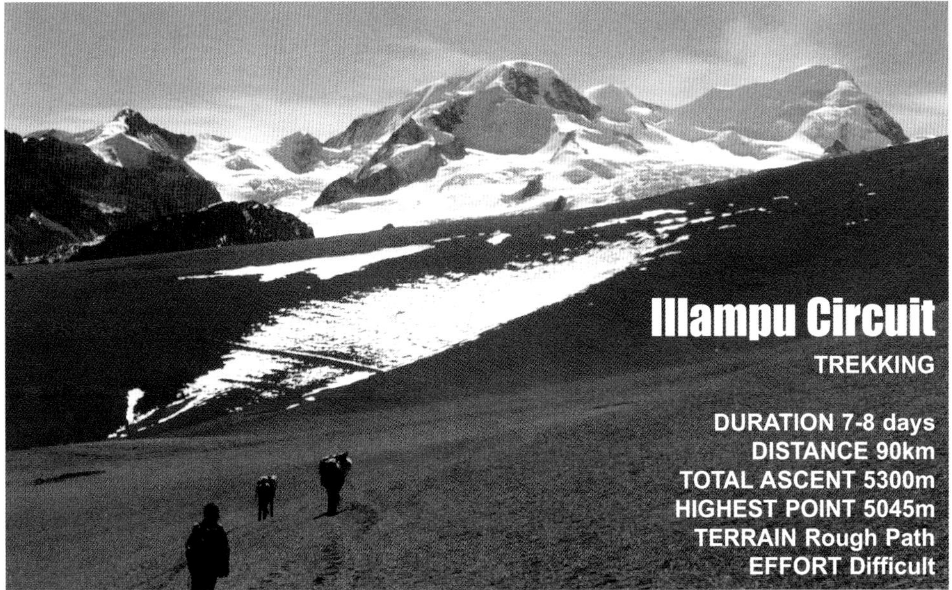

Illampu Circuit
TREKKING
DURATION 7-8 days
DISTANCE 90km
TOTAL ASCENT 5300m
HIGHEST POINT 5045m
TERRAIN Rough Path
EFFORT Difficult

ILLAMPU CIRCUIT

This is a remote and tough trek but it is also very rewarding as it takes you to some spectacular mountain scenery. The route does a complete circuit of the Illampu and Ancohuma massif at the north end of the Cordillera Real crossing over 6 very high passes. The highest of these is the Abra de la Calzada at 5045m. The trek can also be done anti clockwise but it is described clockwise here.

ACCESS

Sorata is a pretty village based around a central plaza, sitting at 2700m beneath the Illampu massif. It can be reached in 4 hours from La Paz by taking a bus from the Cemetery area. There is one stop on the journey when you may need your passport handy. There are two places for guide and mule hire: the Sorata Guides Club off the plaza and the Hotel Copacabana, less than 1km from the plaza down the steep steps and past the football pitch.

WARNING

At Laguna San Francisco it appears there are three brothers who extract money (and goods) from trekkers passing by. They take it in turns to man a site at the top end of the lake the other two remaining at the outlet. They are armed with rifles, and reports indicate that the local police cannot touch them. You will be safer with one of the Sorata guides as the imposition on them is light. From unaccompanied hikers the brothers are reported to take up to $40.

MAPS TO USE

Alpenvereinskarte (German Alpine Club) Cordillera Real Nord (Illampu) 1:50,000 combined with the Mountain Maps: Cordillera Real, 1:150,000, by Liam O'Brien which covers the whole range. The Bolivian IGM sheets Sorata and Warizata at 1:50,000 cover the western side of the range - IGM maps of the east side are not available.

THE ROUTE

1. 5 hours. From Sorata the way up to the settlement of Estancia Lachathiya is a maze of paths through woodland and farming country. Either use the maps recommended, or ask the locals for directions, or use a Sorata guide at least for this section. It is a rising traverse of the slopes directly east of Sorata for **4 hours**, Once you have rounded the shoulder the last hour is a little less steep. Carry plenty of water for this first day as it is a long and hot ascent. It is possible to camp just above Estancia Lachathiya or in around **1**

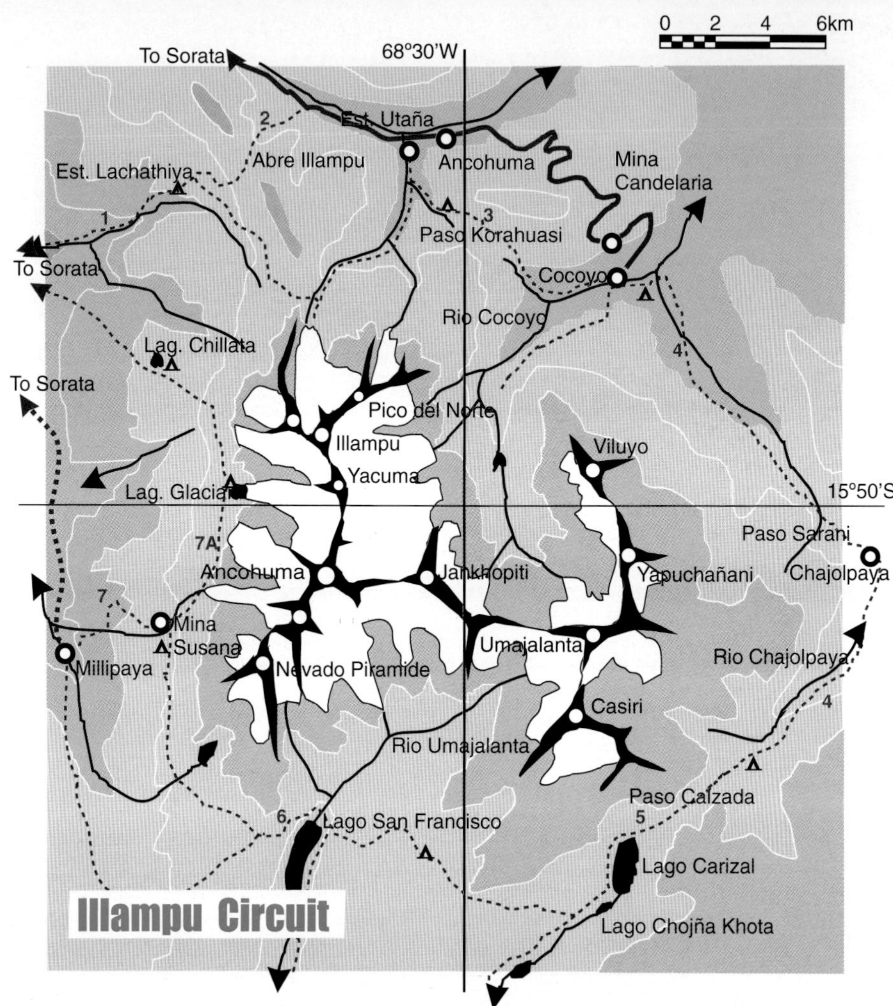

hour beyond the settlement where the main valley widens. From here there is a long view back down towards the shoulder that Sorata nestles behind. If camping here cross a low hill to the north the next morning to regain the main route.

2. 5-6 hours. The route to the Rio Illampu valley (Rio Chucha Jahuira) climbs through a pass called Abre Illampu at 4741m. From Estancia Lachathiya, cross the river and take its left fork on a good path into the valley above. The route rises steadily up this long shady valley then curves to the right round the top of the valley, and onto a high ridge with a steep drop on the right hand side. Tread carefully as there is a lot of loose heavy shale near the top of the pass, **2 hours**. Work your way easily down the other side of the pass in a side valley. Turn right (southeast) when you reach the main Illampu valley onto the track leading to the settlement of Ancohuma, **2 hours**. Turn off right at Estancia Utaña Pampa, up the valley heading southeast. After 1km ascend the steeper hanging valley

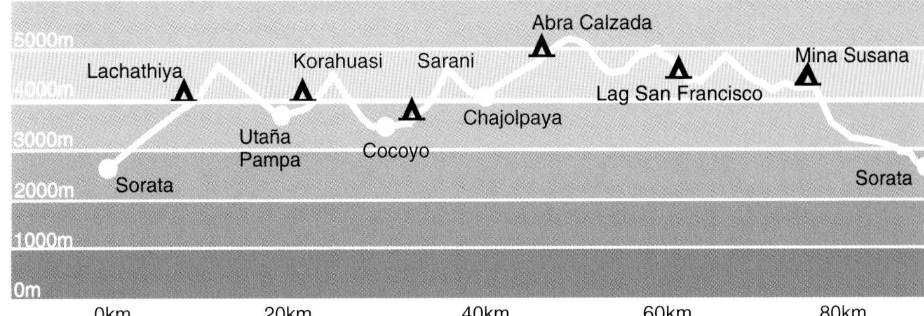

on your left. Climb gently up this valley for a further **1 hour,** where it is possible to camp in various places.

3. 4 hours. As the valley steepens cross to the left (northern) side of the stream and a good path. After **1 hour** the Paso Korahuasi 4480m is reached. The descent from Paso Korahuasi is initially very gentle. Do not be deceived: it gradually turns into a very steep descent indeed - but there is a clear path. From the top of the steep section you can see the flood plain of a stream leading down to the idyllically situated Cocoyo village at 3500m. Once in the valley it is a swift flat walk down to Cocoyo where it is possible to buy basic supplies, **2 hours.**

From Cocoyo the route turns right (southeast) out of the village and up the road. The route becomes a long but gentle uphill walk with many places to camp only **½ to 1 hour** further.

4. 5-6 hours. The trail is a steady **2½ hours** up to Paso Sarani 4500m. On the other side of the pass drop down steeply to the remote Chajolpaya settlement reached after a further **1-1½ hours**. Walk upstream and southeast in the valley of the Rio Chajolpaya for a gentle **2 hours** or so. There are many opportunities to camp on this section. Closer to the Paso Calzada there is a spectacular campsite beside the river shortly before the valley becomes steeper.

5. 7 hours. This section is an enjoyable day for the views from the Abra de la Calzada the highest pass on the trek at 5045m. The pass is reached after a further **3 hours** ascent. There is a particularly good view of an unnamed peak to the right, with a big glacier on its south slope. From the pass the descent is very steep - as bad if not worse than that from Paso Korahuasi. There is also an excellent distant view out towards Lake Titicaca and during the descent you walk along the right hand side of Lago Carizal, which has the most extraordinarily deep blue colour. **1 hour** from the pass you reach the smaller Laguna Chojña Khota. 2km

The Illampu massif from the north

beyond this lake the route (which is now unmarked) heads up to the right across and over a long ridge, 5000m. Turn up the slope and head westwards over the most amazing rounded sandy and barren ridges. There is no distinct path and it is a long **3 hour** trek, but the view, which stretches to the saw-teeth of the Nevado Ancohuma range on the far horizon, is spectacular. Drop down on the far side of the hills to camp at a fork in a high valley about 1 hour before reaching the north end of Laguna San Francisco. There is an alternative longer but lower option to walk down the valley from Lag. Chojña Khota to Lag. Cacha, then north up the San Francisco valley to the lake.

6. 5-6 hours. Read the warning about robbers in the introduction to this trek. Descend to the Laguna San Francisco and walk across the flat boggy area at the north end and ascend the ridge opposite, with no path now, **2½ hours**, to the top of the ridge. From the top of the ridge head in a northwest direction crossing over a series of ridges and valleys. Then there is a long and very gentle downhill trek to a flat valley just below Mina Susana. It is possible to camp below the old mine by a stream and small lake at 3900m. The miners' old concrete huts are right under the mountain at the head of the valley.

7. 4 hours. The long downhill walk back to Sorata passes through the first farmed land since day one. Head down the mine track to Millipaya village, **½ hour**. There is occasional transport from this village to Sorata and La Paz or you can walk back to Sorata on the east side of the river or out to the La Paz road to flag down a truck.

TO LAGUNA GLACIAR FROM MINA SUSANA

Optional extension

7a. 6-7 hours This alternative and much harder last day takes you up to the spectacular Laguna Glaciar, high on the west slopes of Ancohuma. Laguna Glaciar lies at 5038m and this is a very tough day's walk without any path. From the campsite below Mina Susana, walk up a steep path to the mine itself - the vehicle track takes the normal snaky route up the side of the mountain. This is an altitude gain of 200m. Follow the ridge behind the mine northeast; then make a long contour walk round the side of the hillside in a northerly direction, but with much up and down. Be extremely careful over the vast rock slides here: three times the route is interrupted by great slides of rock, leaving a channel some 6m deep. This traverse round the mountain and climb to the lagoon will take a total of **4 hours**. The last 500m up is up a bare rock face and is a scramble with the outlet stream to your left and out of sight. The Laguna is however a stunning sight, with a glacier tumbling in, and often a thin film of ice with small birds hopping about on it.

To return to Sorata from here make a direct descent of the slopes below past the Laguna Chillata, **2 hours**, where it is possible to camp. From Laguan Chillata walk down into a valley. When the valley opens out pick up a path heading northwest to Sorata **2-3 hours** away.

LAGUNA GLACIAR TREK FROM SORATA

The Laguna Glaciar can be walked as a three day trip from Sorata return.

1. Sorata to a camp at Laguna Chilata, 5-6 hours
2. 5-6 hour return day trip to Laguna Glaciar.
3. Return to Sorata in 3 hours.

Campesino Woman and child

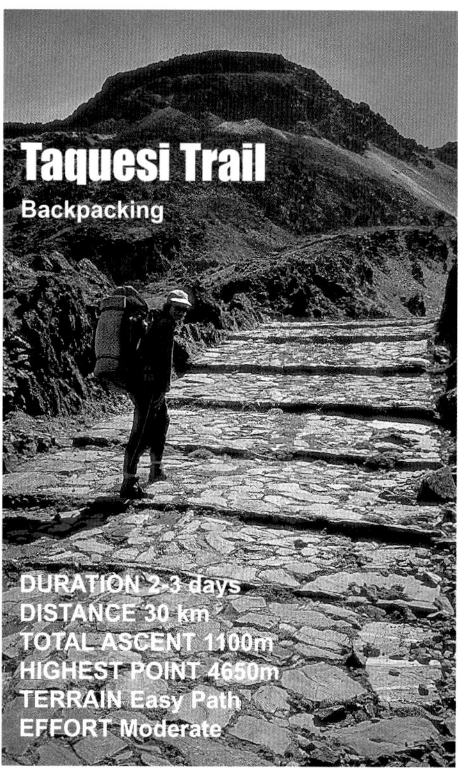

Taquesi Trail
Backpacking
DURATION 2-3 days
DISTANCE 30 km
TOTAL ASCENT 1100m
HIGHEST POINT 4650m
TERRAIN Easy Path
EFFORT Moderate

TAQUESI TRAIL

This is an enjoyable short trek from the high Altiplano down into the Yungas with greatly contrasting vegetation changes and some long and exceptionally well preserved pre-Inca paving complete with excellent drainage. This trail has become popular and can be very busy at the weekends. Cafes have sprung up in some settlements. The walk would be hard work in reverse.

ACCESS

From La Paz there are regular buses to Ventilla, 3 hours, or it is feasible to hire a taxi to the village. Buses leave from Calle Max Paredes above Calle Rodriguez in La Paz. Ventilla has only basic supplies available so you are best to buy all you need in La Paz.

MAP TO USE

Bolivian IGM sheet 6044-IV 'Chojlla' and 6044-III 'Palca' both at 1:50,000 or Liam O'Briens 1:150,000 Cordillera Real map.

THE ROUTE

1. 5-6 hours. From Ventilla walk up the track on the left-hand side of the valley heading north. After **1½ hours** you pass the settlement of Choquekota. Crossing the side stream here continue on the track, passing the church and cemetery, and in a further **1½ hours** the track crosses a river. Camping is possible here. Shortly afterwards you will see a sign and map of the trail. From the track (which goes to Mina San Francisco) you must turn off right on a footpath and ascend the steep slopes above. Soon you are walking on the well preserved and wide pre-Inca paving. Ascend for **1 hour** to the top of the pass, at 4650m. If the cloud has not yet come up from the Yungas you will be rewarded with great views. Continue on the fine paved path, passing a small lake where camping is possible. The trail descends more gently for **½ hour**, passing a larger lake, to the abandoned Mina David. At the mine take the path heading down the slopes to reach the settlement of Taquesi in **1 hour**, crossing the river once. It is also possible to camp just above Taquesi. Some really fine engineering and drainage have gone into making this section of the path.

2. 4 hours. Continuing down the Rio Taquesi valley the path crosses back to the right hand side and starts contouring around the slopes to the east leaving the river far below. You leave the cold mountain

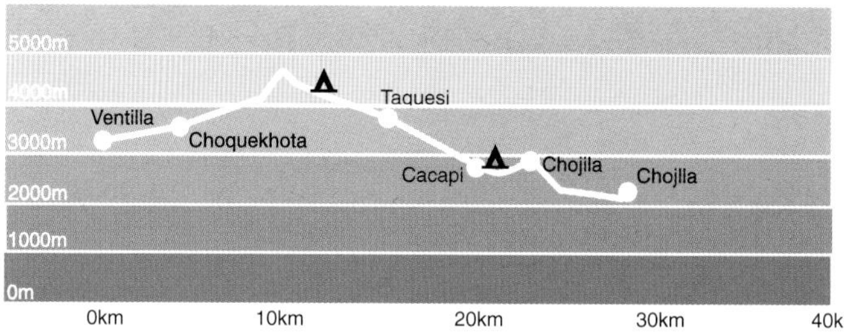

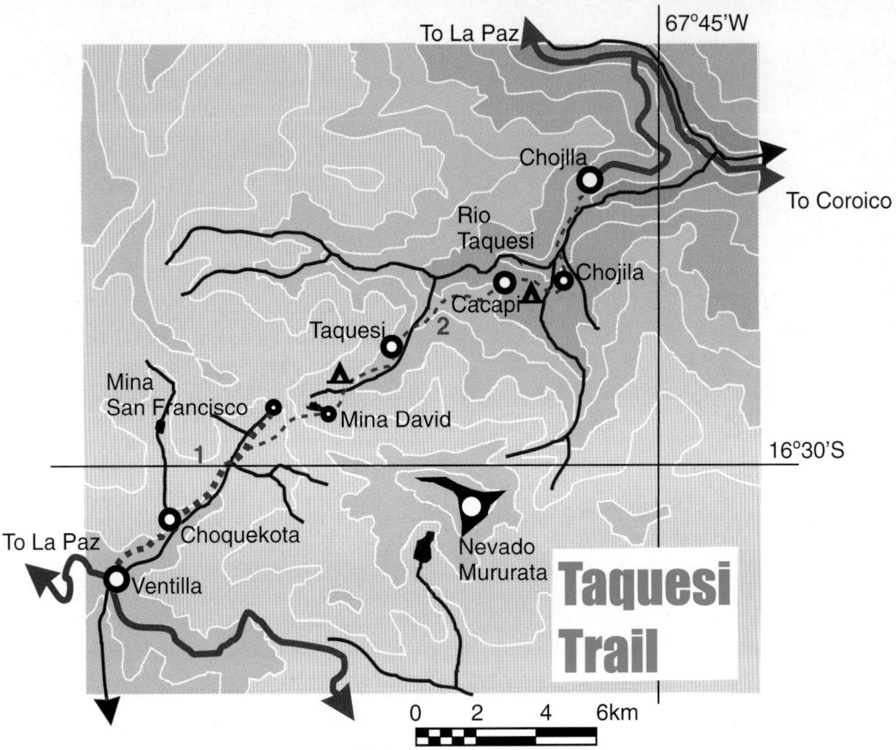

Taquesi Trail

To La Paz
67°45'W
Chojlla
To Coroico
Rio Taquesi
Chojila
Cacapi
Taquesi
2
Mina San Francisco
Mina David
1
16°30'S
To La Paz
Choquekota
Ventilla
Nevado Mururata
0 2 4 6km

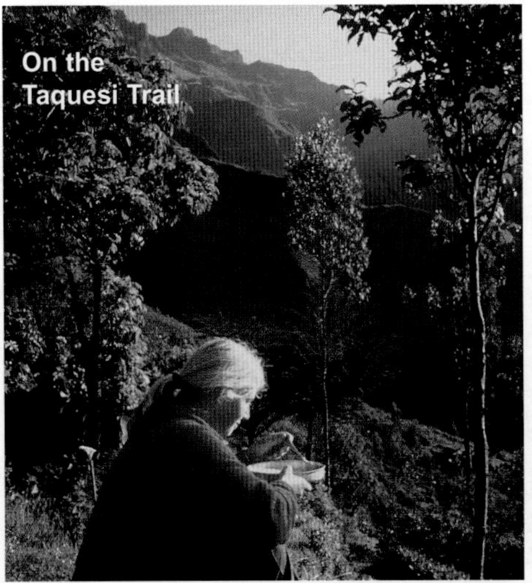
On the Taquesi Trail

environment, with its hill grasses, for warmth and sub tropical vegetation such as ferns, orchids and begonias. Continue round the slopes passing through Cacapi, 2700m in **2½ hours**, where camping is possible. At a stream just beyond the village camping is also possible. Continue around the hillside as the football pitch below Chojila comes into view nestled on the only flat space for miles (but now slowly disappearing under the encroaching vegetation). Rise gently into the village on a good path, then descend down a spur northeast into the main valley, crossing the Rio Taquesi once again to pick up a path by an aqueduct which leads towards Chojlla, 2100m. When the aqueduct ends follow the road around and walk up into the village, **1½ hours** Buses and lorries leave from the village daily for La Paz. If you continue down the valley you will reach the settlement of Yanacachi after 5 km where there is a greater choice of transport and basic accommodation.

Choro Trail
BACKPACKING
DURATION 4 days
DISTANCE 60km
TOTAL ASCENT 470m,
but 3400m of descent
HIGHEST POINT 4900m
TERRAIN Easy Path
EFFORT Easy

CHORO TRAIL

The Choro trail offers a long descent from the La Cumbre pass on the edge of the Altiplano down to the village of Coroico, with its subtropical vegetation. It is an easy route to follow. The walk offers a stark contrast in temperature and vegetation and you need to be prepared for both a snow covered pass at 4860m and for walking through the heat and humidity at 1300m fending off the insects which at time can be a nuisance. Route finding is easy with the exception of finding the start of the trail. In the reverse this trek would be very hard work!

ACCESS

From La Paz take a bus (from Avenida de las Americas 344, Villa Fatima) for the 1 hour journey to La Cumbre which is a main road summit, marked by a statue of Christ, on the way to Coroico. It is also possible to take a lorry or hire a taxi in La Paz to take you here reasonably cheaply. Buy all your supplies in La Paz.

MAP TO USE

Bolivian IGM sheet 5945-II 'Milluni' and 6045-III 'Unduavi' both at 1:50,000 or Liam O'Briens 1:150,000 Cordillera Real map.

THE ROUTE

1. 6-7 hours From La Cumbre at 4700m follow a jeep track northwest until beyond the large lake Jachcha Huampuni, then ascend the scree slope to the north. Look out for paint splashes on the rocks. From the road to the summit of the Apacheta Chucura pass,

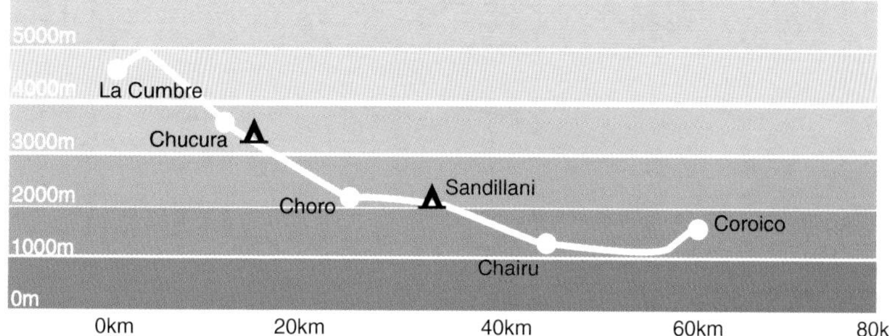

4860m takes around **1 hour.** The descent now follows a clear stone path high on the left of the valley and loosing height rapidly. It is **4 hours** to walk to the village of Chucura (Achura) where it is possible to camp. If possible walk on a further **1-1½ hours** to camp at the next settlement called Challapampa. Its a nice spot and this will also split the daily distances more evenly.

2. 6-7 hours Continue down the left hand side of the valley on an easy trail to reach the Choro bridge after **2 hours**. The trail now stays on the right hand side of the main valley, often quite high above the river for a further **5 hours** through shrubby vegetation to the village of Sandillani at 2000m. You can camp in the garden of an amazingly friendly Japanese local here. His well kept garden really is remarkable.

3. 5-6 hours Follow the valley down on the paved track now to the village of Chairo at 1500m, which is reached in **2-3 hours**. Basic supplies can be bought here. From here the walk follows a quiet road through agricultural plantations of bananas and citrus; however it is usually possible to find transport along the road to Coroico. This last 25km will take around **6 hours** if you're walking. After crossing the river the road climbs to Yolosa and then up into the village of Coroico.

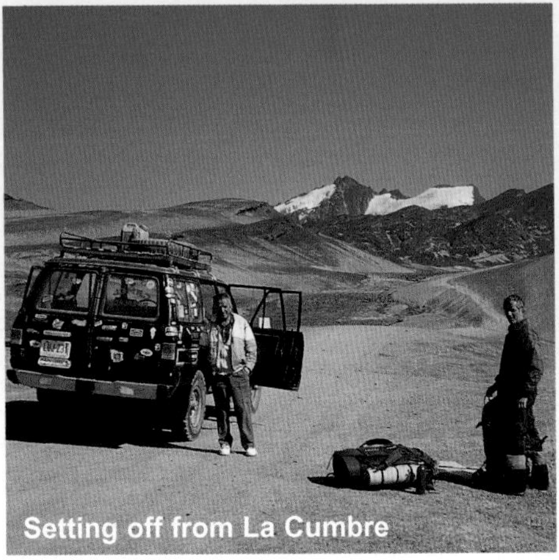
Setting off from La Cumbre

Coroico is a beautiful and relaxing town and it is well worth staying for a night or two to unwind before returning to the smog of La Paz. From Coroico buses and trucks leave regularly every day for La Paz, 4 hours, up the infamous Yungas road with its precipitous drops, sombrely lined with crosses of those who have gone over the edge, and the occasional waterfall to drive under!

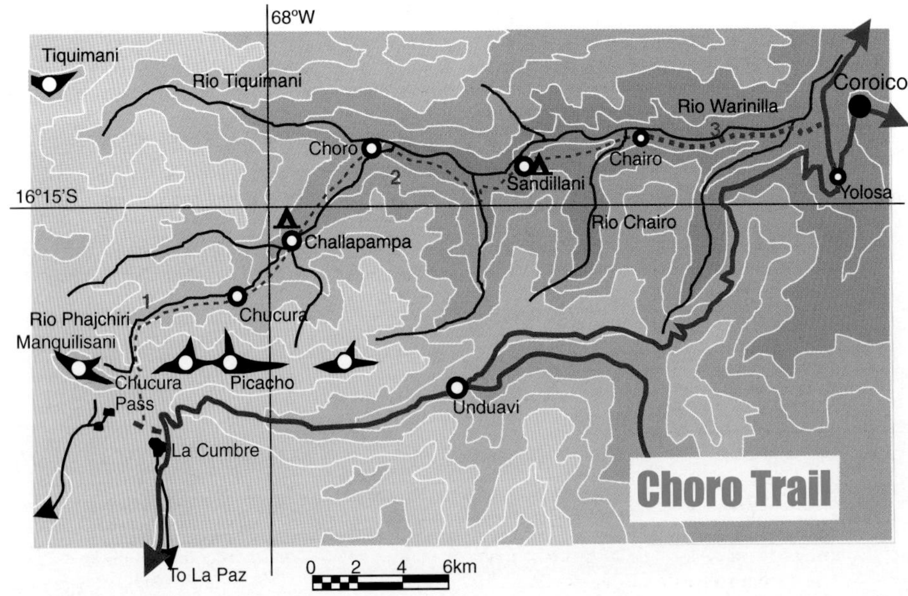

Cordillera Apolobamba
TREKKING
DURATION 7-8 days
DISTANCE 95km
TOTAL ASCENT 6200m
HIGHEST POINT 5100m
TERRAIN Rough Path
EFFORT Moderate

CORDILLERA APOLOBAMBA TREK

North of the Cordillera Real and straddling the Peruvian border are the remote Cordillera Apolobamba. The Apolobamba lie to the northeast of Lake Titicaca, about 250km north of La Paz and some 300km south-east of Cuzco in Peru. They are a lower range of peaks with just one peak, Chaupi Orco, of over 6000m. The Apolobamba are a remote mountain range and just getting to the start of your trek will prove to be quite an adventure. There are a number of good treks but that featured here probably offers the best combination of scenery and adventure. This is one of the best areas of the Andes for seeing wildlife, particularly good for condors and vicuñas. The Apolobamba are prone to slightly poorer weather than the Cordillera Real.

Described here is a popular five day trek from Charazani (or Curva) in the south to Pelechuco in the north via Hilo Hilo. The walking is easiest done from south to north but is fine to do in reverse.

ACCESS

The trek can be started either at Charazani, 3200m, or if you have private transport, at Curva at 3900m. Curva is a four hour walk from Charazani. There are buses most days from La Paz to Charazani village, 10 hours. Accommodation and food are better in Charazani than in Pelechuco at the north. The beautifully situated village of Curva has no accommodation and only very basic supplies, but a great view of Acamani, the sacred mountain of the Kallahuaya people who inhabit the Apolobamba. Mule hire may be difficult in these villages, and if starting in the south, it may be safer to arrange this with a La Paz agency, who can get a Pelechuco mule driver to meet you.

The friendly wee town of Pelechuco lies in a mist shrouded valley at 3600m at the northern end of the route. It is a good base for organising a trek. If using public transport it is easier to start your trek here since there are fewer buses in and out of Pelechuco. There are only very basic shops and facilities. You can hire mules and get some information at the Hotel Llataymanta on the main square.

MAP TO USE

There is a 1:100,000 sheet of the northern Apolobamba published by the Bolivian IGM, but it appears to be hard to get a copy at the IGM office in La Paz. It is sheet 3041, titled ‘Pelechuco’. There are no useful maps available for the rest of the trek.

THE ROUTE

1. 4 hours. Charazani to Curva. If you have a vehicle you can drive this section in one hour. From Charazani drop down the hillside to the north to the hot springs, **10 mins**, then cross the river and climb up to rejoin the road to Curva on the other side of the valley. Go right for short way on the road then climb up left to a small church and a great view of Acamani, then drop down on the other side of the hill to find a good path cutting down across fields to a bridge. Cross the bridge and climb up steeply up to Curva.

2. 2-3 hours. If you arrive in Charazani early this section can be combined with section one quite easily. Leave Curva and contour round a hill to the north to reach a river, **1 hour.** You can camp anywhere beyond here. Cross the river and continue upwards through walled enclosures until you reach a good path. Follow this uphill to a camping area known as Jatunpampa at 4200m, or carry on further to higher sites.

3. 3 hours. From Jatunpampa continue uphill to a gap in a ridge, then continue leftwards round the head of the valley to the first pass at 4700m, with excellent views of Acamani, **1½ hours**. A long descent to the right from this pass will get you to the stone bridge and scenic campsite at Incacancha 4100m.

4. 4-5 hours. From Incacancha the route goes up a steep scree gully to a col at 4800m, **1½ hours**. Traverse leftwards, climbing a wee bit, then drop down to a lake with pleasant campsites. Cross a final ridge to reach another valley and the village of Viscachani, **1½ hours**. From Viscachani climb steeply to a pass at 4900m then descend to the right to meet a jeep track. Follow this track down to Sunchuli where there is a gold mine and a small village. From the last pass it is possible to avoid dropping down to the mine by contouring left around the head of the valley by an aqueduct towards the Sunchuli pass.

5. 5-6 hours. Follow the road for **1½ hours** up to the top of the Sunchuli pass, the highest point on the trail at 5100m. Follow the road down for a short while until you see a steep path cutting down on the right. Take this path and cross a boggy area to reach possible campsites, **1 hour**. Continue down the valley to rejoin the road just above Piedra Grande, then follow the road down to Hilo Hilo at 3900m, **3 hours**. Look out for a possible shortcut on the right, where the road takes a long bend left into a valley just above Hilo Hilo. You can buy basic supplies in Hilo Hilo.

6. 6 hours. The route to Pelechuco is well used. After descending gently to the Rio Hilo Hilo the path climbs

Loading mules at Pelechuco

the valley, passing many good campsites. When the valley bends to the west after about **2 hours** you'll see the steep final climb up the right hand side of the valley. Another **1 hour** will get you up to the top of the pass at 4750m. The route down the other side is obvious, descending to join another valley on the left, then staying on the left side of the valley before finally descending leftwards around the hillside to Pelechuco, **3 hours**.

EXTENSION TO NACARA VALLEY AND ASCENT OF MIRADOR

This worthwhile extension takes in another beautiful high valley and gives a chance to climb an easy glacier peak with great views of the central Apolobamba.

7. 7 hours. From Pelechuco follow the path on the north side of the river downstream to the east. After a short way you contour round to the left and enter the Nacara valley. The path up the valley is obvious, passing a few small houses, to reach campsites in the head of the valley at about 4600m after 7 hours. Mirador is the rounded snow peak that can be seen at the head of the valley.

8. 6-7 hours return. Climb up to the col that lies to the east on an obvious path in the moraines on the left side of the valley, **3 hours.** Get on to the glacier on the right, either by a short steep route or by walking further up till the angle eases. Mirador is the low peak to the north, reached easily in another **1-2 hours**. There are some crevasses on this glacier but otherwise it is an easy ascent with great views of the steep pyramidal peak of Ascarani to the south and the fluted Soral peaks to the north and east.

9. 5 hours. Walk back to Pelechuco as for day 7.

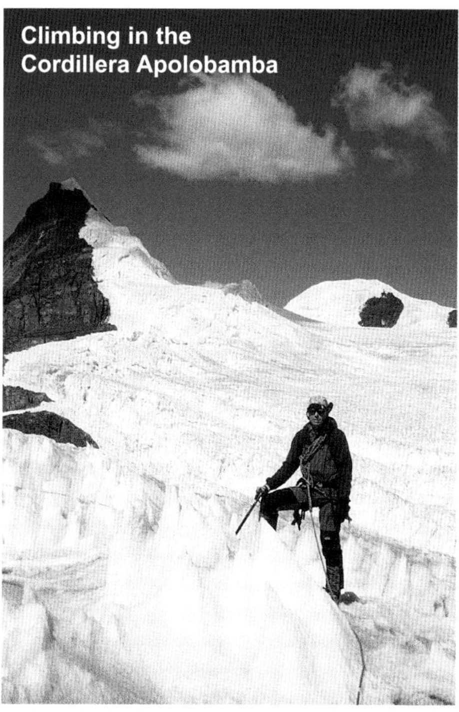

Climbing in the Cordillera Apolobamba

Camp below Sunchuli pass

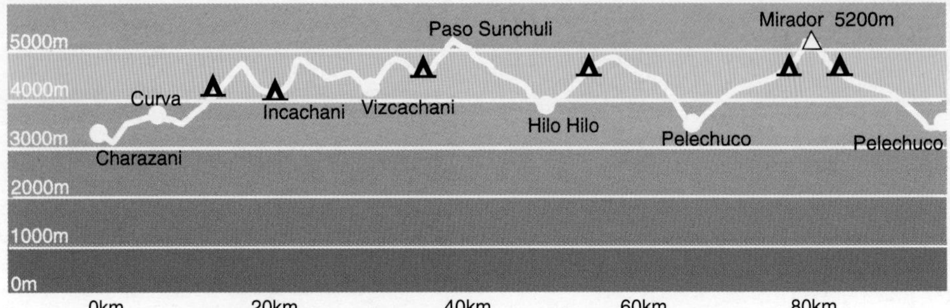

Querra
8
Mirador
Palomani
Ascarani
7
Lag. Suches
Catantica
Nacara
Pelechuco
Paso Pelechuco
6
Antaquilla
Huanacuni
Cololo
Hichocollo
6
Hilo Hilo
15°S
5
Paso Sunchuli
Ulla Ulla
Sunchuli
4
Acamani
Incacancha
3
2
Curva
1
Charazani
To La Paz
69°W

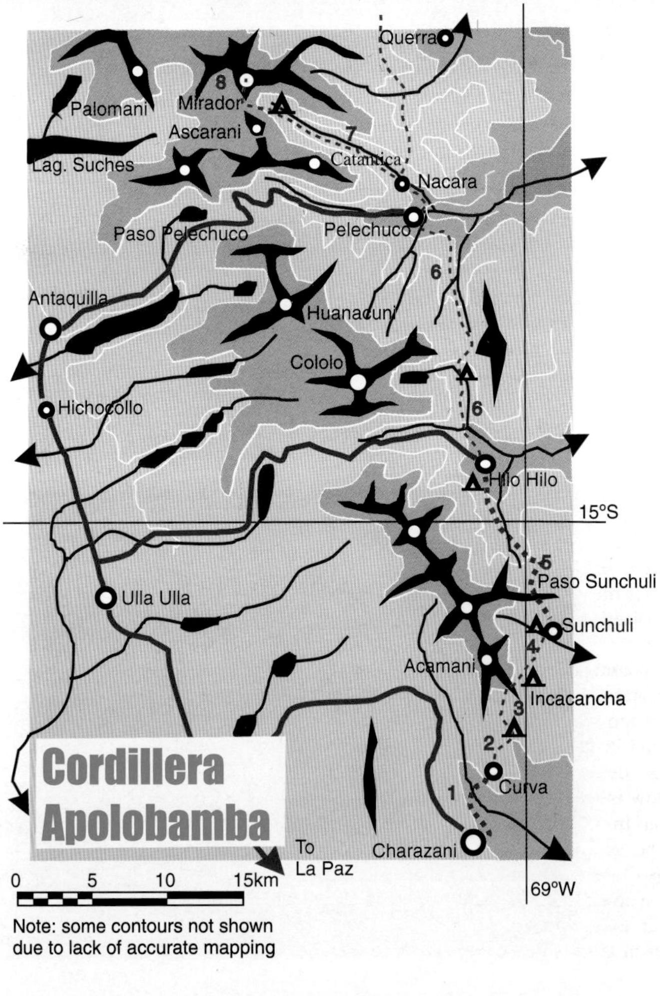

Cordillera Apolobamba

0 5 10 15km

Note: some contours not shown due to lack of accurate mapping

Pomerape Circuit
TREKKING
DURATION 4-5 days
DISTANCE 55km
TOTAL ASCENT 1700m
HIGHEST POINT 5400m
TERRAIN No Path
EFFORT Moderate

POMERAPE CIRCUIT

The Cordillera Occidental are a range of isolated volcanic peaks on Bolivia's western border with Chile. They contain the country's highest peak, Nevado Sajama 6542m. This area has some of the most desolate but beautiful scenery in the Andes and is a good place to see wildlife. Particularly famous is the Lauca National Park (actually in Chile) where you will easily see condors, vicuñas and flamingos and possibly even the rhea. On the border is the beautiful Volcan Parinacota 6342m, a perfect volcanic cone covered in pure white snow. This is an easy ascent though you will need an ice-axe and crampons. If that seems too much there are magnificent walks around the base of the mountain passing high altitude lagoons rich in bird life and eerie volcanic formations such as fresh lava flows and cinder cones. A complete circuit of Parinacota and its twin volcano Pomerape can be done in 5-6 days depending on where you start. The description below is for a circuit from the village of Sajama, 4200m in Bolivia, but the circuit could equally well be started in Parinacota village or Caquena on the Chilean side of the border. However donkeys will be much more easily arranged in the village of Sajama. You'll also get basic food and accommodation in the village of Sajama. Access to this remote mountain area is by the La Paz-Arica bus along a brand new tarred road.

ACCESS

Access to this route is equally easy from La Paz in Bolivia or from the northern Chilean city of Arica. Because the trek is almost entirely above 4500m, there is an advantage in coming from La Paz at 3500m rather than Arica at sea level.

From La Paz take a bus to Arica, daily departures from the central bus station.

If coming from Arica travel by bus to the village of Sajama, or the village of Parinacota in Chile where the trek could also be started. If coming from Arica it might be a good idea to spend a few days at Putre (3600m) for the purposes of acclimatisation.

MAP TO USE

Bolivian IGM sheets 5739-I 'Nevados Payachata' and 5839-IV 'Nevado Sajama' both at 1:50,000 are the best combination though they don't cover the Chilean side of the border.

If coming from Chile then Chilean IGM sheet 1800-6845 'Arica' at 1:250,000

Parinacota 6342m
6000m
Lag. Chiar Kota
Lag.Casiri
5000m
4000m
Sajama
Sajama
3000m
2000m
1000m
0m
0km
20km
40km
60km
80km

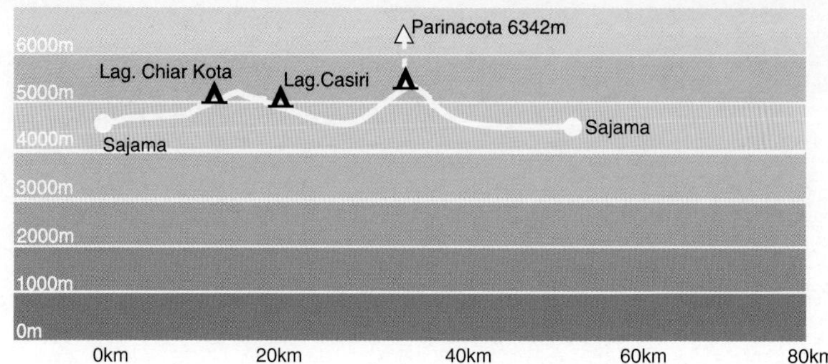

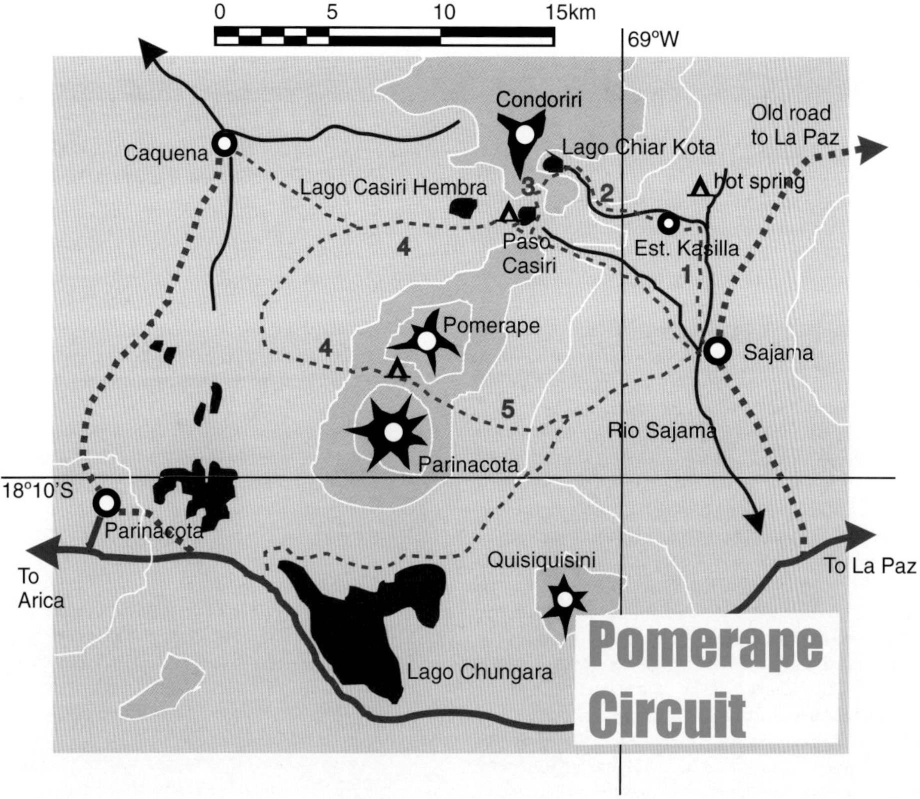

0
5
10
15km
69°W
Condoriri
Old road to La Paz
Caquena
Lago Chiar Kota
hot spring
Lago Casiri Hembra
3
2
Est. Kasilla
4
Paso Casiri
1
Pomerape
Sajama
4
5
Rio Sajama
Parinacota
18°10'S
Parinacota
To Arica
Quisiquisini
To La Paz
Lago Chungara
Pomerape Circuit

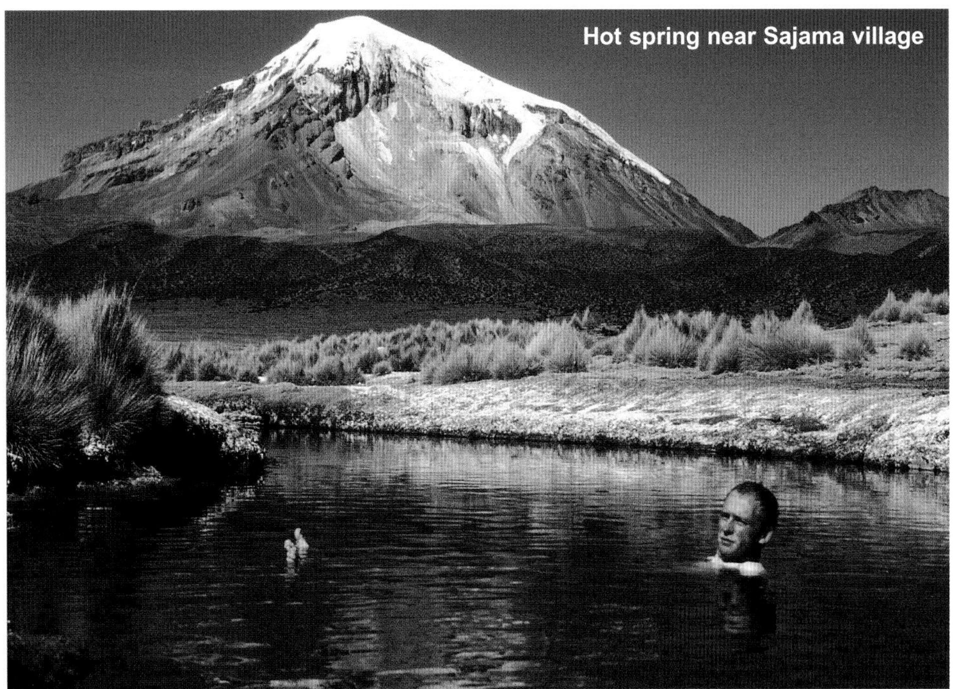
Hot spring near Sajama village

THE ROUTE

A full circuit of Pomerape volcano is described, though there is an option to return to Sajama village after stage 3 giving a shorter trek of only two days. The trek could also be started from Parinacota village in Chile, joining on day 4 after a one day walk.

1. 2 hours. From Sajama at an altitude of 4200m ask for directions to the hot springs 'termales' which lie about 6km north of the village. They are about 100m from the west bank of the Rio Sajama and you should be able to find them if you keep your eyes and nostrils open. You can camp here but take care not to pollute the water.

2. 5 hours. From the hot springs walk up the valley to the west (Rio Milluni) passing a few houses at the Estancia Kasilla. Continue up this dramatic glaciated valley, which bends to the north and then climbs steeply to the Laguna Chiar Kota at an altitude of nearly 5000m. Giant coots 'Taguas' are a common sight on the usually frozen lake. It makes a spectacular, if high camp site.

3. 2 hours. From the Laguna Chiar Kota head southwest over desolate pumice and rock fields and gradually up to a pass of 5050m, with a few cairns. On the other side of the pass drop down, there is a great view of Pomerape volcano and two smaller round lakes below. Go down the valley past the first lake to the second lake, Laguna Casiri. From this second lake you can climb the Paso Casiri (4850m) to the east to return to Sajama village in 3-4 hours if you want to do a shorter trek.

4. 7-8 hours From Laguna Casiri head down the valley to the west passing to the south of a larger lake called Casiri Hembra (possible camps), **2 hours**. From this lake the route is poorly defined. Head generally west and then southwest across pumice fields and lava desert for about 10km until you can see a way up to the broad col between Pomerape and Parinacota volcanoes. You may need to drop as low as 4700m on this section. There is little water, though occasionally melting snow patches may provide some. Once you can see a way up to the col climb as high as necessary to get snow for water supply, **5 hours.**

5. 6-7 hours. Continue up to the col at 5400m on sandy ground. From the col you descend southeast through a field of huge boulders which have rolled down from Parinacota volcano (don't camp here) to an altitude of about 4700 or 4600m, when you will be able to turn to the east and head directly to Sajama village, about **5-6 hours** from the col. There is little or no water on this section until near the village, and there is no definite trail, however once you have descended from the pass it is generally easy to find a way over a series of low sandy ridges until you reach the flatter grassy plains, usually with huge herds of grazing llamas and alpacas, that stretch to the village.

Pomerape volcano from Sajama church

ASCENT OF PARINACOTA VOLCANO

An ascent of Parinacota volcano is highly recommended because of the spectacular crater on the summit, over 200m deep and 1km across.

8-10 hours return. From a camp in the pass between the two volcanoes at an altitude of about 5300-5400m ascend the steep north slopes of the volcano. In most years there are usually only small snow patches. Try to stick to these snow patches (for which you may need an ice-axe and crampons) or the lava ribs where the ground is more stable. The descent can be made very quickly on scree.

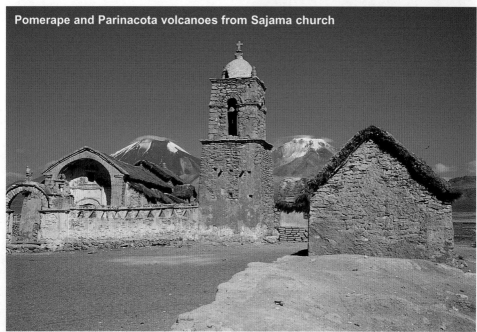

Pomerape and Parinacota volcanoes from Sajama church

The High Andes

Walking towards Aconcagua from the east

INTRODUCTION

The Andes are at their highest in northern Chile and Argentina. The highest peak is Aconcagua, a 6959m giant that towers over the surrounding peaks, yet it is just a short way from the Pacific ocean. This part of the Andean chain is much narrower and the mountains in many places form a single distinct chain, except in the area known as the Puna de Atacama where many volcanoes rising from an extremely high plateau. The greatest concentration of high peaks in the Andes is found in the Puna, with over thirty 6000m summits and six of the ten highest peaks.

Some of the highest summits in this area were climbed at the time of the Inca empire, over 400 years ago. Remains and ruins (as well as treasure and sacrifice victims) have been found on numerous peaks and have given rise to the unusual sport or science of high altitude archaeology.

The walking in this area is very adventurous, but several routes are described which should appeal to the more experienced trekker or backpacker. In the Puna de Atacama the main difficulties for trekking are the lack of water and the sheer remoteness. This area of the Andes could easily be considered as the best place in the world for high altitude hillwalking - with little specialist equipment you can easily climb some of the highest peaks in the Andes. A downside is the high cost of using mules and 4x4 transport for access to these remote mountains. The routes described in the Puna de Atacama area include the rewarding **ascent of Licancabur** in northern Chile, a difficult backpacking route in the **Nevados de Cachi** in northwest Argentina and a challenging high level **Puna Traverse** passing many of the highest peaks.

Further south in the Aconcagua area we give descriptions of difficult routes such as the **Marmolejo Traverse** as well as several easier and shorter walks such as the **Aconcagua Treks** and the **ascent of del Plomo**.

GETTING THERE

There are two main options for reaching this area, depending whether you want to be based on the Chilean or Argentine side of the mountains. For the Argentine side it is quickest to fly to the Argentine capital Buenos Aires and then on to either Salta, Catamarca or Mendoza, all large cities which lie nearer the mountains. For the Chilean side it is best to take an international flight to Santiago, the capital of Chile then either fly or bus north to the cities nearer the mountains. There are direct flights to both Buenos Aires and Santiago from most European capitals, including London, Paris, Madrid, Frankfurt and Amsterdam. Aerolineas Argentinas offer good deals on internal flights if you fly into Argentina with them. There are daily flights from Miami, New York and Houston to Santiago and Buenos Aires as well as less frequent flights from Toronto and Los Angeles to Buenos Aires. There is also a weekly Aerolineas flight from Sydney to Buenos Aires.

CLIMATE AND WEATHER CONDITIONS

The summer months of November to April are the best season to go into the mountains in this part of the Andes. At this time of year the climate is in general very dry and stable. Storms lasting a few days occur once or twice a month in summer and these can bring heavy snowfalls as low as 4000m. Persistent strong winds are common all year at higher altitudes and Aconcagua has a particularly bad reputation. The further north you go the drier the climate is and in the Puna de Atacama obtaining water can sometimes be a problem. Around Aconcagua the climate is still very dry but there are big rivers in all the major valleys, so no real problem obtaining water to drink.

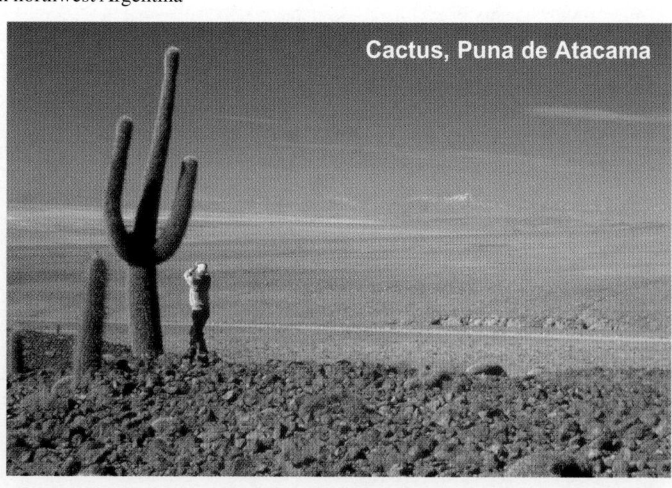

Cactus, Puna de Atacama

The Puna de Atacama

The Puna de Atacama is a high plateau mostly over 4000m above sea level and over 300 kilometres wide. Rainfall is very low and there are many peaks over 6000m with little or no permanent snow on them. The bleak surroundings and constant desolate wind of the Puna de Atacama are not to everyone's taste, but the immense views and the wonderful clarity of the air leave a deep impression on everyone who visits the area.

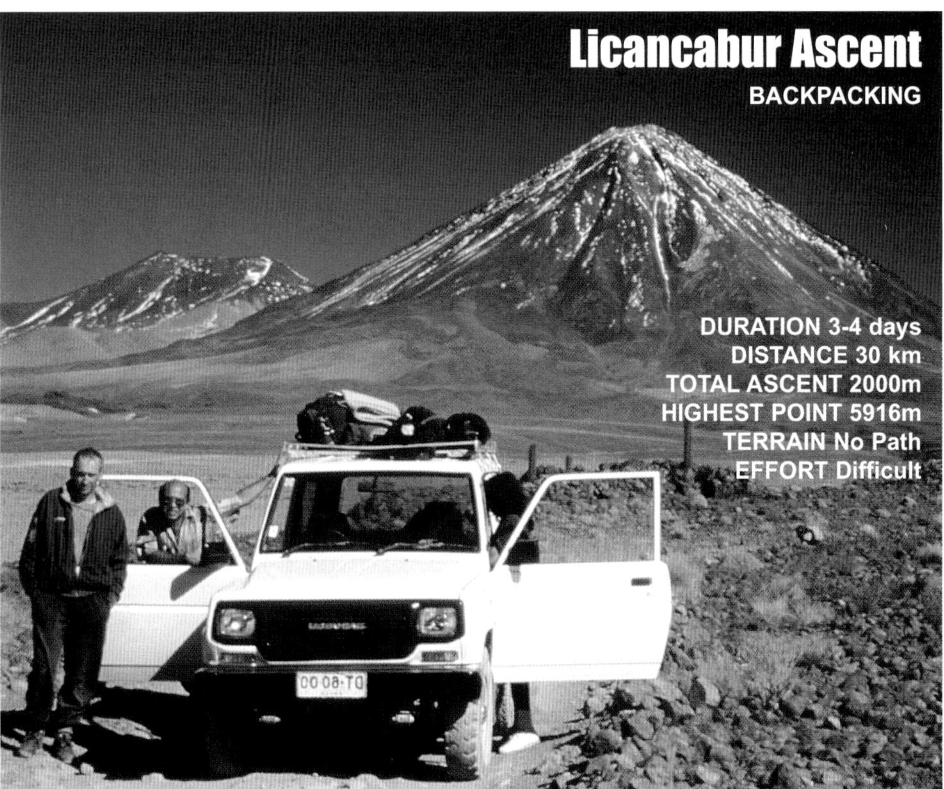

VOLCAN LICANCABUR

In all the wild terrain of the Puna de Atacama one mountain stands out as an easy mountain to reach and climb; Volcan Licancabur 5916m. This is one of the few entertaining outings for walkers in the deserts of northern Chile as it is impractical to trek in many areas due to the extreme aridity. Licancabur is a beautiful active volcanic cone which rises above the oasis village of San Pedro de Atacama, where it has now not rained in 400 years! There are archaeological remains on the summit of the volcano and a crater lake which is usually frozen. The world's highest sub-aqua dive was done here in search of Inca treasure.

You can find a local guide in San Pedro to arrange a trip to the mountain, but make sure you go for at least four days to give yourself time to get used to the high altitude. There is no drinking water anywhere on Licancabur and usually no snow either. You'll need to take all the water you need in plastic containers - allow at least 5 litres per person per day. The ascent is a straightforward and direct route though quite hard work. In the area around the base of the peak you can also walk to and around the beautiful Laguna Verde.

SAN PEDRO DE ATACAMA

The usual start for a trip to Licancabur is the wee village of San Pedro. This beautiful village is very popular with tourists. It sits in a small oasis at a height of 2450m on the edge of a huge salt flat. 4x4 vehicles can be hired here very easily and you can also arrange fully organised trips to Licancabur here. There are lots of cafes and you can take a stroll round the fields of the oasis in the evenings when the heat has died down. You can buy supplies in San Pedro but there is a much better choice in Calama, (see page 183).

To get to San Pedro from the nearest city of Calama is very easy - there are regular buses which take just two hours. To reach Calama from Santiago either fly or take the bus north via Antofagasta. Calama is a small city with a good range of services.

Other highlights of the Chilean Atacama which you should not miss if you are in San Pedro are a dawn trip to see the steaming Tatio geysers at 4500m and a jeep trip out over the huge salt flat of the Salar de Atacama to see the flamingos at the Laguna Chaxa. These trips are well worth doing before you go to Volcan Licancabur as this will allow you some time to acclimatise before the jump to the high altitude of 4500m at the base of Licancabur.

MAP TO USE

Chilean IGM sheet SF-19-11-12, 'Calama', 1:250,000 is adequate, though roads and tracks marked are not up to date. 1:50,000 maps are not currently available.

ACCESS TO VOLCAN LICANCABUR

From San Pedro there are two commonly used approaches to Licancabur, both will require hiring a jeep. The best approach is a very rough track which runs up the west side of the mountain to the col (4400m) between Licancabur and the peak of Sairecabur to the north. It is passable in a 4x4 vehicle to about 3900m, but from here you'll have to walk a further 2-3 hours up the track to a high camp at about 4200m on the northwest side. Watch out for minefields in this whole area - when Chile and Bolivia were less than best friends in the 1970's this area was mined by the military. Most areas are fenced and labelled 'Zona de Minas'.

THE CLIMB

From the camp at 4200m you can walk through the Portezuelo de Chaxas to the Laguna Verde in about **2 hours**. A side walk around the lagoon will take about **4-5 hours**, over some quite rough lava and boulders.

Try to climb Licancabur by a lava rib where the ground is surprisingly stable, composed of large boulders. From the camp at 4200m the summit will be a long day of perhaps **12-14 hours return**, but this very much depends on how well acclimatised you are. The descent is very quick on the loose ash between the ribs. Another option is to bivouac at about 5000m, splitting the long climb to the summit into two days. There is nowhere to pitch a tent here but as long as the weather is good a bivouac can be very comfortable. You'll only need a sleeping bag and mat - you won't need a bivvy bag because the air is so dry.

It is also possible to climb Licancabur from the northeast after travelling up from San Pedro de Atacama via the Portezuelo del Cajon.

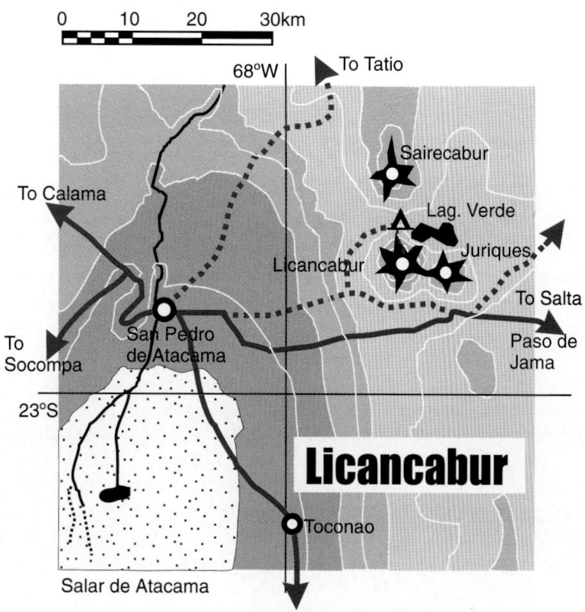

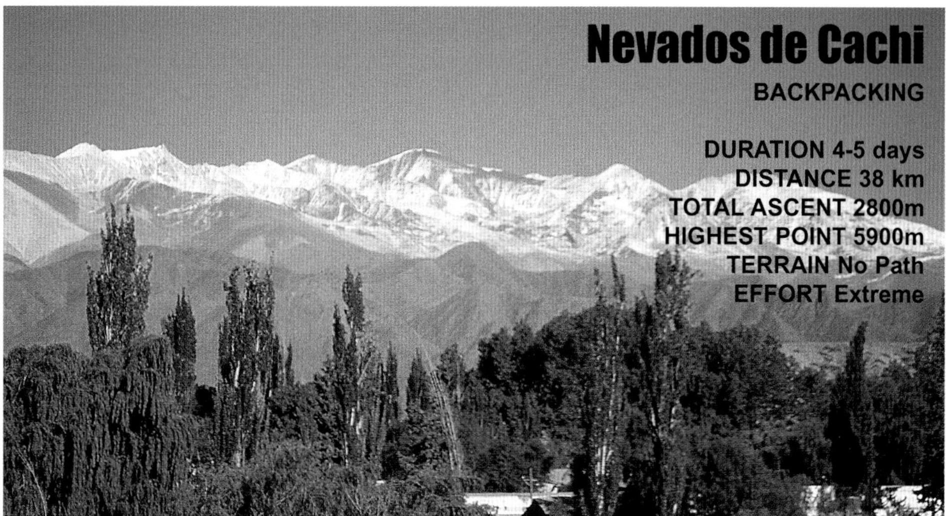

Nevados de Cachi

BACKPACKING

DURATION 4-5 days
DISTANCE 38 km
TOTAL ASCENT 2800m
HIGHEST POINT 5900m
TERRAIN No Path
EFFORT Extreme

NEVADOS DE CACHI

This walk through the highest peaks of the Nevados de Cachi, in Argentina, takes in some of the best scenery in this very quiet mountain range. It is one of the toughest walks in this book but there are some beautiful valleys with magnificent cactus groves to see. It is also a good place to see lots of wildlife such as vicuñas and vizcachas and condors. Although almost unknown to most foreign walkers and climbers this range is quite popular with locals from Salta.

The Nevados de Cachi, which are also known as the Sierra de Cachi are an isolated range on the edge of the Puna de Atacama. The highest peak, Nevado de Cachi, 6380m is also known as Libertador or San Martin after the liberator of Argentina. These mountains are much wetter than the rest of the Puna, though that still leaves them with a very dry climate. The mountains have the same wet and dry seasons as Bolivia. The spring months of October to December are reckoned to be best for walking in the Cachi range though the walk described could be done most of the year with the exception of the very cold mid-winter months of June-September. There will be some snow on this route even in the summer, though an ice-axe should not be needed.

The walk can be done either way around but is described from Las Pailas to Las Cuevas as the high mountain section will be easier this way.

ACCESS

From the city of Salta (see page 184) there are regular buses to the beautiful and sleepy wee town of Cachi at the foot of the Nevados de Cachi. Cachi is approximately 6 hours from Salta by bus (daily). The town has shops, cafes and hotels. The surrounding area has many opportunities for walks in the semi-desert and some wonderful cactus groves. In Cachi it may be possible to arrange mules to help with the first two or three days of this walk whichever way round you do it, though they won't be able to cross the high plateau in the central section. Try asking at the cafe in the main square.

To start the trek travel from Cachi by local bus via Cachi Adentro to the small school in the village of Las Pailas at 3000m, or hire a vehicle to take you here or even a little further up this valley.

MAP TO USE Argentine IGM 1:250,000 sheet 2566-I 'San Antonio de los Cobres' and sheet 2566-III 'Cachi' .

THE ROUTE

1. 4 hours. From the school in Las Pailas walk up the track for 2 km to a track junction. Cross the river on a poor road then take the footpath along the north bank. Cross the wide valley (beautiful cactus forest) to the north side and another stream, then follow this stream uphill. Be sure not to go up the first deep valley on the

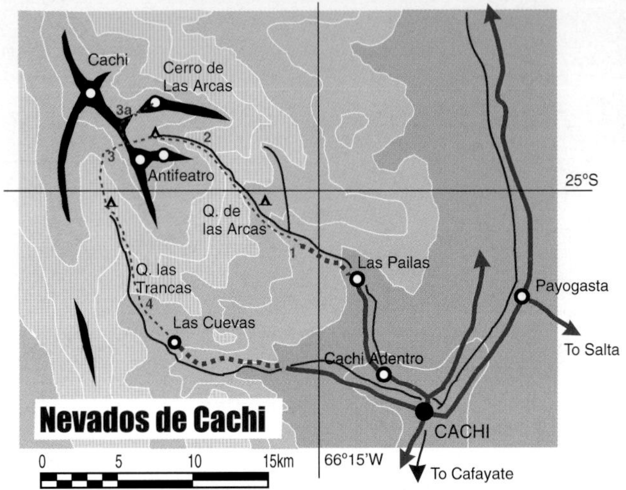

right at an altitude of 3400m. Stay in the main valley and continue up to a less well defined valley and good campsites at 3600m. This valley is the Quebrada de las Arcas.

2. 7-8 hours Follow this valley more steeply going left at the fork at 4200m and on to reach moraines at 4700m, **4 hours**. There is water here and there are other good campsites all the way. Continue through the moraines to a high camp at about 5400m beneath a circular headwall, **3 hours**.

3. 6-7 hours Climb the steep headwall, using one of the rockier ribs to avoid loose scree, **2-3 hours**. Cross the wide plateau above heading almost due west. After a further **1-2 hours** you'll drop into the head of the valley of the Quebrada las Trancas (sometimes called Q. Chinchillar) running away to the south. Walk down this valley to several possible camps at 4600-4800m, **2 hours**.

4. 4 hours. Continue down the Quebrada las Trancas to the track at Las Cuevas at 3600m, **4 hours**. From here it is a further 14km walk downhill to Cachi Adentro if you haven't got transport pre-arranged to collect you.

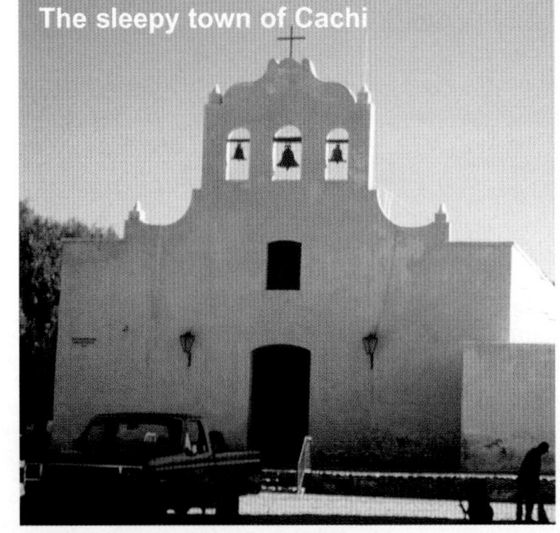
The sleepy town of Cachi

ASCENT OF CERRO LAS ARCAS

From the high camp in Quebrada las Arcas or even from the high point crossing the plateau on section 3 the peak of Cerro de Las Arcas 6050m can be climbed easily. It lies to the northeast and the ascent is a straightforward walk over scree slopes with occasionally a little snow patch.

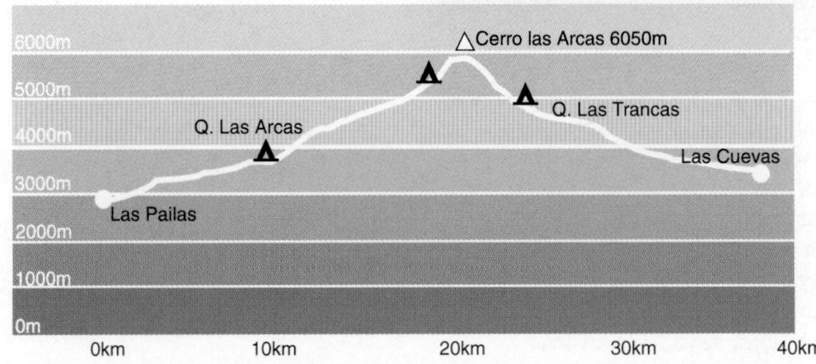

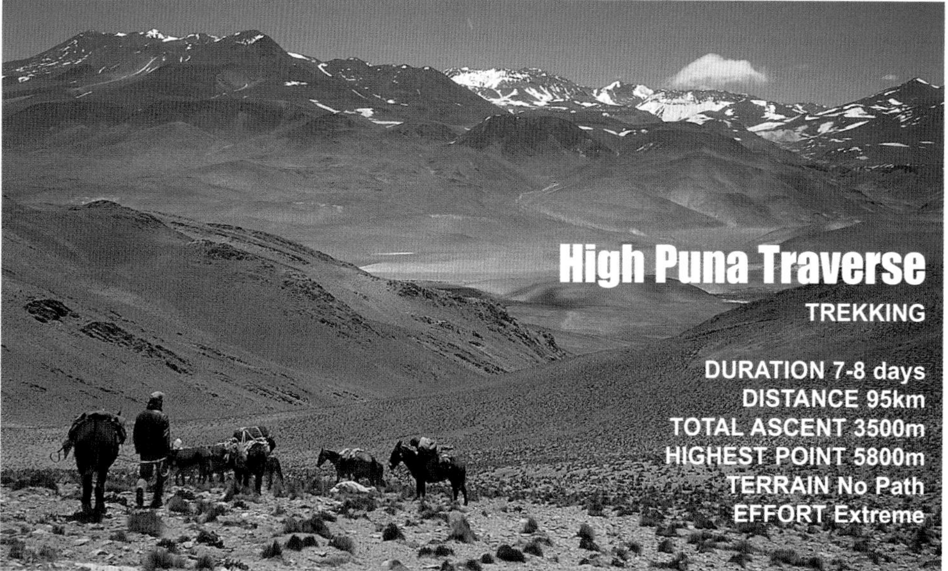

High Puna Traverse
TREKKING
DURATION 7-8 days
DISTANCE 95km
TOTAL ASCENT 3500m
HIGHEST POINT 5800m
TERRAIN No Path
EFFORT Extreme

HIGH PUNA TRAVERSE

This is a trek into the heart of the Puna de Atacama and the remote and sensational Laguna Caldera del Inca, a huge blown out volcanic crater at 5500m above sea level, surrounded by 6500m high peaks. This is one of the most ambitious walks in this guidebook and the full eight day trek should only be undertaken by those with enough experience. There are no mountaineering difficulties whatsoever, but the terrain is very remote and there is always the possibility of bad weather. This is an extremely beautiful but untamed area. It is high desert rather than dramatic peaks which are the attraction here, and wildlife such as vicunas, flamingoes and vizcachas will almost certainly be seen.

There are lots of different opinions about when its best to be in this area. The wetter winter means a lower snowline and more water, but quite serious difficulties due to the cold and the possibility of access roads being closed and mules not being able to pass. The summer is drier and possibly too hot lower down. The spring months of October to December are probably the best on balance. Wind is likely to be the biggest weather problem encountered on this walk - expect 2-3 very windy days per week and be sure to have a tent that will stand up to potentially ferocious winds.

This trek would be quite feasible in reverse.

WARNING

This is an ambitious high trek, with two main potential problems. The weather can be very windy, so a good mountain tent is a necessity. Secondly, several sections require water to be carried if snow cannot be found to melt.

ACCESS

The area described is easiest to reach from the small and sleepy Argentine town of Fiambala. There are basic hotels, shops and facilities for organising an expedition into the Argentine Puna here. There are daily buses to Fiambala from the provincial capitals of Catamarca (page 185) and La Rioja both of which have airports with daily connections to Buenos Aires. Food and fuel can be bought in Fiambala and mountain transport and mules can be arranged through Sr. Jonson Reynoso, who knows the Puna very well. He can be contacted through the offices of the radio station FM Fiambala on the main north-south street in Fiambala.

MAP TO USE

The entire trek is on Argentine IGM 1:250,000 sheet 2769-IV y III 'Fiambala'. Just watch out for those 200m contour lines!

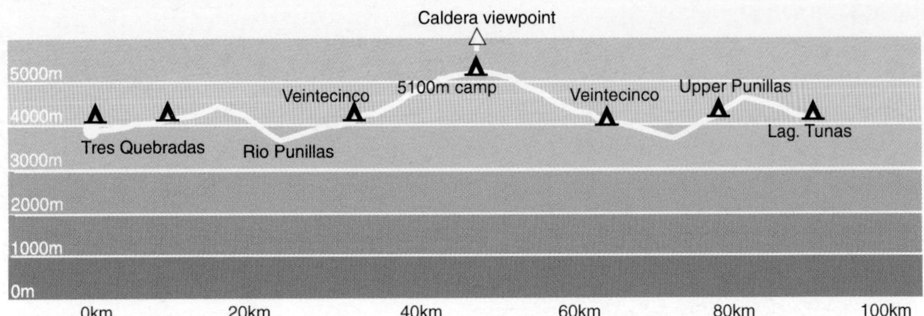

THE ROUTE

A 4x4 vehicle will be needed for the approach. The approach from Fiambala is up the spectacular gorge of Quebrada la Angostura with its bright red canyon walls. After about 60km, at Chaschuil, turn off south and follow a rough track for 20km to the Rio de la Tamberia, then follow this river up westwards as far as you can go, usually with some very rough driving. It is normally possible to get to about 3800m, where the Quebrada Aguas Blancas joins form the northwest. This area is known locally as Tres Quebradas.

1. 4 hours. Follow the main river (Rio de la Tamberia) for 12km to a major valley junction. There is fresh water in the river all the way and the walking is very easy.

2. 8-9 hours. Take the left fork here, walking nearly due west, then **½ hour** later take the right fork to reach a high basin. Go over the col at the back of the basin from the top of which there are great views of the high peak of Bonete 6759m to the west. Continue down the other side of the col on a dusty path to the Rio Punillas (salty), **4 hours**.

Walk westwards across a large grey stony plain and up the valley on the other side, this is the Quebrada Veintecinco. There is fresh water. Several places can be used for camping between 4000m and a valley junction at 4200m, **4 hours**.

3. 7-8 hours. From the junction at 4200m continue up the right hand to another fork beneath a rounded hill. In some years, if there is a lot of snow, this may be as far as mules can go. Take the right fork again and continue northeastwards between two mountain massifs for about 10km to a broad sandy plain at over 5100m. There is a 300-400m high hill in the middle of the plain and a great view northwestwards to Pissis, a 6882m peak. Camping here is truly a wilderness experience!

4. 8-10 hours return. From this camp you can do a return trip to the Caldera del Inca in one day. From the bottom of the 300m hill head west then southwest across a desolate high desert to reach the northwest rim of the Laguna Caldera del Inca. The best view is from a 5800m high hill which lies at the southeast end of a 2-3km long ridge. The caldera is a truly spectacular crater over 5km wide and over 600m deep. There is a glacier on the far side of the crater wall and a deep blue lake in the bottom of the crater, at an altitude of nearly 5200m.

5. 5 hours. Reverse day 3 to the camp at 4200m.

6. 5-6 hours. Continue down the Quebrada Veinticinco to the Rio Punillas, **2-3 hours**, then walk north up the Rio Punillas for 8km to a stream junction at 3900m, with views to the east flanks of Monte Pissis. The water coming down the north branch of the Punillas is fresh. **3 hours**.

7. 7-8 hours From here walk north-north-east, at first following the river upstream, then crossing a shallow watershed at 4550m. Descend gradually through a wide valley, to reach the Laguna de los Tunas (no fresh water). There is sometimes an arrieros camp here. Arrange beforehand to have your 4x4 transport meet you here.

Vicuña, Puna de Atacama

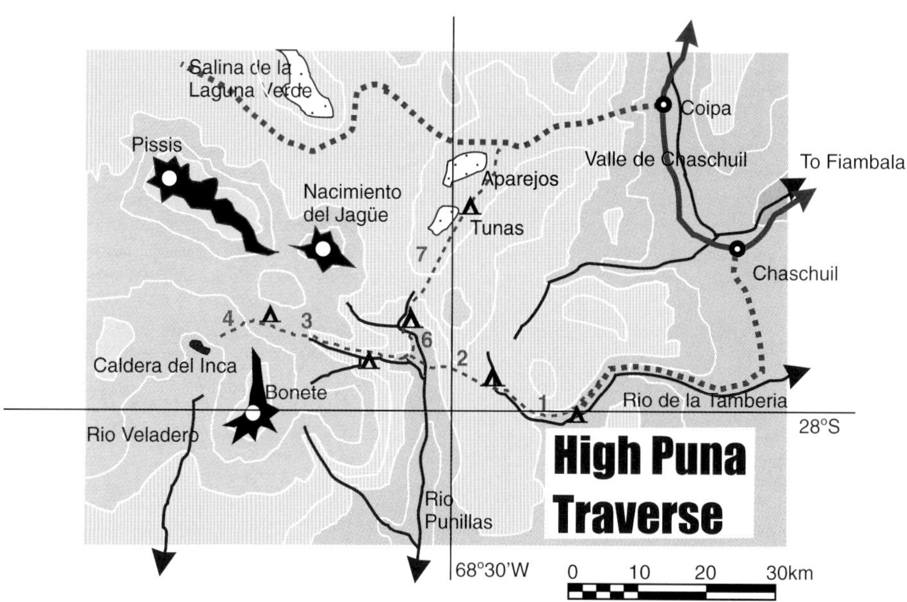

The huge crater of the Caldera del Inca

Aconcagua Area

We use this name for the area of the Andes between Santiago in Chile and Mendoza in Argentina. These are the highest peaks in the Andes with Aconcagua 6959m, lying entirely in Argentina but not far from the Chilean border. The mountains have a very dry climate, though not so dry as the Puna de Atacama to the north. The best time of year to be in these mountains is definitely the austral summer of November-March. The walking here is mostly very adventurous with few easy routes. River crossings are a major hazard on several of the routes described.

Several **Treks around Aconcagua**, are described as well as an **Ascent of Aconcagua**, since this is technically the highest trekking peak in the world. If conditions are good it is just a walk to the summit, mostly on a good path. However Aconcagua is a very big mountain and the challenges of surviving for many day at high altitude (and sometimes in bad weather) should not be underestimated.

In Chile, near Santiago we describe two other challenging trips, either of which would make a good acclimatisation trip if you were planning to walk up Aconcagua. Firstly there is the **Ascent of del Plomo** and secondly the **Marmolejo Traverse**.

Santiago

MENDOZA

Mendoza is one of the biggest and most prosperous cities in Argentina and the normal base for climbing and trekking in Aconcagua provincial park. Permits need to be obtained here in person, whether you are trekking or climbing. Mendoza is a very pleasant, clean and modern city with many tree lined avenues and pavement cafes. In the summer season it is normally very hot and dry, though big thunderstorms are common. There is nothing special to see in Mendoza but tours to the nearby wineries can be enjoyable and are easily organised. A walk round Parque San Martin to the west of the centre, with good views of the city from **Co. La Gloria** and the nearby zoo is a good half day trip. Otherwise hang out in the pavement cafes on Sarmiento or San Martin.

For more information on Mendoza see page 185.

SANTIAGO

Santiago the capital of Chile is a bustling city which lies at the foot of the Andes. On clear days (most common in spring and summer) it is possible to see the great humpbacked peak of Cerro del Plomo 5424m, from the city centre. Access to the mountains around Cerro del Plomo and the Maipu valley is very easy but the low altitude of Santiago can lead to acclimatisation problems.

The city is built along an east-west axis road, known as the Alameda (or O'Higgins) under which runs the main metro line. The smart suburbs and shopping areas are nearest to the mountains and the poorest areas are in the west near Estacion Central.

There is some nice architecture around the older part of town near the Presidential Palace. Near the centre of the old town **Co. Sta. Lucia 634m**, makes a worthy ascent for a view of the city and surrounding mountains, **½hour**. The hill is a maze of pathways and bizarre architecture that is a delight to explore on your first day of 35°C, January weather! **Co. San Cristobal 880m,** with its funicular, gondola and huge statue of the virgin is another pleasant escape from the city fumes.

For more information on Santiago see page 182.

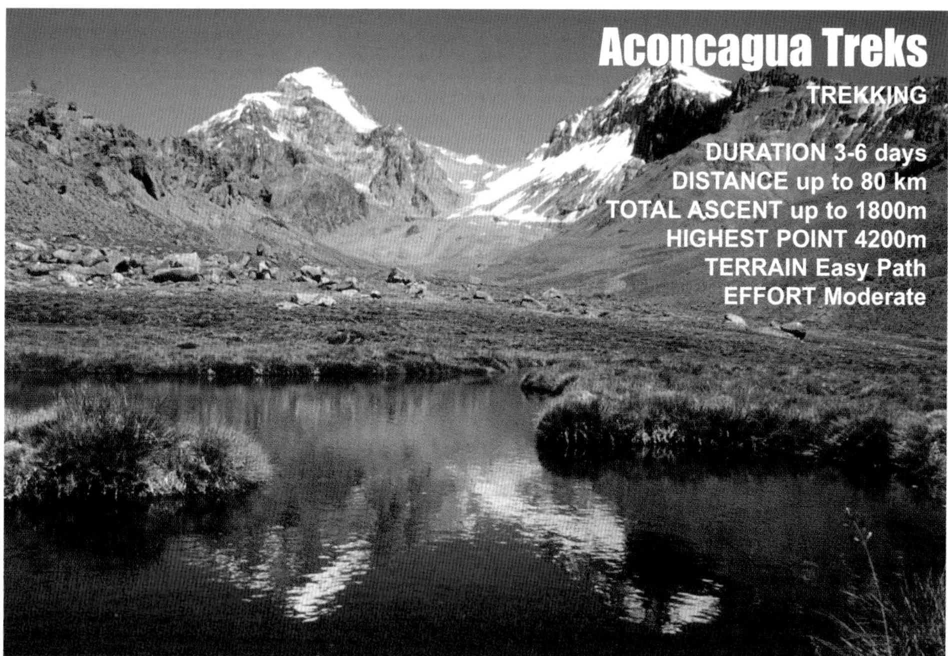

ACONCAGUA TREKS

Because it is an easy climb and the highest peak in the Americas, Aconcagua is now the busiest mountain in South America.

If you aren't interested in climbing Aconcagua the easy three day trek to see the spectacular south face of this mountain is still highly recommended. The trek up the Vacas valley is also worthwhile to see some great scenery and wildlife such as guanacos and condors. The only disadvantage of these treks is that you have to come out the same way you went in. Both these treks are described here. The normal ascent route on the peak, which takes most people about two weeks, is described below. It is also possible to do a 'traverse' of the mountain by walking in up the Vacas valley and out down the Horcones valley or vice versa.

Permission is required to climb the peak or even just to trek in the Provincial Park that surrounds the mountain, but this is easy to arrange in Mendoza.

REGULATIONS

The regulations change regularly. At present they are very simple. A permit needs to be obtained for each member of the group from the 'Subsecretaria de Turismo' at San Martin 1143 (normally open even on Sundays). This requires basic personal details and a fee of \$20-\$40 for a trekking permit and up to \$200 for an ascent permit, all depending on the time of year. (Christmas and January is the high season and most expensive) These fees were current in 2000-01 but may well rise in future. The process takes only an hour at the most. The fee is perhaps justified as the mountain is kept very clean and the base camps are staffed by friendly and helpful rangers with radio communications.

ACCESS

From Mendoza take a bus to either Punta de Vacas for the Vacas valley or Puente del Inca for the Horcones valley. It is about 3 hours by bus to Punta de Vacas, 3½ to Puente del Inca. This is the main bus route to Santiago in Chile and there are frequent departures every morning. Mules to carry your bags can easily be arranged overnight in Puente del Inca, though the mule drivers are very busy with organised groups over Christmas. At Punta de Vacas you can also arrange mules, but it might be better to do this in advance in Mendoza because this route is much less frequented.

MAP TO USE

Despite being the most popular peak in South America it is hard to get a good map of the mountain. The best map, though hard to find, is the 1:50,000 sketch map published in 1987 by the American Alpine Club but it only covers the area around the peak itself. The Argentine IGM sheet 3369-I, 'Cerro Aconcagua' at 1:250,000 is a bit dated but otherwise all right. The 1:100,000 IGM sheets are useless - don't buy them.

THREE DAY WALK TO THE SOUTH FACE

3 days, 32km return, 1600m ascent, Moderate, Good Path

A short trek to see the spectacular 3000m high south face of Aconcagua with its hanging glaciers and huge rock walls.

Go by bus from Mendoza to Puente del Inca at an altitude of 2700m. Mules to carry your gear can usually be arranged on the spot here as there are many climbers going to the base camp for Aconcagua. The natural bridge nearby is worth a look if you have time to spare. There are cafes, hotels, bunkhouse and camping at Puente del Inca.

1. 2 hours. The walk to the south face usually takes three days with a camp at Confluencia (3350m). The trail actually starts at the ranger station at Laguna Horcones (4km west from Puente del Inca on the main road then 2km north on a track). Start on the left side of the river but cross by a bridge and go up the right hand side on an easily followed path. Cross the Lower Horcones river by a bridge and continue for 15 mins. to the Confluencia camp (3350m).

2. 8 hours return. From Confluencia you can walk to Plaza Francia in one day return to see the south face. Go back to the bridge and then up a path on the right side of the Lower Horcones river for about 10km to a ruined hut and Plaza Francia, 4300m, the usual base camp for climbers trying the extremely difficult and dangerous south face routes. Good views of the south face start about half way to Plaza Francia.

3. 2 hours. Reverse day 1 to Puente del Inca.

SIX DAY WALK UP THE VACAS VALLEY

5-6 days, 80km return, 1800m ascent, Moderate, Good Path

A highly recommended longer trek to the quieter eastern side of Aconcagua, reaching the Plaza Argentina base camp at 4200m. There are great views of Aconcagua and the upper Vacas valley is a good place to see wildlife. It is best to arrange mules in advance in Mendoza as far fewer climbers use the Vacas valley approach and you might have to wait a few days to find mules at Punta de Vacas.

1. 5 hours. The route starts at Punta de Vacas (2400m) where there are a couple of cafes. A good path starts on the west side of the river and is very easy to follow. The valley can be very dry, with water sometimes available only once, about half way. The first camp at Las Leñas is reached after a long slow climb and then a sudden descent. There is a bridge over the river Vacas here, ranger station and pit toilets.

2. 5 hours The serious river crossing at Las Leñas is much safer now due to a new bridge 800m upstream from the camp. Once across the river the second day is up the east side of the valley on a good and easily followed path (often no water) to Casa de Piedra, a lovely scenic campsite where the Relinchos valley joins the main valley. If you are just here for the trekking this is a good place to base yourself for several nights before walking back out via Las Leñas.

3. 6 hours From Casa de Piedra the third day is then up the Relinchos valley to the Plaza Argentina base camp. The braided Vacas river is easy to cross at Casa de Piedra to gain the north bank of the Relinchos. Follow the Relinchos on a good but steep path, crossing twice (very narrow but fast and quite deep).

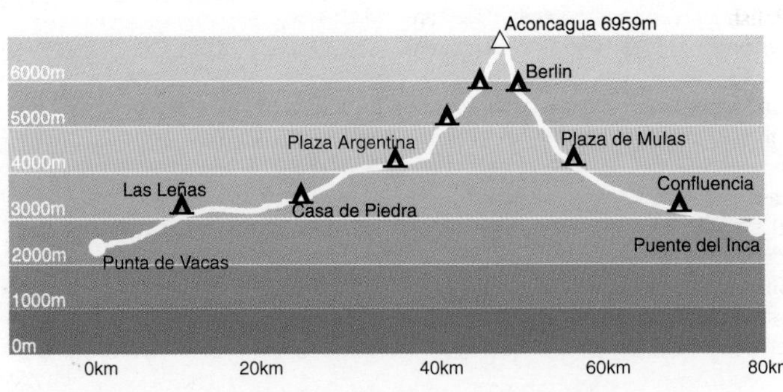

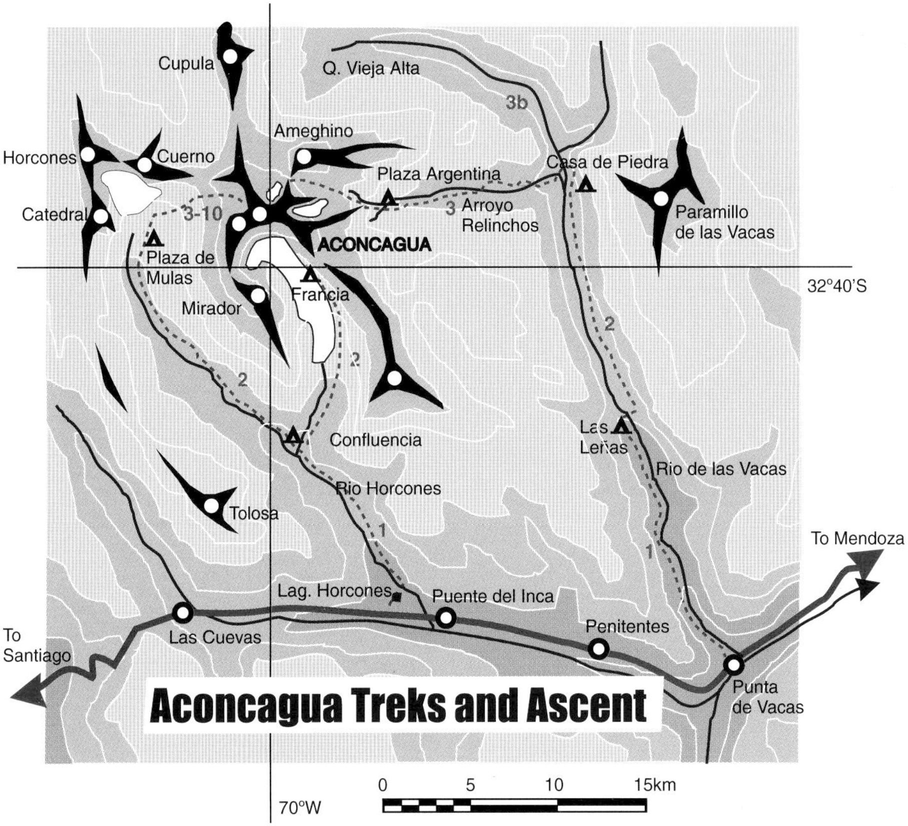

Cupula
Q. Vieja Alta
3b
Ameghino
Horcones
Cuerno
Casa de Piedra
Plaza Argentina
Catedral
3-10
3 Arroyo Relinchos
Paramillo de las Vacas
ACONCAGUA
Plaza de Mulas
Francia
32°40'S
Mirador
2
2
2
Las Leñas
Confluencia
Rio de las Vacas
Rio Horcones
Tolosa
1
1
To Mendoza
Lag. Horcones
Puente del Inca
Penitentes
To Santiago
Las Cuevas
Punta de Vacas
70°W
0 5 10 15km

Aconcagua Treks and Ascent

After a steep climb cross the Relinchos river again and follow the wide flat valley to the Plaza Argentina base camp in the moraines (4200m). There are pit toilets, beer tents, and usually a satellite phone available at this base camp. Climbers come here to try to climb the more difficult Polish glacier route, though others are here to traverse over the mountain and try the normal route.

3a. 7-8 hours return. You can do the walk up to base camp described above in as a long day trip.

3b. Up to 10 hours. Another great day walk from Casa de Piedra is to carry on up the main Vacas valley, after 2-3 hours you'll get good views of the peaks of the Cupula range. It is also a good place to see wildlife as few climbers come this way.

4. and **5.** Reverse your route over days one to three from Plaza Argentina to regain the road.

Sunrise on the east face of Aconcagua

ACONCAGUA ASCENT
Aconcagua is widely regarded as the highest peak in the world which can be walked up. While Aconcagua can indeed be climbed without special mountaineering techniques, the ascent can often be in difficult environmental conditions (high winds and sometimes snow) and should only be tackled by experienced trekkers. The main reason people fail to reach the summit is poor expedition organisation.

First there is a two day walk from Puente del Inca to the base camp at Plaza de Mulas at 4200m. From here the ascent is over scree with some snow patches and three or more higher camps will be needed before the final climb up the north-west ridge and a steep scree gully known as the canaleta.

In most years no technical equipment is needed, but snow is common higher on the mountain and occasionally an ice-axe and crampons may be needed above the Independencia hut. In all conditions a very good pair of boots (preferably plastic), gaiters, full windproof clothing, several hats, thick gloves and mitts and a down jacket are all pretty much essential for a safe ascent.

The route is described below over 12 days, but many groups may need a few days more to allow for acclimatisation on the mountain. Access from Mendoza is described above under 'Aconcagua Treks'

1. 2 hours. As for day one of the walk to the south face described above, to the Confluencia camp at 3350m.

2. 6-7 hours. Continue up the dry and dusty Horcones valley on a very easily followed trail. Sometimes this requires crossing some of the channels in the Horcones river. Soon after you reach a ruined building at 4000m

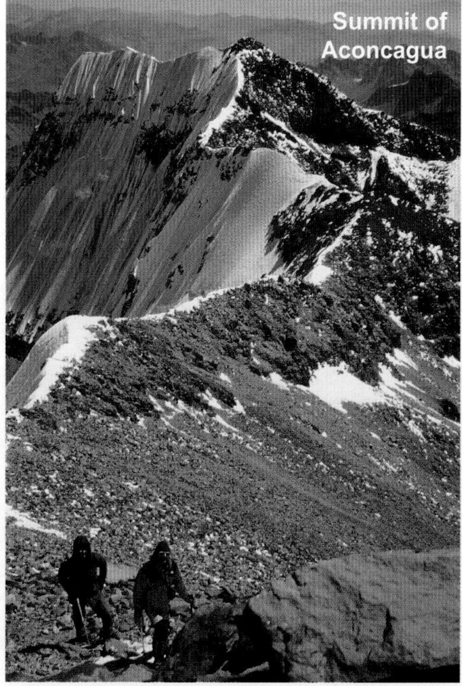
Summit of Aconcagua

you begin the last steep climb to the Plaza de Mulas base camp, where there are toilets, meal tents, a hotel refugio and many other facilities for climbers.

Days 3 to 6. Above base camp the route is very obvious, starting up to the right of the Horcones glacier. Above this the trail is a wide path that climbs the scree slopes of the northwest flanks in a long series of switchbacks. The first camp above base that is regularly used is the big flat area at Nido de Condores at 5350m, though camps are also possible at Canada, 4900m and Alaska 5200m. Your progress will depend on your acclimatisation but it is likely you will need days 3 to 6 to rest at base camp, carry loads and establish a camp at Nido. The walk to Nido can take anything from 4-10 hours up, depending on acclimatisation and load carried, and as little as one hour to descend.

Days 7 to 9. These days will get you to the Berlin (Plantamura) camp at 5950m on the normal route. The path from Nido is again obvious, going eastwards then following a slight rib to the huts at Berlin. Nido to Berlin takes from 2-4 hours depending on acclimatisation and load carried.

Day 10. Summit day. 10-16 hours. From Berlin you can climb to the summit in one very long day, but it is also possible to camp a little higher at White Rocks, 6000m Though there is no permanent snow and the route can be entirely over scree, an axe and crampons may be needed and they should perhaps be carried. Follow the path up the left hand side of the ridge to the White Rocks camp. From White Rocks the path weaves up the ridge to the Independencia ruin at 6500m. From here to the summit hard snow and ice might be encountered but most years the path is free of snow. Continue over the Cresta del Viento and then on a path across the top of the Gran Accareo past a very prominent vertical rock to the foot of the notorious Canaleta. This is an appalling and unstable boulder slope which leads to the summit ridge at 6900m. The climbing is easiest on the right of the Canaleta. Turn left at the top of the Canaleta and follow the ridge a short way to reach the summit, **7-10 hours** of ascent from Berlin camp, plus **3-4 hours** to descend.

11. 3-4 hours. From Berlin the descent to Plaza de Mulas is obvious. Drop quickly down the 1800m to the base camp and a beer.

12. 7-8 hours. The walk out to the road the way you came in takes one day.

High Camp on Aconcagua

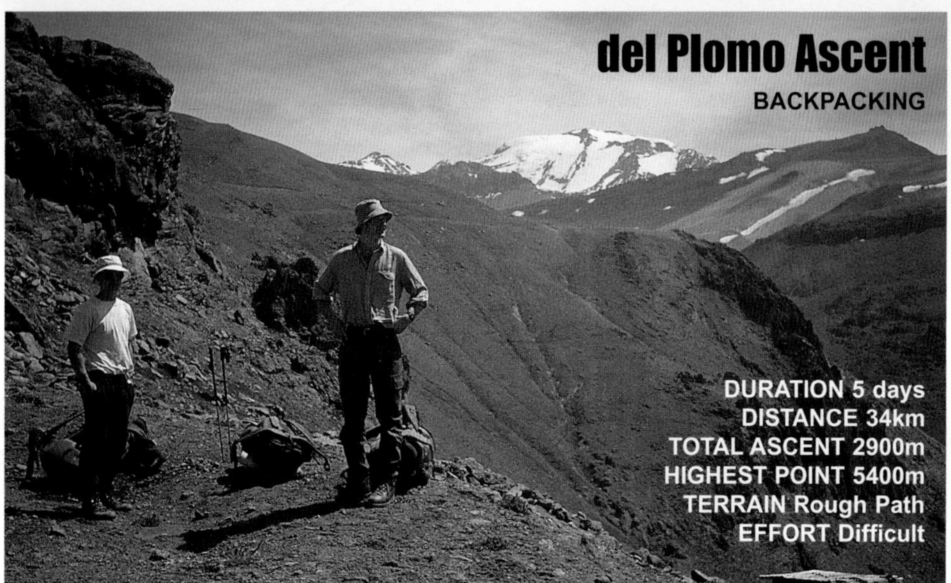

DEL PLOMO ASCENT

Cerro del Plomo 5424m, is the peak seen prominently from Santiago as a curving snow dome. It makes a fine ascent with easy access and is one of the easiest peaks of the High Andes to climb. The ascent is popular in summer with Santiago students. There are excellent views from the summit to the giant peaks in this area including Aconcagua and Tupungato. The summit was reached by the Incas many years ago and a mummy was found buried near the summit in 1954, the first such discovery. This body proved that warts existed in the New World before Columbus arrived!

We describe two different access possibilities and two routes, but in practice you can choose either of these routes to reach and leave the mountain. The route as described requires an ice-axe and crampons even during the high summer months of January and February because of a short icy section high up.

ACCESS

The route is described starting out from the Valle Nevado ski resort and finishing at La Parva ski resort, but it can be done in reverse or you can walk back to the same ski resort you started from.

Drive from Santiago to the Valle Nevado ski resort (this has no facilities in summer). A taxi will cost $40-50 from Santiago, 2 hours drive. If you can't afford a taxi it might be easier to start and finish the walk at La Parva. For travel information on Santiago see page 182.

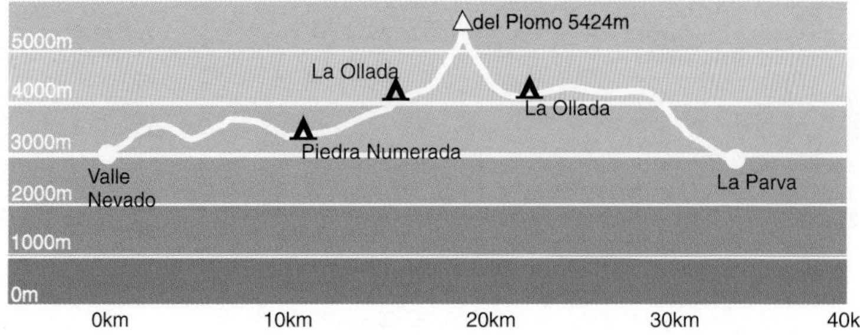

MAP TO USE

Chilean IGM 1:50,000 sheet 3300-7000 'Cord. de los Piuquenes', sheet 3315-7000, 'Rio Olivares' and sheet 3315-7015 'Farellones'.

THE ROUTE

1. 5-6 hours From Valle Nevado follow vehicle tracks to the hill at the top of the 4 person chair known as El Mirador then descend the other side of the ridge to reach the Estero las Bayas valley which lies behind. Descend into the Estero las Bayas to a point where two ski tows leave from either side of the valley floor. From here walk up the right hand fork of the valley on a track and cross a col at the top, 3550m. On the other side of the col descend the valley of the Estero Las Yaretas to the east, now following a faint path, to reach the main valley of the Estero Cepo. Turn left here and follow this river upstream to a camp by the large boulder at Piedra Numerada (3400m). If you are not acclimatised it is a good idea to have a rest day either here or at the next camp before making your ascent.

2. 3-4 hours Follow the valley upstream on a path to the base of the southwest glaciers of del Plomo. There are various campsites here between 4200m and 4300m. This area is known as La Olla. Camping one or two hours higher will make the long summit day shorter.

3. 8-10 hours From the La Olla camp at the foot of the glaciers climb the right hand (and broader) of two ribs on rock and scree. There is a clear path that zigzags up here but it is quite loose with scree in places. There are a couple of rundown huts on the route at 4600m. At 4900m the path steepens and becomes looser. Move left to reach the ruins of some Inca walls at 5150m, then cross a short icy section and climb up the ridge behind over gradually less steep ground to summit. **5-7 hours** up plus **2-4 hours** down.

4. Either reverse your route back to Valle Nevado or follow the description here to reach La Parva.

6-7 hours. From the high camps descend the Estero del Cepo slightly to about 4000m and then make an ascending traverse for 100-150m out of this valley to reach the broad ridge running from Cerro Leonera to Pintor. Follow this ridge southwards passing near the summits of Pintor 4180m and Cerro la Parva 4070m. Between Cerro La Parva and Cerro Falsa Parva you can drop off the ridge to the left, so that you bypass the summit cliffs which lie south of Cerro La Parva and reach a small col at the top of the ski area. Follow the tows and chairlifts down to the resort of La Parva. Though this high route back to La Parva has excellent views and easy walking it is also possible to make a lower route back to La Parva by walking out past Piedra Numerada and Estero las Yaretas, then heading west to reach the ski slopes of La Parva at the top of the Franciscano chairlift. If setting out to Plomo from La Parva this lower route is recommended.

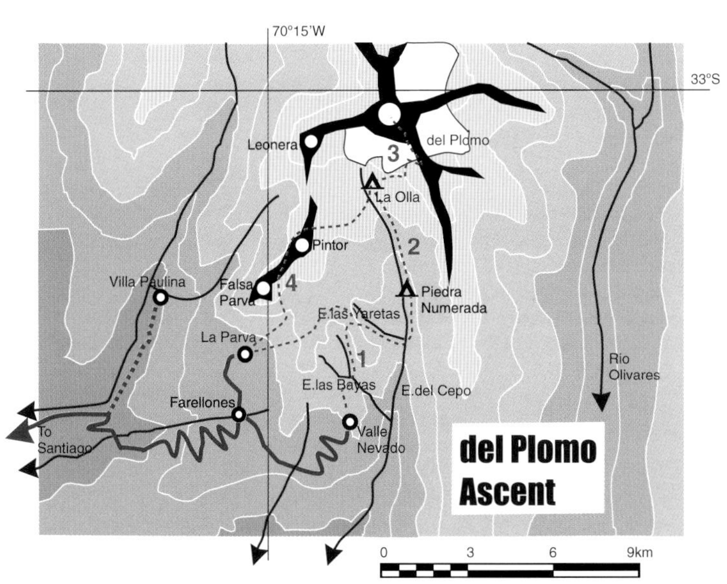

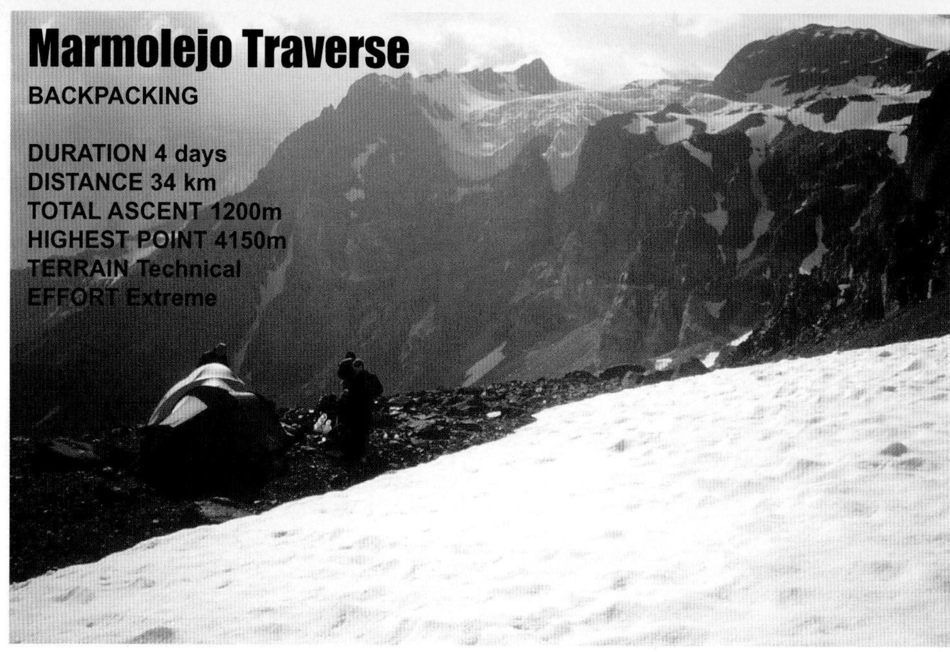

Marmolejo Traverse

BACKPACKING

DURATION 4 days
DISTANCE 34 km
TOTAL ASCENT 1200m
HIGHEST POINT 4150m
TERRAIN Technical
EFFORT Extreme

MARMOLEJO TRAVERSE

This is one of the more difficult and rewarding routes in this guidebook, a relatively short but high walk over a 4150m pass with the option to climb to one of the easiest 6000m summits in the Andes. And all this is just two hours drive from Santiago. Marmolejo is the southernmost 6000m peak in the Andes and, indeed, in the world. It has impressive faces on many sides with a huge hanging glacier on the north face.

The steep snow slopes on the south side of the pass will probably require an ice-axe (and possibly crampons) most summers, and there are several river crossings for which a rope may need to be carried. The walk should be planned so that the river crossings can be done as early as possible in the day. It is better to do the walk from north to south as there is an altitude advantage and transport is much easier to find at Baños Morales.

ACCESS

From Santiago (see page 182) travel to the road end at the Termas del Plomo on the Rio Yeso. Turn off the main road to Baños Morales at the village of San Gabriel in the Maipo canyon. There is no public transport beyond San Gabriel so you will need to arrange to be dropped off by a tour agency. The road is quite rough and will probably require 4x4 for the last few kilometres. There is nothing at Termas del Plomo apart from the hot springs, which are worth a quick visit - it may be best to camp overnight here to cross the river early in the morning.

MAPS TO USE

For the traverse Chilean IGM sheet 3330-6945 'Rio Yeso' and sheet 3345-6945 'Volcan San Jose' both at 1:50,000. For the day walk up the Morado valley use sheets 3345-7000 'El Volcan' and 3330-7000 'Embalse El Yeso' at 1:50,000.

THE ROUTE

1. 3-4 hours. Make a difficult river crossing at the Termas del Plomo, best early in the day. Then walk south up the west bank of the Estero del Plomo valley to a more open and grassy meadow at 3300m with excellent views of the north face of Marmolejo. The first part of this section is quite rough going over moraines cut through by the river.

2. 5 hours Go south across the meadows with more good views of Marmolejos northern glaciers. Then walk up the smaller valley on the right towards a col to the southwest. There are good campsites just before the col at 4050m but water only from snow melt. Marmolejo can be climbed from this camp in two days.

3. 4-5 hours To continue the main walk cross the small col behind the campsite (marked as 138 on the 1:50,000 map but obviously 4138m). Descend steep slopes for 200m on the south side; these may have considerable snow cover and require an ice-axe and perhaps crampons. These slopes are easiest to the east. Then walk down the Estero Colina, at first over wide rubble strewn slopes then down a narrow gorge staying mainly on the west bank but making several crossings. After **3-4 hours** the slopes open out and you'll see the broad green pastures of La Engorda in front of you. There are many good campsites here, the best are about 1-2 km further on once the valley has turned to the west. This is a particular scenic spot under the slopes of Volcan San Jose, 5856m.

4. 2-3 hours. Follow the valley down, keeping to the south side and pick up a path which descends around the prominent ridge of El Morro to meet a mining track coming up from Baños Morales. Follow this track down to the village, a small mountain resort where there are several hostels, shops, beer and a camp ground. Buses from Baños Morales back to Santiago are very busy in summer, but you should at least be able to arrange one for the next day. Hitching is also possible; even a lift a short way down the valley will give you more public transport options.

ASCENT OF MARMOLEJO

2a. 2 days. The ascent is very straightforward with only a short section over a largely crevasse free glacier. From the col at 4138m follow the broad west ridge on scree and rock to a higher camp on small rock platforms at 4500m just before the glacier, **3 hours.** From this high camp follow the ridge up and across the glacier (very few crevasses) to reach the easy final summit cone of screes. **6-8 hours up** and **2-3 hours down.**

DAY WALKS FROM BAÑOS MORALES

There are several good day walks which can be done from Baños Morales. The most notable is the walk up the Estero Morado valley into the heart of the Loma Larga range.

Another good day walk is to reverse day 4 of the Marmolejo traverse, reaching the scenic La Engorda valley.

Estero del Plomo valley

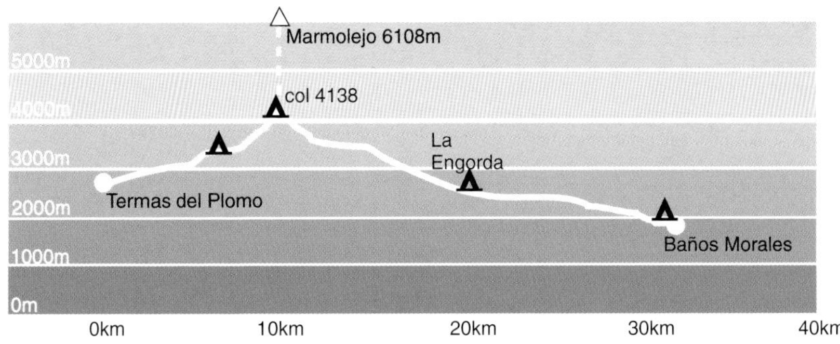

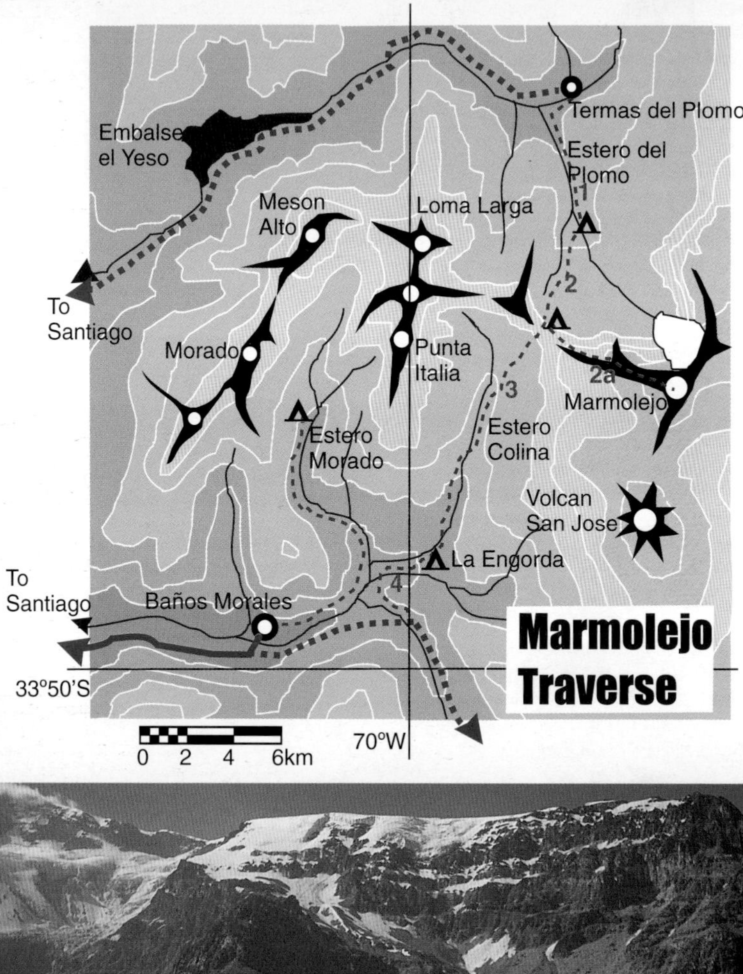

Termas del Plomo
Embalse el Yeso
Estero del Plomo
1
Meson Alto
Loma Larga
2
To Santiago
Morado
Punta Italia
2a
3
Marmolejo
Estero Morado
Estero Colina
Volcan San Jose
La Engorda
To Santiago
Baños Morales
4

Marmolejo Traverse

33°50'S
0 2 4 6km
70°W

Walking towards Marmolejo from the north

Campsite below Volcan Villarrica

INTRODUCTION

The northern section of the Patagonian Andes is better known as the Andean Lake District. It is a stunningly beautiful region of blue lochs, thick forests and snow capped volcanoes which straddles the Chile-Argentina border. This is without a doubt the most underrated area of the Andes, with great weather, easy travel and access and absolutely superb scenery. There are some excellent long distance walks and backpacking trips in wild and untouched forests as well as plenty of shorter hikes. The area also has some superb areas for mountain biking, horse-riding, rafting, skiing and a selection of easy volcanoes to climb including the spectacularly active **Volcan Villarrica.** When you are not active there are hundreds of tea rooms serving excellent cakes. Its pretty close to paradise.

In the Chilean Lake District all longer trips will need to be done as backpacking trips. The majority are forest based walks, often through stands of the unusual monkey puzzle trees. In the north of the region the **circuit of Volcan Antuco** takes three days and you can add another day to climb the peak. This walk is mainly through lava deserts and volcanic wilderness. In the Villarrica National Park the **Villarrica traverse** offers varied walking through monkey puzzle forest, grassland and volcanic plateaux with great views of several snow capped peaks.

To take you between Chile and Argentina we describe the **Paso de las Nubes** hike with great views of Tronador's spectacular glaciers.

On the Argentine side of the Andes the rugged Cerro Catedral group of peaks offer good mountain walking. They are one of the few areas of the Andes where you can do a hut to hut tour as you would in the Alps. The route that has come to be known as the **Nahuel Huapi traverse** is described here. Many other hut based walks are possible in this very accessible and popular area of the Andes.

GETTING THERE

For the Chilean side of the mountains (Villarica and Antuco) the best way to get to the area is an international flight to Santiago (page 182) and then either fly or take a bus south to the cities of Los Angeles or Temuco. For the Argentine side of the mountains it will be quickest to fly to Bariloche via the capital Buenos Aires (page 184), though there are also bus services on this route. Bus transport on these long distance routes is very comfortable and efficient in both Chile and Argentina.

CLIMATE AND WEATHER CONDITIONS

The whole area is far enough south to experience full temperate summers and winters, so December to March is the best time to walk in the whole area. The weather during this period is generally very good and similar to the weather in a northern European summer. The Chilean side of the mountains are wetter than the Argentine side and even in summer it can sometimes rain for several days at a time. Because of the lower altitude of the peaks in this part of the Andes the weather is rarely very extreme.

The view down into Volcan Villarrica's active crater

Villarrica's crater

Antuco Circuit
BACKPACKING
DURATION 3 days
DISTANCE 40km
TOTAL ASCENT 900m
HIGHEST POINT 2050m
TERRAIN No Path
EFFORT Moderate

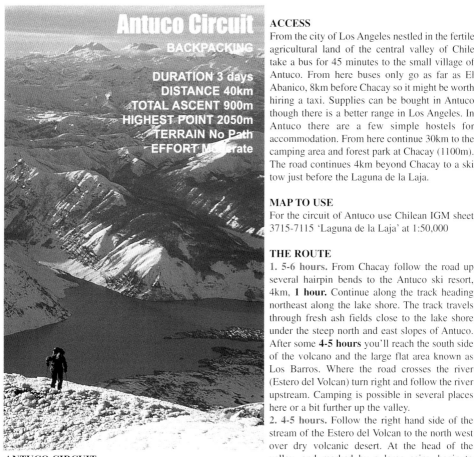

ANTUCO CIRCUIT
Volcan Antuco is a 2985m high active volcano whose recent eruption formed a 200m high lava dam creating the beautiful blue Laguna de la Laja. This area is now protected by a national park. A circuit of the mountain is described here, along with an ascent to the crater by the north slopes. There are good views from the circuit and the ascent of the neighbouring peak of Sierra Velluda. Volcan Antuco was first climbed in 1828, the earliest recorded mountain ascent in Chile. The route is described clockwise as the descent from the pass is probably easier this way, but could be done equally well in reverse.

ACCESS
From the city of Los Angeles nestled in the fertile agricultural land of the central valley of Chile take a bus for 45 minutes to the small village of Antuco. From here buses only go as far as El Abanico, 8km before Chacay so it might be worth hiring a taxi. Supplies can be bought in Antuco though there is a better range in Los Angeles. In Antuco there are a few simple hostels for accommodation. From here continue 30km to the camping area and forest park at Chacay (1100m). The road continues 4km beyond Chacay to a ski tow just before the Laguna de la Laja.

MAP TO USE
For the circuit of Antuco use Chilean IGM sheet 3715-7115 'Laguna de la Laja' at 1:50,000

THE ROUTE
1. 5-6 hours. From Chacay follow the road up several hairpin bends to the Antuco ski resort, 4km, **1 hour.** Continue along the track heading northeast along the lake shore. The track travels through fresh ash fields close to the lake shore under the steep north and east slopes of Antuco. After some **4-5 hours** you'll reach the south side of the volcano and the large flat area known as Los Barros. Where the road crosses the river (Estero del Volcan) turn right and follow the river upstream. Camping is possible in several places here or a bit further up the valley.
2. 4-5 hours. Follow the right hand side of the stream of the Estero del Volcan to the north west over dry volcanic desert. At the head of the valley, and marked by a large cairn, begin to climb the slopes to the right to reach a col (2054m) which lies southwest of Antuco, **3 hours**. This section may have some snow on it. Drop steeply down into the valley below and pick-up and follow the small stream westwards as it is forced around the edge of a fresh lava flow to a camp on grass by the stream at 1530m, **2 hours**.
3. 2 hours. Follow the path downstream for ½ **hour** to reach a lava flow. the path continues down to the left of this lava, marked by cairns, then moves away from the stream. Continue downhill for another hour to reach Chacay, emerging by the park rangers hut (In reverse this path is signposted ' Los Zorros'.)

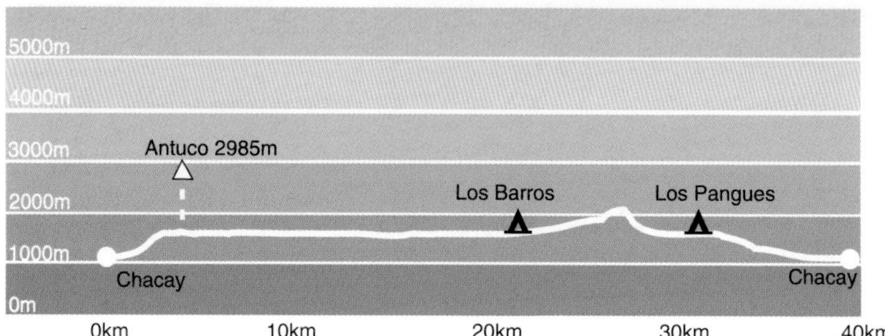

ANTUCO CLIMB

The climb can be done on day 1 of the trek, or as a separate day.

6-8 hours return Climb by the north slopes from the ski tow at 1400m. Follow the tow to start with then head rightwards and upwards towards a slight ridge running north from the summit. Either climb this ridge or stay on the west side of it, up unstable lava scree to the small (and still warm) summit crater. There is normally no snow on this route, but there is a glacier on the southeast slopes.

Descend the same way.

Spring Ascent of Antuco

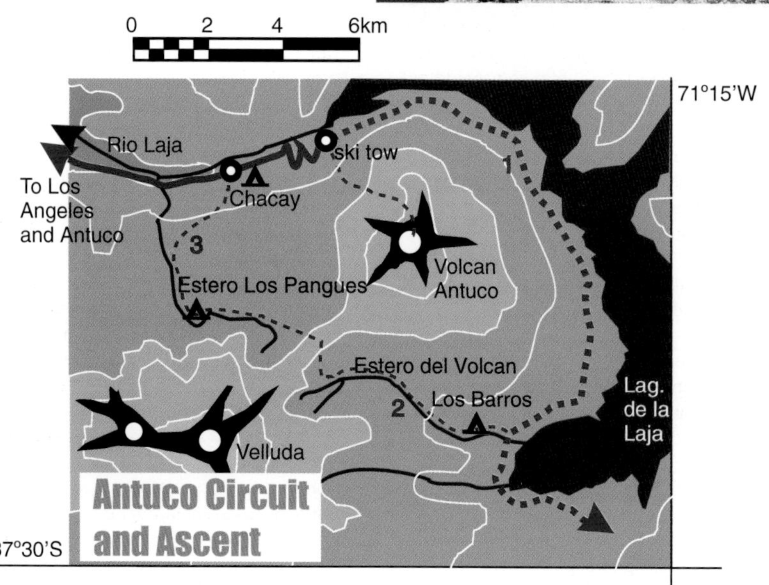

Antuco Circuit and Ascent

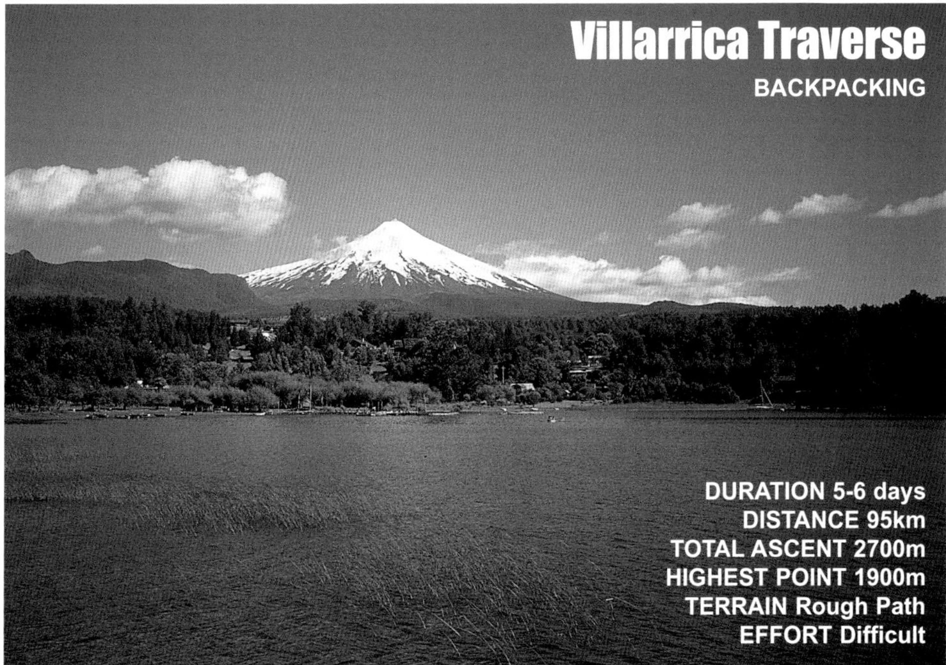

Villarrica Traverse
BACKPACKING
DURATION 5-6 days
DISTANCE 95km
TOTAL ASCENT 2700m
HIGHEST POINT 1900m
TERRAIN Rough Path
EFFORT Difficult

VILLARRICA NATIONAL PARK

Volcan Villarrica is a spectacularly active and very accessible mountain. It is one of the most interesting ascents in the whole of the Andes and should not be missed if you are anywhere in southern Chile. The level of activity varies from year to year but is never disappointing. In recent years there has been a pool of molten lava in the bottom of the crater, frothing and bubbling and occasionally spurting up the sides of the crater before slopping back down. This is probably not completely safe but it is totally overpowering to witness. This is the earth boiling and you can smell, feel, taste, see and hear it. Don't miss it.

Day trips up the volcano are available in Pucon for about $40 including lunch and all equipment necessary including an ice axe and crampons. Because of recent accidents (in crevasses, not hot lava pools) the authorities do not normally allow unguided ascents.

If you are in the area for any length of time it is well worth walking the full traverse of the Villarrica National Park as described below. This is a varied and interesting route passing through temperate rain forest, barren ash plains and fresh lava flows. The route is a combination of a semi-circuit around the west and south sides of Villarrica volcano and then a traverse of the high ground south of Quetrupillan volcano. There are great views of these two volcanoes and the much higher Volcan Lanin to the west. The north and east sides of Villarrica volcano can also be walked (though the volcanic scenery is less interesting) giving a different start to the traverse or allowing a full circuit of Villarrica to be done.

PUCON

Pucon is probably the most booming outdoor tourism centre in South America. Every summer thousands of Argentine students and Chilean families seem to descend on this tiny lakeside town to experience the great outdoors. In ten years time it may have been ruined by its popularity, but at the moment it is still quite a small and pleasant place. The big tourist attraction of Pucon is Volcan Villarrica's spectacular crater, but there are also lots of opportunities for enjoying yourself rafting, biking, windsurfing or just sunbathing on the black volcanic sands of Lago Villarrica.

For Pucon travel information see page 183.

ACCESS TO VILLARRICA VOLCANO AND THE TRAVERSE

From Santiago travel by bus or plane to Temuco then on by bus to the small village of Pucon at the foot of the mountain. This is a more convenient place to organise a trip from than the neighbouring town of Villarrica. There are also a few direct buses from Santiago to Pucon.

From Pucon by a good road to the National Park entrance station. There is a barrier to prevent vehicle access at night. Continue to the base of the ski resort above the forest at 1200m on the northern slopes. Start both the climb and trek a little higher at the ski refugio at the foot of Volcan Villarrica at 1400m, access by taxi for $10. No public transport.

MAP TO USE

JLM mapas sheet 7 ´Pucon´ which although topographically quite good shows the trail in the wrong places, available in Pucon.

VILLARRICA ASCENT

Due to large numbers of tourists climbing the peak and several fatal accidents in the 1980's the authorities control the mountain quite strictly. However you can easily join a guided group in Pucon, for about $40-50. It is still possible to climb without hiring a local guide if you can prove that you are a 'qualified' climber, requiring a (photo) ID card or just a club membership card. Flashing a few bits of shiny climbing gear around at the national park entrance station may also help convince the park rangers. At times in the past proof of insurance has also been asked for.

If you wish to climb Villarrica without a guide and can't get past the rangers the best option is probably to avoid the park rangers i.e. climb the mountain by another route, or walk through the forest to avoid the park entrance station or (possibly) walk past the entrance station late at night. It should be stressed that it is not known what penalty (if any) there might be for making an illegal ascent.

5-8 hours return. Follow the chairlift that starts about 400m to the east of the ski refugio to the highest lift station then take a more or less direct line to the summit. There are sometimes very small crevasses, easily avoided and not normally requiring the use of a rope. The top 100m can be icy and crampons and an ice-axe may be needed. Organised groups usually travel very slowly, taking up to 6 hours. Fit walkers can make the climb to the summit in just 3 hours.

THE VILLARRICA TRAVERSE

The trail is generally very dry under foot except a few sections in the forest and there is often a lack of drinking water on the high lava sections. The high section around Laguna Azul can have a lot of snow on it and there will always be at least some snow. Fresh snow can also fall above about 1600m any time.

The trail is probably best done in the direction described, to have any bad weather coming from behind and a small height advantage, but it could easily be done the other way round. It should be possible to arrange to climb the volcano with an agency, return your hired ice-axe and crampons, then set off on the trek.

THE ROUTE

1. 4-5 hours. About 200-300m before the ski refugio the road bends left at two maintenance huts. There is a sign saying ´Challupen 15km´. The trail starts here passing just above the two huts. A clear path then traverses the hillside southwest over gullies and lava flows, rising and falling but generally staying at the same level. After about **2½ hours** the trail drops into the forest and the large gully of Voipir Seco. From Voipir Seco the trail ascends, crosses a small gully,

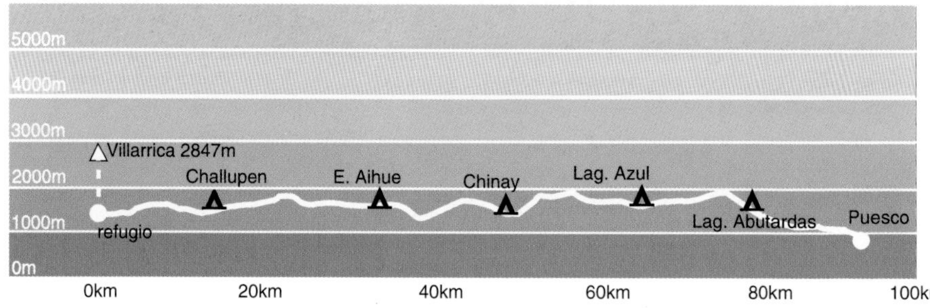

then descends for quite a long way, now in monkey puzzle forest to a second large gully, Pino Huacho, **1 hour** (water from springs in the north bank - camp possible). The path continues through forest for ½ **hour** to another canyon which has been filled with fresh lava. Take a left turn here (signpost Chinay) and walk up the valley for about 500m then look for a path on the right (south) bank. After a few hundred metres climb the steep bank (look for sticks or paint splashes on the rocks) and then a five minute walk through the forest to the scenic Lagunillas de Challupen Camp.

2. 4-5 hours From the Challupen camp follow the path south through the forest, crossing a number of gullies and rising slowly. After about **1 hour** the path leaves the forest and crosses the Estero Ñilfe (usually running water). Carry on across the lava of the Valle del Fuego passing just north of a low red hill. Cross a long barren section then descend slightly to the Arroyo Coñaripe before rising slightly and passing just north of a second (and larger) red hill. From the col here are the first views of Quetrupìllan, Lanin and the way ahead. About half an hour beyond this hill the path crosses the large stream of the E. Ahien coming from Villarrica's south glacier (water and campsites **3 hours**). Continue for **1 hour** across lava and ash on a well marked trail to a second large stream, Estero Aihue.

3. 4 hours. Soon after leaving the E. Aihue camp you reach the first trees. After the first big isolated cluster of monkey puzzle trees the trail crosses a small dry gully. From here the trail rises a little and traverse open hillside to the northeast. (Be very careful no to get drawn down into the forest too soon by false paths). After traversing open grassy slopes for about 2km descend right into scrub and follow the path down through monkey puzzle trees then more steeply into bamboo and ñirre forest to reach the Rio Pichillaneahue (camps possible). You have to ford this stream. Go ½ km down the east bank then over a low ridge on a well cut trail to reach the Coñaripe-Palguin 4x4 road about 2km south of the pass. Turn left and walk over the pass then another ½ **hour** down to the picnic and camping area at Chinay (coming the other way look for a signpost on the right ´Challupen 28km' about ½ hour south of the pass.

4. 7-8 hours. ½**hour** down the road from Chinay is the Porteria Quetrupillan national park office (you can ask here about the state of the trail ahead, which can have large amounts of snow on it even in high summer). A minute further down the track turn right (Lag. Azul signpost) onto a path. Go down to the river and cross

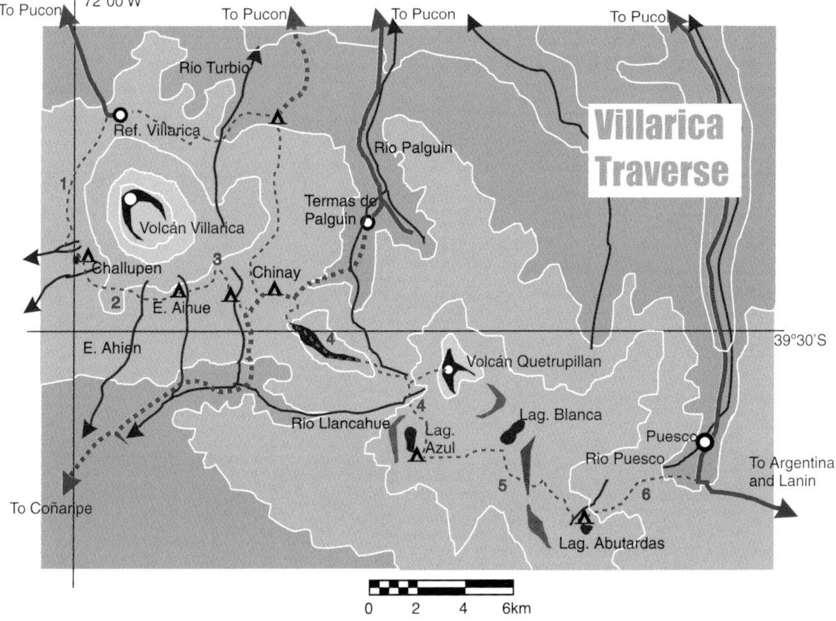

it on a bridge, then the trail begins climbing an open hillside in a series of zig-zags with nice views back to Villarrica. The path continues up a ridge in forest, emerging briefly at 1550m then finally emerging from scrub at 1600m, **2½-3 hours**.

Traverse right just above the scrub to a small stream in a valley, then climb the left hand side of this valley to a col at 1680m. Turn right along the ridge, going over the first peak, around the north side of second peak (highest) then traversing in scrub on the north side of the third peak. Then stay mostly on the crest over several low rises, each lower than before, finally zig-zag down through forest to a broad col at 1400m, **2 hours.**

On the other side of the col the path joins a larger trail (coming from the other direction look for a recently cut trail on the left leaving just before the col). The path ascends more gently to a stream bed, camps possible. Go a short way up the left fork, then back right and cross the stream again and follow a path ascending grassland on a small ridge between streams to a low wide col. From here head south across the flank of the mountain, crossing two streams, often containing snow, then make a rising traverse south and then southeast to a ridge at 1850m. Traverse southeast across the head of a snow filled valley beyond and continue traversing. 10mins after a large square boulder you reach a small pass (1900m), the highest point on trek, then begin descending, turning to the southwest. Follow a ridge down to Lag. Azul and beautiful campsite - **2½ to 3 hours** from the broad col.

Volcan Quetrupillan 2382m can be climbed easily over scree and snow fields from the low wide col above the stream campsite in about **2-3 hours** return.

5. 5 hours. From the camp at Lag. Azul the path goes to the left of the lava but after 5 mins crosses the lava (sticks show way). Once across the lava turn left and go up to a low col then cross more lava and begin rising leftwards to a low ridge. Follow a shallow gully with lava on the left for 10 mins then leave it on the left and cross more lava for 10 mins to a stream. Cross this and head east across a flat sandy plain to a hillside, **1 hour** from Lag. Azul.

Go up a small valley then down a very similar valley on the other side to the plain above Lag. Blanca (5mins to lake and campsite on the left) **½ hour**.

Turn right and follow the big valley south away from Lag. Blanca for **½ hour**, then turn left and climb a hill on the right of a lava flow onto a crater rim. Climb the rim for a while then leftwards up a gradual valley to a col at 1700m. The path rises gradually on the left hand side of this col then traverses east to a small basin. Cross this basin and climb to a higher col, 1780m, **1 hour**.

From this col descend slightly right then back left to a path on the left of a stream. Descend to a boggy area. Traverse the bog away to your left then zig-zag down a short steep slope. Traverse back right under the cliff, rising slightly and crossing several rivers. When you get onto a bare ridge heading towards a small hill - turn down right into the trees at a marshy area just before the hill ahead.

When down near lake level the path branches. Go right and down across stream, then through lenga and marshy grass heading for the big trees just left of the lake (Lag. Abutardas). There are nice campsites just inside trees, **1½-2 hours** from col.

6. 3 hours. The path continues in trees on the north shore of Lag Abutardas. Leave the lake eventually from the northeast corner of the grass meadow east of the lake. After ½ hour cross a stream then rise to a long thin marshy area. Go 400m down this marshy area and then find a path (paint flashes on tress) on the right. Follow this good path over a couple of low hills, to the top of a steep descent (**1 hour** from lake). **½hour** of steep descent brings you to a wider trail (Coming the other way this is signposted Lag. Abutardas 7km). Turn right and reach the road in another **1 hour**. Hitch a ride to return to Pucon, 2hrs drive or walk down the road to Puesco. Buses run from Puesco twice a day - it is about 1 hours walk.

Meadow Flowers, Villarrica Traverse

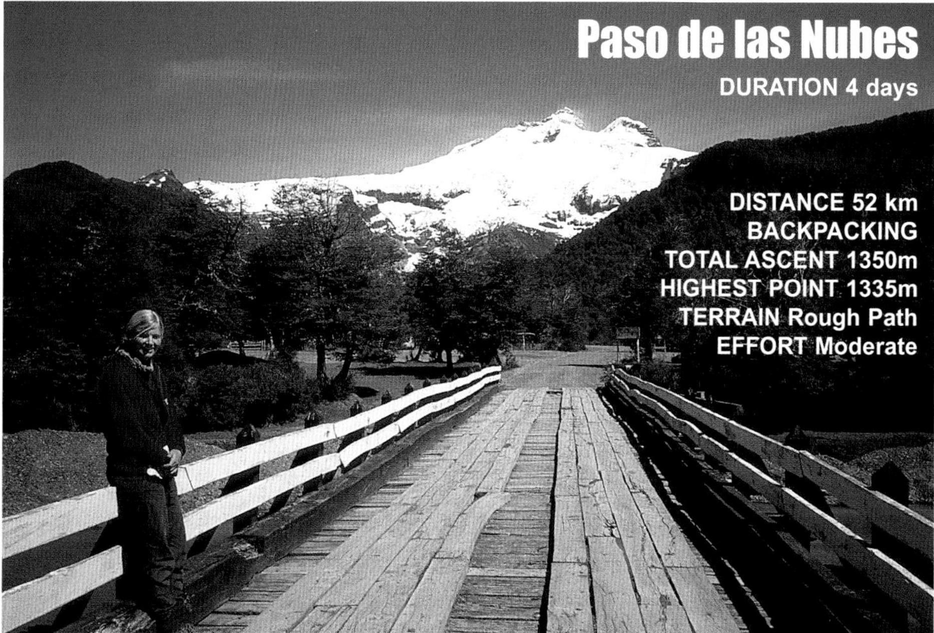

PASO DE LAS NUBES

This is an international walk crossing the border from Chile to Argentina. The route involves crossing one lake by boat, passing through bamboo forest, dense trees and over a mountain pass. It is a wild walk passing through some remote scenery close to the spectacular Monte Tronador.

The walk is described from west to east, starting in Chile, but could easily be done the other way around. It is also possible to start at Pampa Linda, finish at Puerto Frias and return to Bariloche from there.

ACCESS

From Puerto Montt take the bus via Ensenada to the village of Petrohue on the shore of Lago Todos Los Santos. There are hotels, cafes and shops at Petrohue but a better choice of supplies in Puerto Montt (see page 183).

From Petrohue take the pleasant 2 hours boat journey across Lago Todos Los Santos to Peulla. The tourist launch leaves daily Tuesday to Saturday early in the morning and often more frequently in the summer. Peulla also has some accommodation including a campsite.

To start in Pampa Linda take a bus from Bariloche (where you can buy supplies). One leaves from outside the Club Andino office daily in summer taking 2½ hours. Buy your supplies in Bariloche (see page 185).

MAP TO USE

Bariloche Cerro Catedral trekking map 11, (published by JLM mapas). This map is available in Bariloche and in shops in Chile.

THE ROUTE

1. 7-8 hours. From the jetty at the Peulla end of Lago Todos los Santos follow the road for **15 minutes** into Puella and visit the Chilean customs and international police post. After presenting your passport continue on the road north through open grasslands. Turning east the road continues in the wide flat valley then crosses the Rio Peulla on a suspension bridge, **3-4 hours.** Another **25 mins** on you reach the friendly Chilean Carabineros post at Casa Pangue where you get the first views of Monte Tronador. There are possible campsites along all this section, but be discrete. The road continues now steeply uphill through thick forest for **3 hours** to the Perez Rosales pass just over 1000m on the border between Chile and Argentina. There is one possible camp area at the abandoned house on the

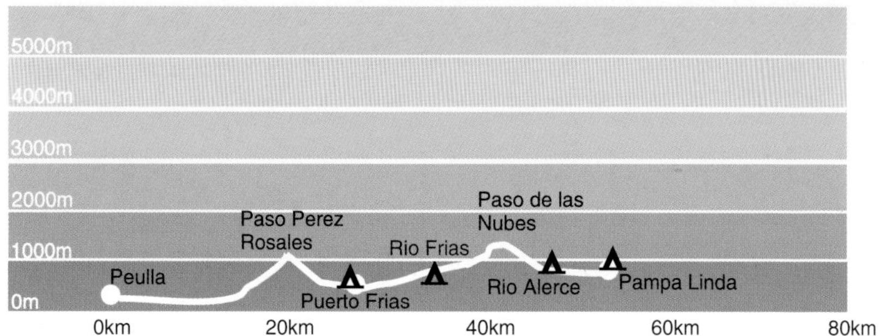

right ½ hour before you reach the pass. From the pass it is ½ **hour** down to the Argentine border post at Puerto Frias on the shore of Lago Frias. There is a campsite here in the trees.

Alternatively, there is transport along this road. The tourist bus meeting the boat at Peulla drives to Puerto Frias, however it is relatively expensive.

2. 5-6 hours. Continue on a track south along the shores of the lake for **30 mins**. The path then heads up the Rio Frias valley through beautiful lenga and alerce forest for a further **30 mins** to a path junction where you need to take the left fork to the large log crossing of the Rio Frias. Cross this with care and continue on the left hand side of the Rio Frias. The path can be hard to find through dense vegetation and some boggy sections. Keep an eye out for way markers. After **4 hours** or more of climbing over or under fallen trees you reach the camping area near the head of the valley. The camp is situated in the trees with views out to Glaciar Frias tumbling down from Monte Tronador. This is a remote and peaceful camp with the only noise the occasional ice fall from the glacier. Puma have occasionally been seen in this area.

3. 4 hours. From the camp continue southwards then zigzag directly up the steep rocky slopes with views of glacier Frias to your right. Head upwards, now through the trees, keeping an eye out for painted markers on rocks and trees. After ½ **hour** cross a stream and continue for a further 1½ **hours** until the steep gradient eases close to the rounded summit of Paso de las Nubes at 1335 meters. Aptly named as it can often be cloudy and can also have snow lying. If necessary take a compass bearing south and look for trail markers to direct you down to the steep zigzags leading down to the Rio Alerce river valley. The path keeps to the right hand side of this river. The path becomes indistinct but heads across a short boggy area. Watch out for markers hanging in trees. Further down the valley the path improves. Cross the side stream coming down from the Laguna Alerce where you will find many places to camp

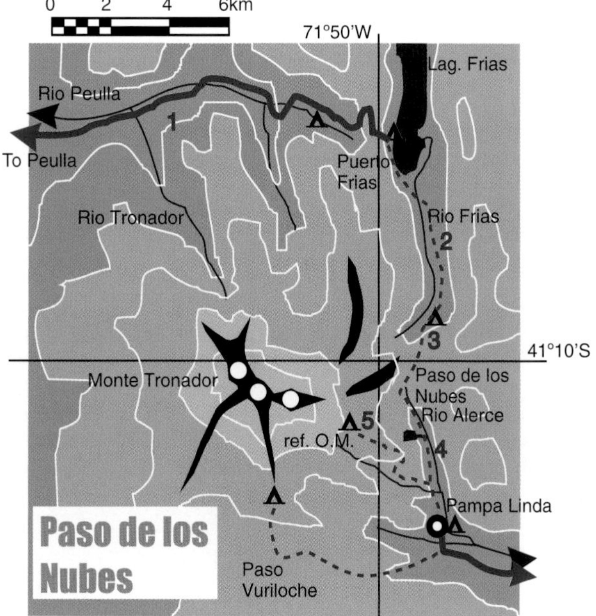

amongst the trees, **2 hours**. The side trip to see the lagoon takes about 2 hours return and is well worthwhile. Start on the left side of the stream.

4. 2 hours. From the camp carry on down the Rio Frias valley on the remains of an old mule trail. After **1½ hours** the junction with the trail heading northwest up the Rio Castanño Overo to the Refugio Otto Meiling is reached. Cross this stream, camping is possible here, and follow the track into Pampa Linda only **½ hour** away. Pampa Linda has camping and basic facilities and meals can be bought at the Hosteria. It is worthwhile popping into the park rangers office to let them know you have arrived in from Chile and to complete passport formalities.

5. 6 hours return 20km, 1200m ascent

A very enjoyable day trip can be made to the Refugio Otto Meiling on the side of Monte Tronador. This can be done as a day walk or you can break the trip with an overnight stay in the hut. Refugio Otto Meiling offers spectacular views of the glaciers on the east side of Monte Tronador. Follow the track north out of Pampa Linda for **½ hour** to the bridge over the Rio Castaño Overo. From the signposted junction on the other side of the bridge a 4x4 track heads up the valley left then swings northeast steeply up through the trees. There are various shortcuts off the jeep track taking a more direct route for walkers. After **1½ hours** the track ends near the treeline. A well marked path cuts off the track shortly before the track ends along the south side of the ridge and leads to the Otto Meiling hut at 2050m on the edge of Tronador's snowfields. The hut has 60 beds and serves meals and drinks when the warden is there in season.

BARILOCHE

San Carlos de Bariloche is the undisputed capital of the Argentine Lake district. It is an affluent and bustling tourist city on the south shores of Lago Nahuel Huapi, full of skiers in winter and families and picnickers in the summer. Bariloche is famous for its chocolate so it is a good place to stock up on trek rations! Though it is a beautiful area there are no particular 'sights' to see, an evening stroll along the lake shore is about as good as it gets in the immediate vicinity. For a short day trip you can climb **Cerro Otto 1405m** by a track up the east ridge, starting 1km west of the town. For further travel information on Bariloche see page 185.

Tronador, the Catedral range and the city of Bariloche from the air

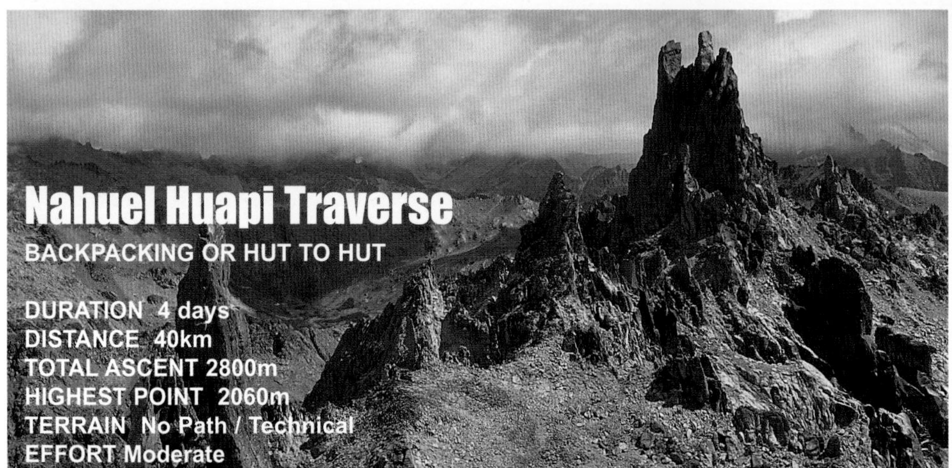

NAHUEL HUAPI TRAVERSE

This is the name commonly given to a high level route through the peaks of the Catedral range in the Nahuel Huapi national park. The Catedral range are a series of dramatic granite peaks and needles lying between the huge bulk of Monte Tronador and the city of Bariloche. The range is very well-developed for walkers with good paths and several refugios (huts).

The range is very popular with Argentine walkers and climbers. The route described can be done either as a hut to hut walk, or a lightweight backpacking and camping trip. The huts cost only a few dollars per night and the camping is free. Although this is the Nahuel Huapi national park there are no permits or entrance fees. Optional side trips are described at various stages and there are also alternative shorter and longer finishes described. The walk is definitely best done in the direction described so that you descend the biggest scree slopes, rather than ascend them with difficulty.

Above about 1800m it can snow in the Catedral range at any time of year.

ACCESS

Drive or take a bus (every hour) from Bariloche to the ski resort of Villa Catedral at 1050m. This is South Americas largest and busiest ski resort. There are two main routes to start the hike from here, either by taking the Refugio Lynch chairlift or by walking up. The chair does save gaining a lot of height, but is actually no quicker than the walk. Another common access point at the other end of the route described is from the village of Colonia Suiza, which can also be reached very quickly and regularly from Bariloche by bus.

MAP TO USE.

Several reasonable sketch maps of the range are available in Bariloche, including one by the Club Andino Bariloche and the JLM mapas sheet 11, 'Bariloche - Cerro Catedral'. The Argentine IGM sheet 4172-IV 'San Carlos de Bariloche' 1:250,000 is also useful.

THE ROUTE

To begin with there are two routes to the Refugio Frey. The uphill walk is really not so bad, the traverse south on the ridge from the chairlift is quite exposed but never too difficult.

1a. 4 hours. Take the Lynch chairlift out of Villa Catedral to the Refugio Lynch at 2050m. From here a well marked trail follows the ridge south, (mostly on the west side of the ridge) with long sections on scree and boulders and a short difficult section around a boulder before finally crossing back over the ridge at a col known as the 'Cancha del Futbol' From here descend east down the valley past the small Laguna Schmoll to the Refugio Frey, **4 hours**. The Ref. Frey, dramatically situated at the east end of the large Laguna Toncek is at 1700m and has 40 beds and will serve beer and meals. There are some tent sites in the bushes on the south side of the Laguna Toncek.

1b. 3-4 hours If you want to walk all the way take the trail which heads south from the car park at Villa Catedral, (well signposted on the southwest side of car

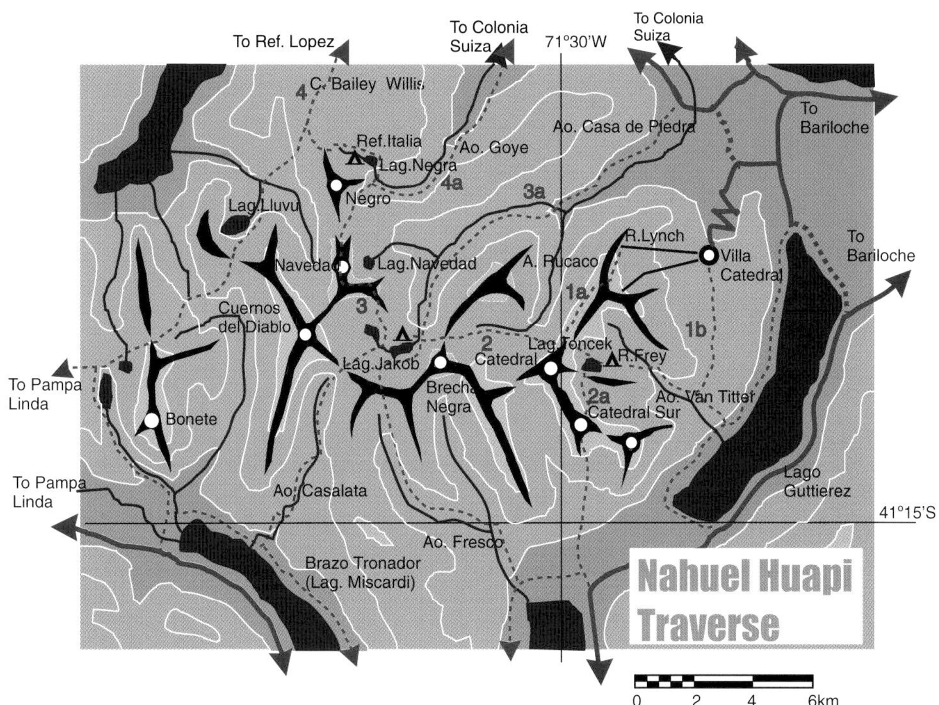

park) rising gradually through scrub and bamboo forest to reach the Arroyo VanTitter in **1½ hours**. Soon after this is a short section of scrambling. Continue to climb up this valley crossing the stream (camping area) then passing the small Ref. Piedrita at about 1300m which was built under a big boulder. Higher up you leave the big trees and climb more steeply up left side of valley through scrubby beech to reach the refugio Frey. The hut is only visible for the last ten minutes of this walk. From the Refugio Frey an intersting side trip can be made to climb the peak of Cerro Catedral Sur.

2a. Cerro Catedral Sur from Refugio Frey 800m ascent, 6 hours return

This is one of the highest peaks in the range and the ascent gives great views of the more dramatic pinnacles such as Campanile Esloveno and the Torre Central The walk is quite rough, with lots of scree. From Ref. Frey go over the low col south of the lake and descend the other side, moving right to pass beneath a big rock slab. From here rise again slightly to a terrace and use this to traverse round the head of the valley to two small streams. Climb up the hillside here to a flat area at 2000m with big boulders. From the far end of this flat area climb a large scree gully directly towards the summit. There are a few metres of easy scrambling just under the summit.

2. 4-5 hours Most of this walk is well marked. To follow the main route from Frey go round either side of the Laguna Toncek. Walk back along the valley until you can see a path and paint marks begin climbing the right hand (north) side. Climb in short zigzags to the right of a stream to reach Laguna Schmoll. Go round the left of this lake then cut back left up a rocky ramp which leads to a col. Cross a sandy area, known as the Cancha de Futbol. Then turn left and follow a path steeply down scree which becomes a dry stream bed that leads to the floor of the Arroyo Rucaco valley. Walk along the valley floor to the west on a good path, mostly in trees, occasionally on grass past a stream and campsite, **2½ hours**. The path continues up the valley westwards then climbs a wide stony hill in the middle of the valley before going up a final steep slope to another col 1850m. This is the Paso Brecha Negra. Descend steeply down the other

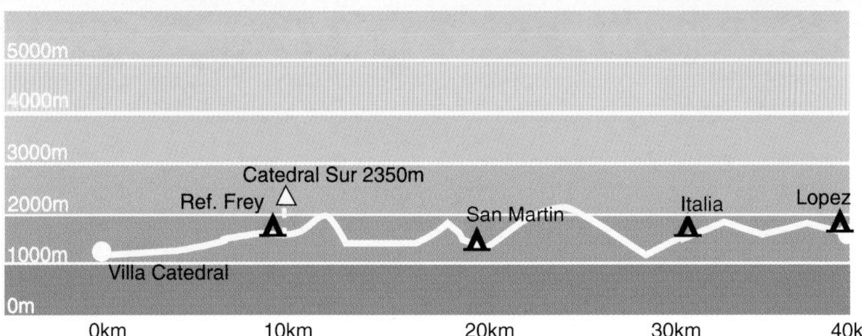

side, going left at first until you have passed a small outcrop of rock. Walk up the valley to the scenic Laguna Jakob at 1500m. The refugio San Martin here has accommodation and serves meals and beer. There is camping in the forest just beyond the hut.

3. 7-8 hours. The long section from Lago Jakob to Lag. Negra has a short exposed scramble and shouldn't be attempted in bad weather or if there is snow.

From Laguna Jakob go up over rock slabs and short gullies on the north side of the lake following paint marks and cairns until you can see the Laguna de los Tempanos. As soon as you see this higher lagoon head right and walk up a rocky ridge which gradually narrows and steepens. At about 1700m under a steeper rock face traverse left for 50m to a gully. Climb the gully for 50m, or drier rocks on the right. This is exposed and about 5.0/Moderate. Then make a rising traverse left over scree to reach a ridge, **1-1½ hours**. Continue up the ridge until you reach a short descent on the right just before a pinnacle. Traverse this scree slope to a col in the next ridge (1950m). From this col traverse around the bowl above Laguna Navedad on scree, keeping about 50-100m below the ridge until you reach another col (1900m). From here climb the ridge north to the top of Navedad at 2060m. **1½ hours**. Go down the north ridge to where it splits into two and enter the valley between the two ridges. Follow this narrow valley down, with difficult sections on snow, scree and moraine. Keep mostly to the left until you get to the vegetation. Then continue down, sometimes on the left, sometimes on the right and sometimes in the stream bed itself. Eventually after **2½-3 hours** you reach a path junction in the main valley at 1200m.

Take the path to the left which climbs steadily in zigzags to the Laguna Negra and the Italia hut, which is also known as the Segre hut, **1½ hours**. The hut has 60 beds and there is camping nearby.

3a. If this days section is dangerous you can always walk out down the Arroyo Casa de Piedra from Laguna Jakob to the road in **4-5 hours**.

4. 5-6 hours. To continue from the Laguna Negra to Refugio Lopez go round the north side of the lagoon past a tricky rock step then continue up and leftwards on steep and loose rock to a small col on the south side of Cerro Bailey Willis. From here the trail heads north along the west side of Cerro Bailey Willis and is usually marked by paint. It then crosses the headwaters of the Arroyo Goye and then eventually makes a long and tiring ascent of a scree filled gully to reach the ridge just south of Pico Turista (which can be climbed easily by the ridge). From the col the path descends over rocks, going left of a lake, and sometimes scrambling to reach the Refugio Lopez at 1600m. The refuge has beds and there are camping areas in the trees just ten minutes below the hut. From the Refugio Lopez a trail leads steeply down the right (east) bank of the Arroyo Lopez to the road in **2 hours**. Buses back to Bariloche pass every 2-3 hours.

4a. The path to the right from below Lag. Negra offers another route out of the mountains. It takes 3 hours to reach Colonia Suiza on an easily followed path through the forest following the Arroyo Goye. There is a short uphill section right at the end and the final 150m down to the road is very steep. Turn right when your reach the road. There are regular buses back to Bariloche.

The other commonly used access points to the range include the Hotel Tronador on the road to Pampa Linda (southwest side) from which you can walk to the Refugio San Martin by the Arroyo Casalata valley in 5-6 hours, and the north end of Lago Mascardi (south side) from which you can reach the Frey or San Martin huts. Most paths are well signposted and there are descriptions of the walks in the locally available guidebooks. See the 'Guia de Sendas y Picadas' published by the CAB (Club Andino Bariloche).

Torres del Paine, Chilean Patagonia

INTRODUCTION

Patagonia is the name used for the southern areas of Chile and Argentina, often applied to anywhere south of about latitude 40º. Perhaps the greatest variety of scenery and mountain types in the world are to be found here at the southern end of the Andes. There are snow covered volcanoes, the huge and imposing granite towers of Paine and Fitzroy, the vast ice fields of the northern and southern Patagonian ice-caps and the forest choked and perpetually wet islands of the archipelago of Tierra del Fuego. Though the highest peaks here are low for the Andes at only 3000-4000m, the glaciers descend to sea-level. Without a doubt this is the least explored and wildest part of the Andes.

The area is very popular for walking and this usually involves at least some backpacking. The most popular venues are the **Los Glaciares** national park in Argentina and the **Torres del Paine** national park in Chile. Relatively easy multi-day backpacking routes are described in both of these parks as well as a number of more serious walks, including a circuit on the southern **Patagonian Ice-cap** and walks through the remote mountains of the **Sierra Valdivieso** and **Isla Navarino** in Tierra del Fuego.

GETTING THERE

Patagonia is a long way from the national capitals of Santiago and Buenos Aires, so unless you have plenty of time it makes sense to fly south. There are two main ways to reach this part of the Andes.

If your international flight arrives in Santiago in Chile you can take an internal flight south to the city of Punta Arenas (close to the Torres del Paine park and also the best way to access Isla Navarino). Puerto Natales near the Paine national park can also be reached by ferry from the Lake District city of Puerto Montt, a beautiful three day voyage if the weather is good.

From Buenos Aires you can fly south to either Rio Gallegos or Ushuaia. From Rio Gallegos there is regular bus transport to Calafate and the Los Glaciares national park. If you want to visit both Torres del Paine and Los Glaciares there are also regular buses in the summer between Calafate and Puerto Natales. From Ushuaia access to the Sierra Valdivieso is very quick.

See the introduction chapter for brief details of international flight options to Santiago and Buenos Aires. For travel information on these cities see pages 182 and 184 respectively.

CLIMATE AND WEATHER CONDITIONS

The area has a climate that is the mirror image of western Europe, with the austral summer from November to March generally the best season to walk. However the climate in Patagonia is colder and windier for any given latitude and the mountains are more exposed to westerly storms than the mountains of Europe. In winter temperatures are not very low and the winds are usually less strong at that time of year.

There is a very rapid transition in the climate across the Andes from west to east. On the Chilean side of the mountains there are some incredibly wet places where rain falls on over 350 days of the year. On the Argentine side of the mountains there are much drier steppes and deserts where it rarely rains but is always very windy.

The whole of southern Patagonia from about latitude 45° to Cape Horn suffers from strong winds and these give rise to the biggest problems when walking exposed routes and camping. Expect gale force winds on one or two days per week, and rain or cloud on half of the days in a week. In general the area gets a fair amount of hot sunny weather and the scenery is so spectacular it is well worth enduring a few rainy or windy days.

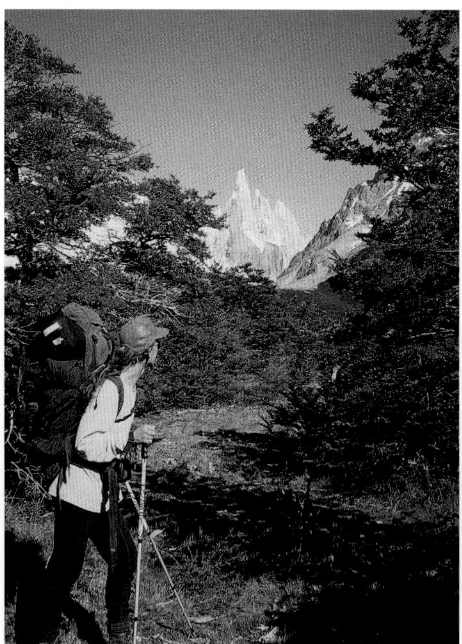

Los Glaciares National Park

Fitzroy at sunrise

INTRODUCTION

The world famous Los Glaciares national park in southern Argentine Patagonia lies on the edge of the southern Patagonian Ice-cap at 49°S. It is over 2700km from Buenos Aires, the Argentine capital. The park includes the famous granite peaks of Fitzroy 3375m and Cerro Torre 3128m and some huge glaciers on the edge of the southernmost of the two Patagonian ice-caps. These mountains and glaciers are among the most impressive peaks in the Andes.

There is good backpacking and walking country in the rich evergreen beech forests at the foot of these spectacular mountains, with beautiful and secluded campsites, particularly in the remote northern part of the park around Laguna del Desierto. We describe a five day backpacking route around the eastern and northern sides of Fitzroy taking in the best of the parks scenery.

Another highlight of this park are the views of the mountains from the glacier lagoons above Chalten; particularly recommended are walks to Laguna Sucia, Laguna de los Tres and Laguna Torre. It is possible to see many of the most scenic areas of the park, including these three lagoons, in day hikes from the administration centre at Chaltén. You must sign in at this centre for any walking in the park.

EL CALAFATE

El Calafate is a pleasant wee town on the shores of Lago Argentino which becomes very busy in summer with tourists from all over Argentina and indeed all over the world. If you've time to spare the one day tourist trip to the famous Perito Moreno glacier is well worth doing, numerous agencies on the main street offer this tour. For a short walk go and have a look at the bird life down by the lake shore - there are usually several species of ducks, geese and flamingos.

Calafate has plenty of accommodation, though it can get busy over Christmas and in January, see page 186.

EL CHALTEN

El Chalten (see page 186) is a rapidly growing village at the entrance to the Los Glaciares national park, now with several hotels and camp sites. You can now buy basic food and camping supplies here but the choice is not great. For a good view of Fitzroy you can take a short walk from El Chalten north on Ruta 23 for 1km to the Cascada del Salto waterfall walk. Follow the stream above the waterfall for another ½ hour to a big boulder which can be seen on the horizon.

PARK FEES

There are no fees but you must sign in at the Park Office just south of the bridge as you arrive in El Chalten. If doing the semi-circuit check with the Guardaparque that the short cut path (section **2** on the map) is still open. It was reopened in January 2000 after a period of closure apparently to reserve a quieter area for wildlife.

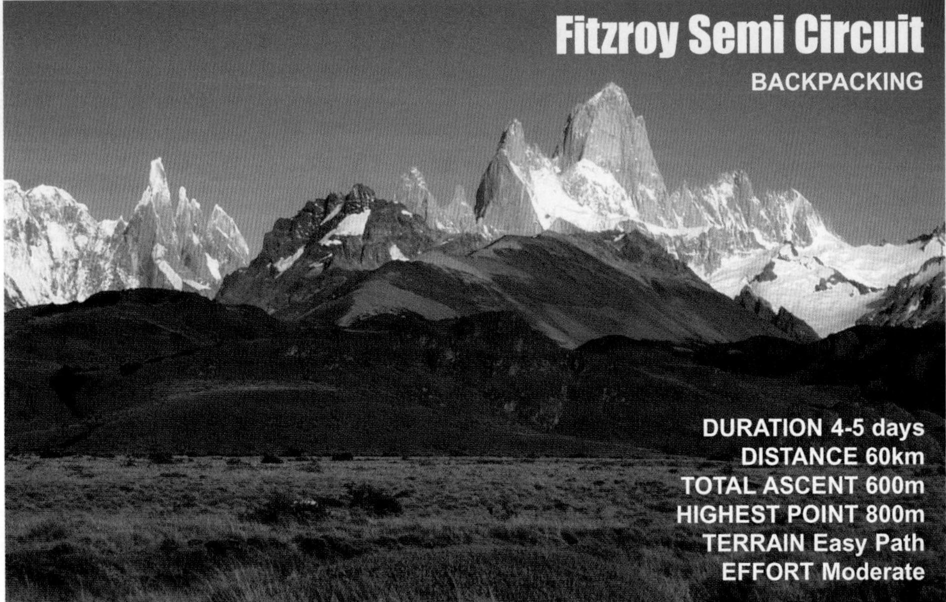

Fitzroy Semi Circuit
BACKPACKING
DURATION 4-5 days
DISTANCE 60km
TOTAL ASCENT 600m
HIGHEST POINT 800m
TERRAIN Easy Path
EFFORT Moderate

FITZROY SEMI-CIRCUIT

The route described below is a sort of half circuit around the east and north sides of Fitzroy. It is a route we feel offers the best choice of scenery and pleasant walking in the Los Glaciares park. There are numerous variations and possible side trips which can be added or taken away from the basic route, most of which are described below. The trails are well marked and sign posted. Most of the campsites are now semi-organised and have pit toilets.

ACCESS

Access is easiest by flying from Buenos Aires to Rio Gallegos. Rio Gallegos has good hotels and some large supermarkets, where it might be worth buying some camping food if you have time. From Rio Gallegos you can travel by bus to Los Glaciares in one long day with a change of bus in El Calafate. El Calafate, a pleasant lake shore town, is another good place to buy supplies and prepare for your walk. There are several daily buses from here to El Chalten in the summer season.

MAP TO USE

Monte FitzRoy and Cerro Torre trekking and mountaineering map at 1:50,000 published by Zagier and Urruty. Readily available in tourist agencies and kiosks in El Calafate and El Chalten.

THE ROUTE

1. 3 hours. From El Chalten the walk up to Laguna Torre offers excellent close views of the impressive rock spire of Cerro Torre. There is a choice of routes out of El Chalten village. **1a.** In El Chalten centre walk northwards on the road through the houses. You will see a path ascending the grass slopes to the west. There is a signpost and a path at the roadside leading off towards a large white house at the foot of the rise. From behind this house the path passes a burnt out tree. Further on you pass small pools to your right and then enter the Rio Fitzroy valley, **1 hour. 1b.** Alternatively from the bridge at the south end of the village follow the path on the northern bank of the Rio Fitzroy to meet the **1a.** route after **1 hour**.

20 mins. on from where these two routes converge the path rises over a lateral moraine from which there is a good view towards Cerro Torre. Continue on a good path to reach a second moraine. Passing the junction to Laguna Hija which is usually signposted. Descend to more open and level ground, then the path goes along the bank of the river to reach Campamento Bridwell, **1½ hours. 10 mins** beyond the camping area the shore of Laguna Torre is reached.

Mirador Maestri, **2 hours return.** The sidewalk to this viewpoint from Campamento Bridwell is very worth while. To walk up to the Mirador Maestri on the north side of Laguna Torre traverse around the lake shore on rough moraine to pick up a more definite path ascending the obvious moraine ridge rising on the north side of Laguna Torre.

2. 4 hours. From Campamento Bridwell an early rise is worth while to see a spectacular sunrise on the granite spire of Cerro Torre. Retrace the path for **1 hour** to the Laguna Hija path junction on the first rise you encounter. Turn left off the main route on this path and rise steeply at first through the forest to reach the higher plateau of the three lakes, **1½ hours**. Pass these lakes on the east side on a less distinct and boggy path, Monte Fitzroy slowly comes into view. The path follows the outlet stream of Laguna Madre to join the main path, coming in from the north of El Chalten and Campamento Madsen, in **1 hour**. Join this path and head towards Fitzroy through more boggy ground. Follow markers to cross a stream into Campamento Poincenot in the trees by the Rio Blanco, **25 mins.** A second camp area is available (although it is used more by climbers) across the river, using a log bridge, called the Campamento Rio Blanco. From these camps there are two worthwhile side trips.

Fitzroy Lookout, 3 hours return. For the Fitzroy lookout make your way on the sign-posted path up through Campamento Rio Blanco. Above the tree line rise steeply for 500 meters on an obvious path to Laguna de los Tres from where there is a great view of Fitzroys huge east face.

Laguna Sucia, **2-2½ hours return.** The low level and less used route to Laguna Sucia heads southwest on the north bank of the Rio Blanco from Campamento Rio Blanco. The path is vague at times but heads over rough boulder strewn ground rising gently towards the

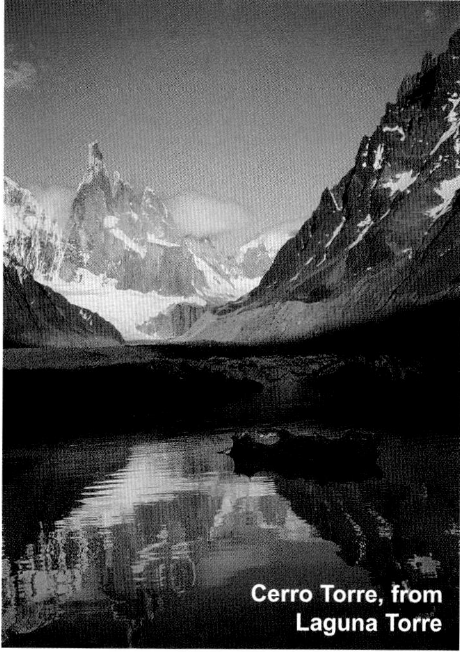

Cerro Torre, from Laguna Torre

lake. There is one awkward step where you have to climb up away from the river. The view of this lake sitting in its deep glacial trough is again spectacular.

3. 4 hours. The next stage of the main circuit to Refugio los Troncos goes down the western bank of the Rio Blanco as sign posted from the Rio Blanco camp. The path is rough under foot with boulders. After **45 mins** the outlet stream from the glacier and Laguna Piedras Blancas is reached. The easiest way across is marked by some small cairns - jump from one big boulder to another. A short side trip up the stream or up the moraine above the north side of this side

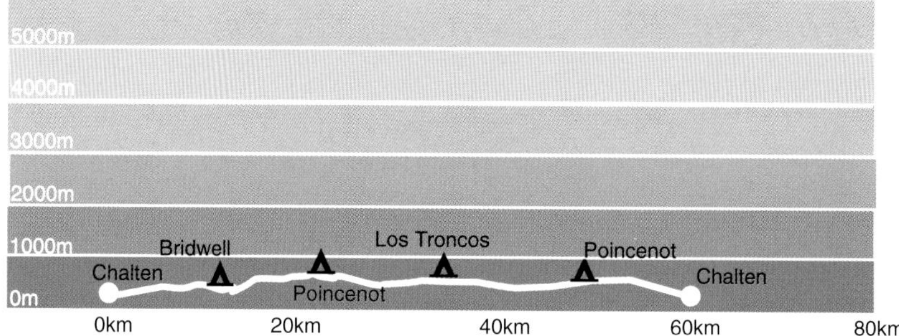

valley (loose scree) can be made for another great view.

From here follow the Rio Blanco for a further 2 km downstream. In around **50 mins,** where the valley opens out, there is a path heading away from the river and into the trees to the left. The path is a bit vague but heads northwest over small rises through tall trees and occasional areas of burnt out trees. This path then joins the main path heading in from Ruta 23 to the east and is now well trodden, by horses too, and easy walking for under **2 hours** to Refugio Los Troncos. This is a privately owned refugio. There is a small charge for camping and there is also some accommodation with basic facilities. The refugio may sell wine and bread but do not rely on this. It can be a wet and windy campsite, with rain pushing down from Laguna Electrico but the camping is sheltered behind the large Piedra del Fraile erratic boulder. From this base two side walks can be made.

Cerro Electrico, 3 hours return. A steep climb on the slopes south of the refugio to the Cerro Electrico lookout at 2200m offers views into the bowl north of Fitzroy and the long line of granite needles running north from Fitzroy.

Glacier Marconi 6-8 hours return. Well worthwhile is a walk along the southern side of Laguna Electrico as far as the glacier Marconi. There is a vague path most of the way though most of it is on rough scree and moraine. One section requires you to leave the shore and rise on a rock band higher above the water. The Rio Pollone valley can also be explored.

4. 5-6 hours. From Piedra del Fraile you can return to El Chalten two ways. For both you need to retrace your path along the Rio Electrico first, **2 hours.**

4a. Continue along the well trodden path east to join Ruta 23 at Puente Rio Electrico, **½ hour** and return to El Chalten on the road from here. Hitching may be possible on the road but cars are not frequent. Walking will take about **3 hours.**

4b. Alternatively retrace your steps up the Rio Blanco to Campamento Poincenot **4 hours** then walk down the Chorrillo del Salto path. From the Poincenot camp take the signposted path up a rise and through the trees to cross the boggy stream outlet by the markers. This path meanders more gently through dwarf lengas until after **1-1½ hours** you will pass the turn off to Laguna Capri. Continuing in a southwesterly direction the path descends a small bluff and then descends gently down through trees to the top of Campamento Madsen at the north end of El Chalten.

THREE DAY WALK TO PASO DEL VIENTO

Another highly recommended itinerary in the park is this leisurely three day walk which will give you amazing views out over the ice-cap. It crosses a very short section of 'dry' glacier on the way up to the pass, but no special equipment is necessary.

1. 5 hours Leaving from behind the Park Office in Chalten follow day 6 of the ice-cap circuit in reverse to Camp Toro.

2. 7-8 hours return. Follow day 5 of the ice-cap circuit in reverse up to the Paso del Viento, then descend back to Camp Toro.

3. 5 hours. Reverse your first day to El Chalten.

River crossing in Patagonia

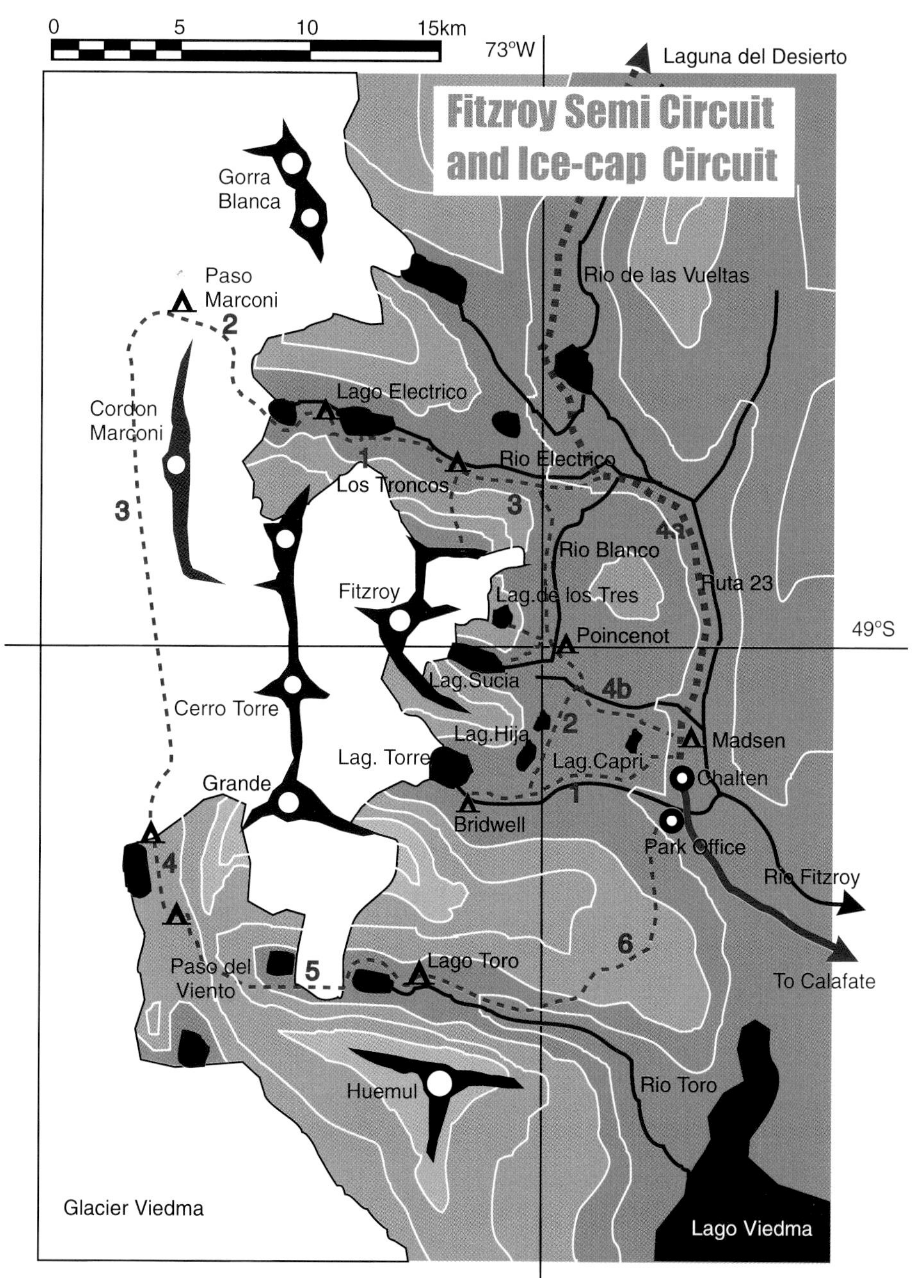
0
5
10
15km
73°W
Laguna del Desierto
Fitzroy Semi Circuit
and Ice-cap Circuit
Gorra
Blanca
Paso
Marconi
2
Rio de las Vueltas
Cordon
Marconi
Lago Electrico
1
Rio Electrico
Los Troncos
3
3
4a
Rio Blanco
Ruta 23
Fitzroy
Lag.de los Tres
Poincenot
49°S
Lag.Sucia
4b
Cerro Torre
Lag.Hija
2
Madsen
Lag. Torre
Lag.Capri
Chalten
Grande
1
Bridwell
Park Office
4
Rio Fitzroy
6
Paso del
Viento
5
Lago Toro
To Calafate
Huemul
Rio Toro
Glacier Viedma
Lago Viedma

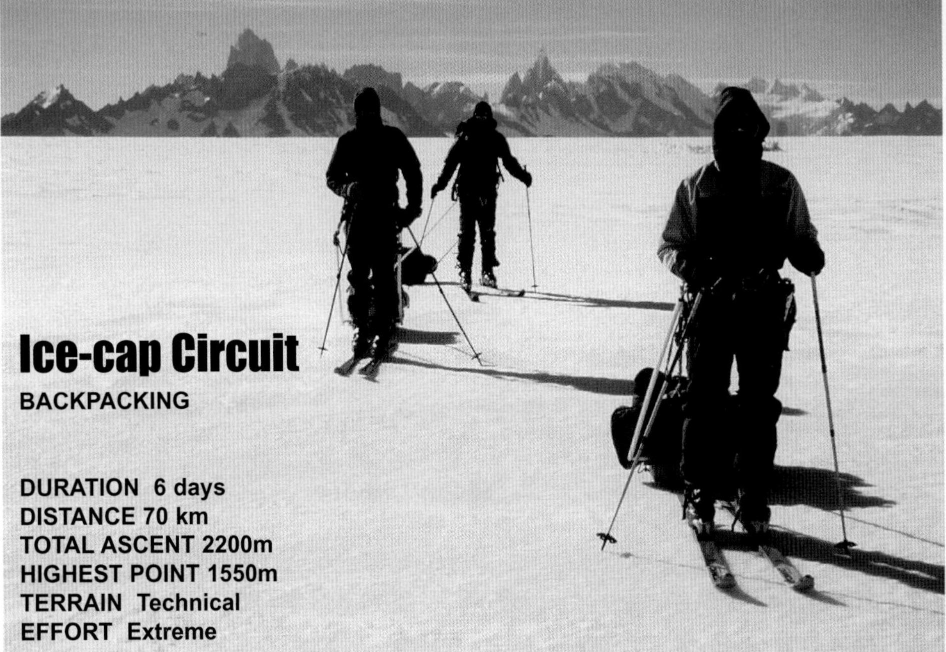

Ice-cap Circuit

BACKPACKING

DURATION 6 days
DISTANCE 70 km
TOTAL ASCENT 2200m
HIGHEST POINT 1550m
TERRAIN Technical
EFFORT Extreme

ICE CAP CIRCUIT

This is without doubt the most serious and committing route described in this guidebook. Although it is essential that someone in the party has mountaineering skills and judgement the route can be completed by fit trekkers. The main hazards of the route are the potentially very serious weather, the difficult route finding and navigation which will require a confident navigator, and the risk from crevasse falls in one or two short sections of the glacier. It is also one of the most strenuous and toughest routes in this guidebook. Not entirely by coincidence it is one of the most rewarding.

The route described below is a full circuit around the Fitzroy and Cerro Torre massif which (if the weather is good) gives fantastic views of the north and west sides of these peaks.

The route will be much easier with snowshoes or skis and it is worth considering using at least one or two sledges in your group. Snow shoes can be rented in El Chalten. It is essential to have very good camping equipment, particularly a storm-proof tent. One snow-shovel for every two or three people should be carried, a compass is essential and a GPS can be useful. Spare food for several days should be carried in case of adverse weather.

This circular route is probably best done in the direction described as navigation will be a bit easier.

ACCESS

As for the Fitzroy semi-circuit to Chalten village.

MAP TO USE

Maps for this trip are unfortunately hard to find. There is an Argentine IGM 1:100,000 sheet of the area but at the time of writing (2000) it couldn't be bought in Buenos Aires. The Zagier and Urruty 1:50,000 map of the area around Fitzroy is good enough for the approaches on and off the ice-cap. Neither of these maps is however completely up-to-date, in particular the glaciers have retreated considerably (e.g. the small lake in the moraine above Lago Electrico is not shown on either map.)

THE ROUTE

1. 4-5 hours. Start from the bridge over the Rio Electrico on Ruta 23. From Chalten you should be able to organise transport to here in a pick-up truck. A narrow path leads off along the bottom of a small cliff on the south bank of the river from the bridge, but soon reaches meadows and widens. You'll cross several small streams then in about ½ **hour** join the path coming down by the Rio Blanco. Continue through forest with views to huge cliffs for about **2 hours** to reach the Refugio Los Troncos (sometimes known as Piedra del Fraile). The path continues along the river bank behind the large erratic boulder and crosses wide open boulder fields, reaching Lago Elecrtrico in ½ **hour**. There is a good path along the south shore of the lake over slabs and outcrops. Drop down to the Rio Pollone and cross it (can be knee deep). Continue along a rough boulder slope, then follow cairns over a steep and rocky outcrop/knoll to reach sheltered campsites at the northwest corner of Lago Electrico, where the main river flows into the lake, **2 hours** form Piedra del Fraile.

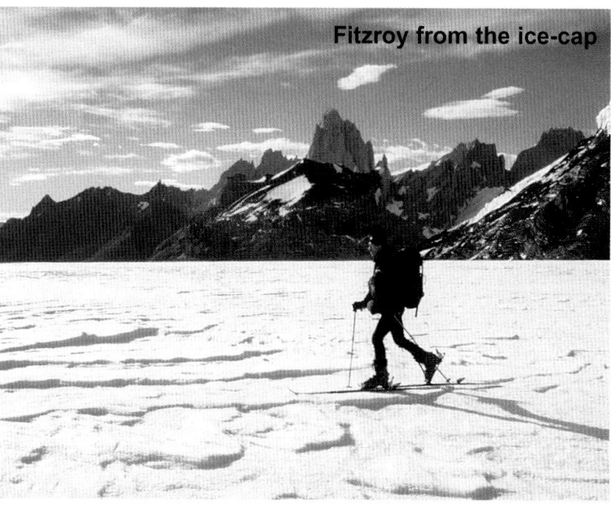
Fitzroy from the ice-cap

2. 6-8 hours. From the Lago Electrico camp go out of the south end of the camp and follow a stream up slabs. Climb about 100m until you see a small circular lake which you go around the south side of on loose and dangerous moraine to gain the glacier at the other end of the lake at an altitude of 700m. Climb the left hand side of the glacier then the right hand stream above the glacier fork (be careful not to get too close to a dangerous serac zone up on the left near here). This climbs steadily to the Paso Marconi with only one short steep section between 1000 and 1200m height. There are a number of narrow crevasses before the pass. There is a final long gradual uphill slope to reach the crest of the pass and magnificent views out over the expanse of the South Patagonian Ice-cap. There is plenty of space in which to camp.

3. 7-9 hours. It is nearly 25km south from Paso Marconi to the edge of the glacier north of Paso del Viento and this should ideally be done in one day with good visibility. There are incredible views from this section of the route which shouldn't be missed, also to get caught here in bad weather could be extremely serious. Take a line parallel to the Cordon Marconi but at least 500-1000m out on to the ice-cap. South of the Cordon Marconi cross the mouths of two large cirques, Cerro Torre rises from the back of the first cirque and Cerro Grande from the south side of the second. There can be quite bad crevasses in this area, but they are often very visible. Beyond the second

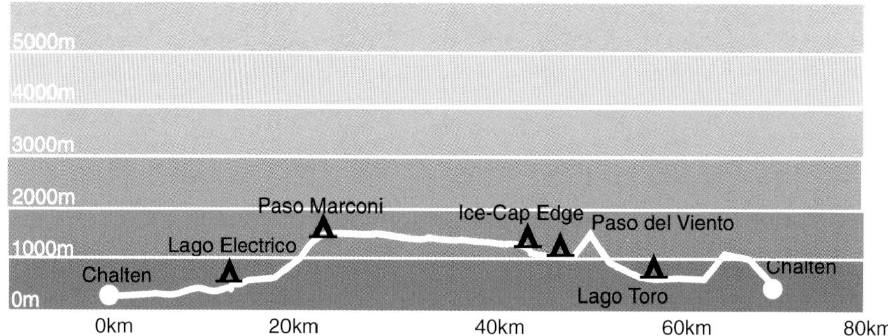

cirque look out for the small glacier coming down from Cerro Grande and go over to the edge of the main glacier where the small glacier joins. It is possible to camp just off the glacier on the left here. The most serious part of the navigation is now over. This point will take from **7-9 hours** to reach from Paso Marconi

4. 2 hours. Follow the left (east) edge of the glacier down for another 4-5km, with one short steeper downhill section where you drop about 100m, and then leave the glacier at the north end of a small lagoon. Go round the east side of the lagoon to the far (south) end and then climb steeply up on boulders past one small level area to a little hanging valley to the east, **1½ hours**. This makes a good camp, but there are also nice camps by a blue lagoon **½ hour** further on. The path is now well marked with cairns. Cross the small valley eastwards and stumble over boulder fields to reach the blue lagoon.

5. 5 hours. Beyond the blue lagoon you will see a diagonal path rising rightwards up the scree to the Paso del Viento. The pass is reached in about **2 hours.** It is very wide with several small lakes; you could camp here but it might get very windy. In front of you is the spectacular Toro valley with two huge glaciers coming down the north slope and throwing up huge moraines on the south slope. Descend into the valley by steep screes with faint paths on the right hand (south) side. After about **1 hour** you will reach the top of a huge 100m high moraine. Double back to the west here to avoid the steep front slopes of the moraine and get on to the glacier below. Walk east along the edge of the glacier until it begins to steepen dramatically and leave it here for the moraine (it may be hard to find a path here as the glacier and moraine are always moving). Continue traversing and descending this hillside to the outwash plain next to Lago Toro. You can go round either side of the lake, both involve a river crossing. For the north side cross the inflow which is fast flowing, about knee deep and divided into several channels, then walk along grass to the Campamento Toro which lies in trees behind an outcrop of rock. The path along the south side of the lake is quicker and more interesting, the river crossing at the lake's outflow is about waist deep but with no significant flow, either way **2 hours** from the top of the moraine.

6. 5 hours. The final day is along the north side of the Toro valley through patches of trees and meadows to a tin shack, **2 hours**. Climb the hillside to the north here on a good path and then follow a fence line up to about 1100m with great views of Lago Viedma. Then continue through meadows and forest and a final steep descent through scrubland to the gate and signpost at the southwest corner of the national park offices, which lie just south of the Rio Fitzroy bridge, in Chalten.

Fitzroy from the ice-cap

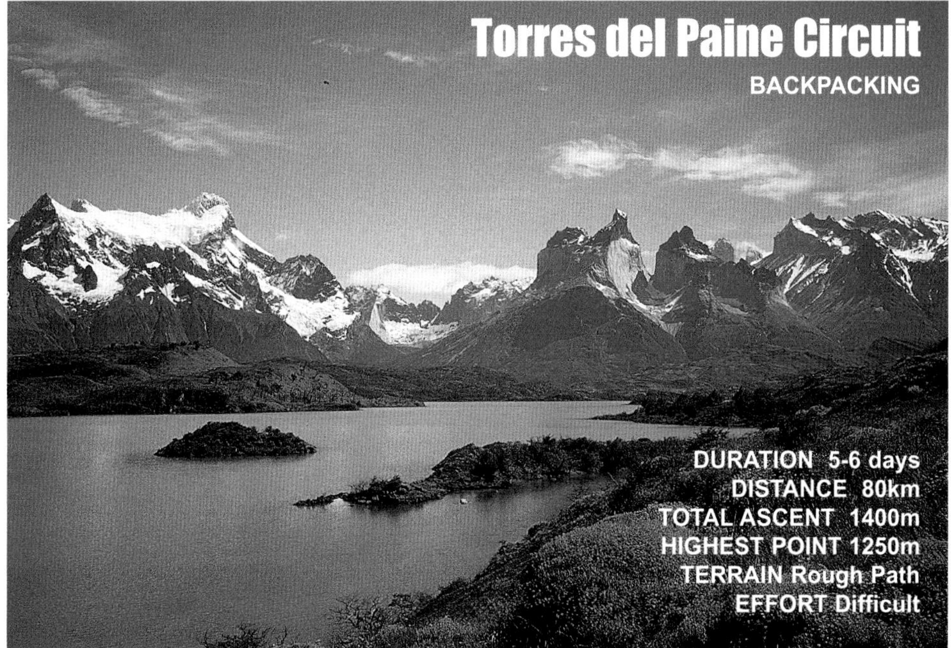

Torres del Paine Circuit
BACKPACKING
DURATION 5-6 days
DISTANCE 80km
TOTAL ASCENT 1400m
HIGHEST POINT 1250m
TERRAIN Rough Path
EFFORT Difficult

Torres del Paine National Park

INTRODUCTION

Even further south in Patagonia and reached from the town of Puerto Natales in Chile, is the famous Torres del Paine national park, named for several steep rock towers (torres is Spanish for towers) rising to around 2500m. There are three Torres, conveniently known as the south, central and north. Nearby are the equally steep Cuernos del Paine and the highest peak in the range, Paine Grande 3248m which is a massive bulk of a mountain guarded by big hanging glaciers.

Like the Los Glaciares park in Argentina, the Paine are a superb area for backpackers who can enjoy walking through evergreen beech forests at the foot of these magnificent peaks. Most walkers like to do the famous circuit around the Paine massif, but many short walks can be done in the park if you don't fancy six days of wilderness backpacking. The best of these has to be the walk up to the small lagoon at the foot of the Torres del Paine. This popular hike takes 4-5 hours from the campsite at Los Torres at the eastern end of the park.

PUERTO NATALES

A pleasant wee town on the shores of the Seno Ultima Esperanza fjord. Puerto Natales (page 184) is the southern terminus for the famous ferry through the Chilean fjords from Puerto Montt. The town becomes quite busy in summer with tourists stopping off on the way to and from the Torres del Paine national park. If you've time to spare the one day boat cruise up the Seno to the foot of Cerro Balmaceda is very worthwhile, with some good wildlife viewing, especially sealions and sea birds, from the boat.

TORRES DEL PAINE CIRCUIT

This is without doubt the most popular multi-day walk in the park. The hiking on the circuit is mostly through open forests or grasslands but there is also a pass of about 1250m which sometimes has snow cover even in January. Horses can't cross this pass so you will need to carry your own pack at least some of the way if you want to do the complete circuit. Maps and up to date information about the route are easily obtained in Puerto Natales or at the national park headquarters. Sadly, but perhaps inevitably, this great wilderness walk is now quite heavily used and the park authorities are having to build toilets, refuges and organised campgrounds on the circuit. We recommend doing the trek clockwise, starting from Lago Pehoe, but it is also quite feasible in reverse. The main circuit will take only five days, but it is worth having at least two spare days on the route for some of the interesting side trips. Some of the campsites charge a small fee of $3-5 per person for the facilities although Chilean pesos are much more popular with the wardens. When facilities are mentioned in the following text they include a basic toilet and shower, drinking water and basic food supplies for sale. However do not rely on the huts to buy food - if the warden is not there the shop will be closed.

ACCESS

Puerto Natales is the base town to reach the Torres del Paine park. You can travel here by bus from the big city of Punta Arenas in southern Chile, from Rio Gallegos in Argentina or (if you have been in the Los Glaciares park in Argentina) from El Calafate. It might be worth buying some camping food in the large supermarkets in Punta Arenas if you have time. From Punta Arenas you can also travel direct to the Paine park in one long day with a change of bus in Puerto Natales.

MAP TO USE

Parque Nacional Torres del Paine 1:125,000 is readily available from tourist agencies and kiosks in Puerto Natales and Punta Arenas.

THE ROUTE

Everyone must sign in and pay an entry fee at the park entrance at Laguna Amarga, public buses all stop here to allow you to do this. If you want to do the walk anti-clockwise head down to the bridge from the Laguna Amarga entrance and take the track heading north.

1a. From the entrance continue on your transport to the launch jetty at Pudeto. The modern catamaran costs $15 single and takes **40 mins** to reach the Lago Pehoe campsite. Camping with facilities is available here.

1b. 4-5 hours. Alternatively take your transport to the park administration centre. Follow the Lago Grey road for 5 minutes and you will see the path, marked with orange sticks, heading off on the right hand side of the road. A flat walk for **2 hours** on open ground leads to the first camp at Las Carretas by the side of the huge Rio Grey. Continue on a good path through scrub and grassland for **2 hours** to join the shore of Lago Pehoe, from where it is **1 hour** more walk to the camp area. From the Pehoe camp there is a highly recommended side trip up Valle Frances.

Valle Frances, up to 8 hours return.

Pick up the trail heading out of Pehoe camping area down by the Lago Pehoe heading east. This good trail passes Lago Skottsberg undulating gently and crosses the Rio Frances on a bridge after **2½ hours.** There is camping **5 mins** further on at Campamento Italiano (no facilities). A little further up the valley the rough path brings you out to an open spot where there are good views of the ice-falls on Glaciar Frances. It is possible to walk further up this valley, reaching the Campamento Britanico (no facilities) after another **1½ hours**.

2. 7-8 hours. From Pehoe the main circuit continues to Campamento Paso with spectacular views over the spectacular Glacier Grey. This is a long day. Find the path leading away from the lake, behind the toilet block. This gently rises until you get a view of Lago Grey. There are usually some icebergs on their journey down to the far end of the lake to be seen. On the next section there are great views of Glaciar Grey. Follow

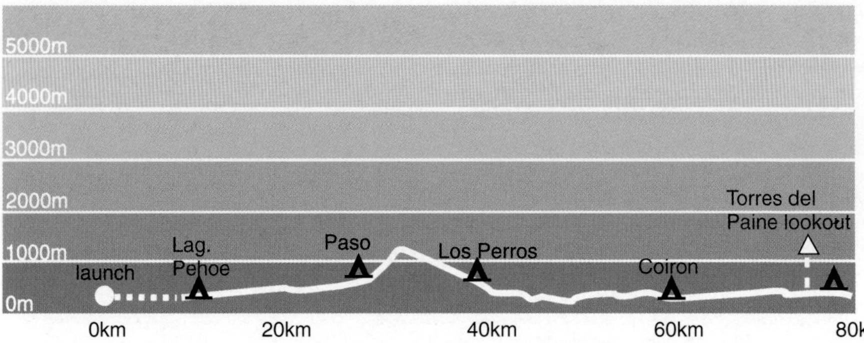

the clear trail until the junction for Refugio Grey is reached, **3 hours.** There is camping and facilities at Refugio Grey. There is also a tourist launch that travels the length of Lago Grey. If you are lucky you may see an iceberg calve from the snout of the glacier. Continue on a path which climbs gently through the trees to Camp Chileno, **1 hour**. After a further **3 hours** or more of hard work you will reach Campamento Paso, no facilities. This last section to the Campamento Paso is a very rough path. There are two loose scree gullies to cross, some trees to climb over/under and one in-situ ladder to descend. Between the Chileno and Paso camps there is a new, but cramped, camp area with recently constructed cooking shelter and toilet.

3. 4-5 hours. From Campamento Paso take the marked path rising very steeply up through the trees. This whole section can be a very difficult battle with mud if it has rained recently. As you rise the vegetation becomes smaller and denser until you come out through the scrub on to scree. Follow the orange marked stones and cairns to the pass which is reached after **2 hours** or more from the camp. The best views are had just before you reach the top of the 1200m "John Garner" pass. Follow the stream down on the other side of the pass with the occasional orange paint on stones or marker posts. There are often small patches of snow on this section. After **1 hour** or so the path crosses the steam to its left hand side just below a small chasm. It then continues gently downhill through short trees and patches of unavoidable and deep bog for a further **1 hour** to the small bridge crossing at Campamento Los Perros, (facilities).

From the camp it is worth taking a short 10 min. walk to the moraine by the Laguna de los Perros, with views of the small glacier behind. There are often icebergs floating in small Laguna de los Perros.

4. 5-6 hours. The circuit continues past the Laguna de los Perros down the valley, crossing the outlet stream, after **25 mins** from the camp, on a good suspension bridge. Continue down the right hand side of the stream, the path meanders easily through more open and larger trees now. There is a side stream to cross on a log bridge after **1½ hours** and you see your last views of the pass. The path continues down the valley now in a northerly direction descending gently to Refugio Dickson, **1 hour.** Camping with facilities is available here.

The circuit follows a clear path past the old refuge with a short steep rise to the south to gain a grassy moraine crest heading east down the right hand side of the wide valley. It is **2 hours** over grasslands to Camp Coiron, also known as Camp Lago Paine, no facilities, situated amongst scattered trees with their host of

Guanaco, Torres del Paine

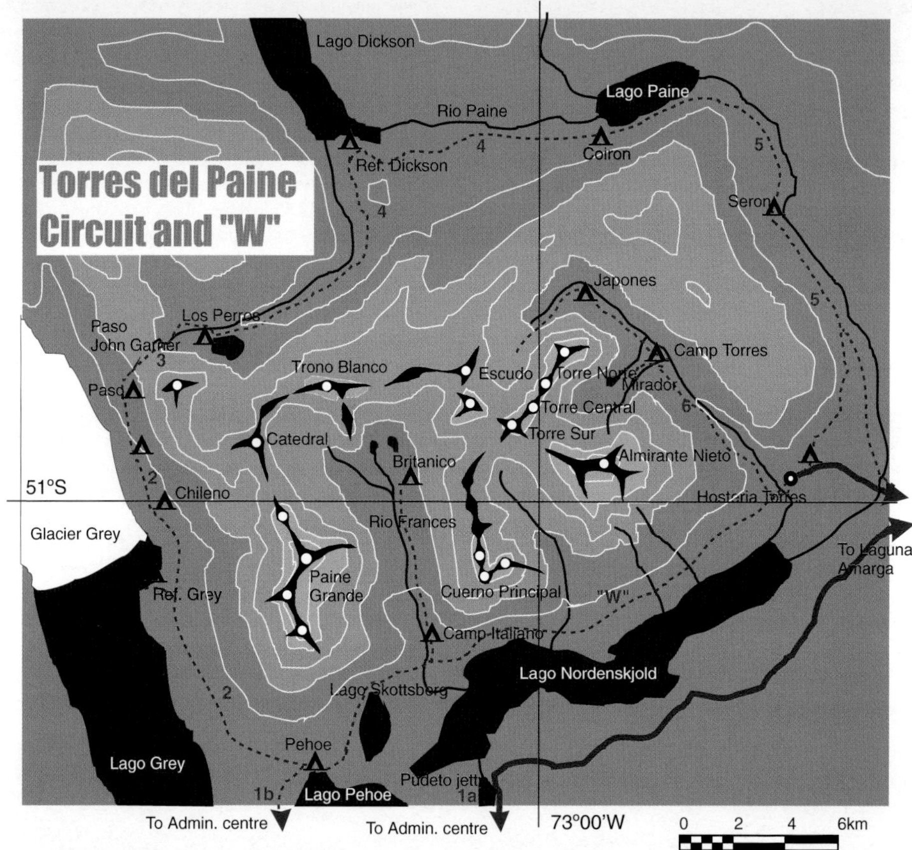

noisy parakeets.

5. 4-5 hours. From Camp Coiron follow the clear trail to a gentle rise and traverse the slopes above Lago Paine, **1 hour,** to descend to a wee lagoon. Continue through patchy trees before heading in a more southerly direction, along the flat open valley by the river for over **1 hour.** The path moves away from the river to encounter a fence and shortly after you pass a small wooden house. The Seron camping area, with facilities (and good hot showers), is 5 mins further on. Continue on the path through meadows. **1 hour** further on, shortly after crossing a small stream on a log, you pass through a gate. Almost immediately through the gate the path splits. The left fork returns to the Laguna Amarga entrance following the Rio Paine. The right hand fork heads gently uphill to traverse higher around to the Camping Las Torres **1½ hours** away. Take this path leading uphill and then undulating through sparse trees before finally descending towards the building complex by the Hosteria Las Torres. The first building you pass is a small farm stead, 10 mins further on an almost dry river bed is crossed to reach the campsite, with good facilities. There is also a hostel for cheap accommodation and for bread and beers. There is a small shop (though not great for camping supplies) and restaurant facilities at the Hosteria Las Torres 1km along the road. Rooms here are very expensive.

From camp the most spectacular area of the park can be reached in a days walk up to the Torres del Paine lookout.

DAY WALK TO TORRES DEL PAINE LOOKOUT

24km return, 700m ascent, 6-10 hours return

This walk is without a doubt the highlight of the park. Six hours return will get you to the Torres lookout, allow up to 10 hours return to see the upper Ascensio valley. It is worth setting off at day break to arrive at the lookout area before the crowds of day visitors. From Las Torres camping area walk through the Hosteria on the track which changes to a footpath and descends to cross the Rio Ascensio over a suspension bridge. Ascend out the river gully to the northwest on a good path, which is flat at first but which steepens as it heads up the slopes to the left of the Rio Ascensio. Once over the first bluff the path contours high above the river which it then rejoins at the new hostel **1½ hours** from the Las Torres camping area. Continue up the west bank for **1 hour,** gently rising and crossing two small side streams. At the third stream, which is in a wide boulder strewn gully, you will see the sign post for the "Mirador", the lookout. The path heads straight up this stream on boulder moraine well marked with orange paint splashes. The spectacular view of the Torres del Paine is reached after **45 mins** of direct ascent. Camping is available in Campamento Torres in the Rio Ascensio valley just beyond the Mirador sign.

If you have time it is well worth exploring further up the Rio Ascensio valley. This area is much less frequented and equally stunning. To do this continue through Campamento Torres staying on the left side of the Rio Ascensio. Cross a channel of moraine rubble following cairns then back into the woodlands on gentle terrain to reach the climbers camp Campamento Japones after **1 hour** or so. Rising more steeply from here the path follows the valley on its south side coming out of the tree line up a small gully. Continue over rough boulders through moraine and small snow patches to increasingly good views, up to **2 hours**.

TORRRES DEL PAINE "W"

This route visits the most scenic valleys between Pehoe and the Hosteria Las Torres as a 4 or 5 day backpacking route. It is described as a "W" since it heads up the three valleys of Lago Grey, Valle Frances and the Torres lookout valley. These valleys are all described in the above text. To link them from west to east the path along the north of Lago Nordenskjold begins near the footbridge crossing below Campamento Italiano in the Valle Frances. It is signposted here. The path rises at first then undulates and crosses several streams to reach Las Torres camp area over **6 hours** later.

Glacier Grey

Daisies, Patagonia

Tierra del Fuego

INTRODUCTION

Tierra del Fuego is a wild and less visited area at the extreme southern end of Patagonia. It is an archipelago of windswept islands, dominated by Isla Grande, on which the big town of Ushuaia is situated. Cape Horn, the southernmost point of south America lies at the southern end of the archipelago. In the highest mountains of Tierra del Fuego, the Cordillera Darwin, there are glaciers reaching down to the sea. We describe a walk at the edge of this range in Argentina and a walk on the Chilean Isla Navarino. Much of the walking involves your own bush whacking and route finding with the benefits of some remote and wild scenery. The North American beaver has been introduced here and there are now many areas of damaged trees where the beavers have made dams forming small lakes and pools.

USHUAIA

At the southern end of Argentine Tierra del Fuego, lies Ushuaia, the southernmost town in the world. It is a scenic town with a Scandinavian or Icelandic feel situated on the coast. Being almost 55°S Ushuaia enjoys long hours of daylight in December and January. There are regular flights here from Rio Gallegos and Buenos Aires. Boat trips down the Magellan Straits are very worthwhile and there are some good day walks in the Lapataia park about 15km west of the town. For further information on Ushuaia see page 186.

Ushuaia

HALF DAY WALK TO GLACIAR MARTIAL

About 7 km, 500m ascent, 3 hours return.

A half day walk to a small glacier snout with views over Ushuaia town to the Beagle Channel. Take a taxi or minibus service to the chair lift base - Aerosilla del Glaciar. From here walk up the clear track crossing to the left hand side of the stream. The track turns into a path as it heads up into the corrie above to reach the glacier snout. Return by the same route. It is easy to walk back into Ushuaia town by many obvious routes or arrange a taxi to pick you up.

HALF DAY WALK - LAPATAIA PARK COASTAL ROUTE

About 8km, 2½ hours.

The Lapataia National Park is 10 km west of Ushuaia. Take a taxi or a regular minibus service. The 'Senda Costera' path from Bahia Ensenada to the Rio Lapataia is signposted on the left from the main road into the park about 1km after the road down to Bahia Ensenada. It follows a well marked route and is a very pleasant half day shore walk. You'll see lots of unusual looking orange tree funguses if you walk the path from the main road down to the shore.

DAY WALK FROM USHUAIA, CORDILLERA DEL GUANACO

About 8km, 950m ascent. 5 hours return.

This is a days hill walk ascending the Cordillera Guanaco ridge (917m) with superb views across the Beagle channel and down towards Cape Horn. From the shore of Lago Roca in the Lapataia park follow the steep well marked path up through trees. Above the tree line the path becomes vague but head straight up to the ridge. Return the same way.

Valdivieso Circuit

BACKPACKING

DURATION 4 days
DISTANCE 52km
TOTAL ASCENT 1250m
HIGHEST POINT 1000m
TERRAIN No Path
EFFORT Extreme

SIERRA VALDIVIESO CIRCUIT

The Sierra Valdivieso Circuit is a remote and wild backpack offering great scenery but requiring good navigational skills and route finding. The walk ascends three passes, travelling through open ground a lot of the time but with the occasional bush whacking through young beech. There are also areas of rough ground damaged by fallen trees and waterlogged by the actions of the introduced beaver which can make walking very slow progress.

This area is much quieter than the national parks further north (Fitzroy and Paine) and you will seldom see anyone else walking here.

ACCESS

You can fly to Ushuaia (see page 186) from Buenos Aires or Rio Gallegos. Supplies can be bought in Ushuaia. From Ushuaia it is easiest to take a taxi for the 15 km journey north on Ruta 3 to the start of the trail at a disused gendarmeria on the road side.

MAP TO USE

No good topographical maps are available. The tourist office in Ushuaia produce an excellent brochure and leaflet 'Area Recreativa Sendas' which is good for exploring the Lapataia park.

THE ROUTE

1. 4-5 hours. From Ruta 3 immediately before the abandoned gendarmeria post take the track which crosses the Rio Olivia towards some houses behind a locked gate. Cross over this gate (Signs may say private but the local residents to date are quite happy for walkers to climb this gate) and continue on the track which turns to a footpath leading north towards the Rio Carabajal valley. After **2 hours** a pool is reached, camping is possible here. The path comes to the Rio Carabajal where if you are lucky it will be possible to cross on tree trunks, but you may need to wade.

Cross the wide valley over open and spongy ground, passing to the west of Laguna Arco Iris, **½ hour**. After another stream crossing, and beaver dam, it is possible to camp or continue to the edge of the woods at the bottom of stream outlet from Lag. Paso Beban **10 mins**. Continue north up this side valley with no definite path on the left hand side of the stream. The ground is steep and densely vegetated with lengas. The next camp space is reached where the gradient eases, after **1½ hours**. This camp area is immediately before where the path rises out of the vegetation and onto scree. Look for a round area of larger trees, containing a house sized boulder, beside the stream and the inevitable beaver dam. It is also possible to camp on the more exposed rocky ground **½ hour** away near the Laguna Paso Beban.

2. 4½-5½ hours. From the camp go along the east shore of the Laguna Paso Beban and rise up to the pass in the northwest side of the valley head. There is often a small patch of snow here. The pass summit can be recognised by the graffiti covered boulders, **1 hour.** On the other side there is a gentle descent down the valley on open rocky ground. Pick up a faint path following the line of the stream. When you reach the dwarf lengas follow the path on the right hand side of the stream. The path continues down to a lake formed by a beaver dam. Pass this on its left through an area of inundation. It is possible to camp in various places down this valley. Continue through more beaver damaged ground to follow a low ridge feature down then cross to the right hand side of the river. After **2 hours,** before the valley turns northward to join Lago Kami, you must cross the river, now wider, and ascend the valley wall, south, up to Laguna Azul, (start climbing 1km after you see the outlet stream from Laguna Azul tumbling down as a waterfall on your left).

The going can look formidable but it is easier than it looks - try to link the visible open grassy areas. Head towards the definite vertical break in the vegetation to rise almost straight up fighting your way through some dense trees. A series of 2 or 3 rock bands with boggy pools on the levels can be used to traverse leftwards until eventually the outlet from Laguna Azul can again be seen. Follow this upward over more false rises before the lake is reached, **1½ hours** from the valley floor. It is possible to camp by a wide fan shaped waterfall on the last one of these rises.

3. 4-5 hours. Passing Lag. Azul on its west shore a pass on a ridge can be seen at the back of the barren bowl behind the lake. There are two inlets to the Lag Azul. Take the main southwest inlet and follow it upwards to a fork. Follow the right hand stream to gain an orange coloured rocky ridge. Climb up this in a westerly direction. From the top of this rounded orange ridge head up to the low point towards the right to gain the pass. Alternatively, in poor visibility or snow cover after the fork follow the main tributary keeping near to the big buttress on your left. From the top of the tributary ascend directly to the ridge then make a short ridge walk north to the low point on the pass, **1 hour.**

From the pass descend in a westerly direction over

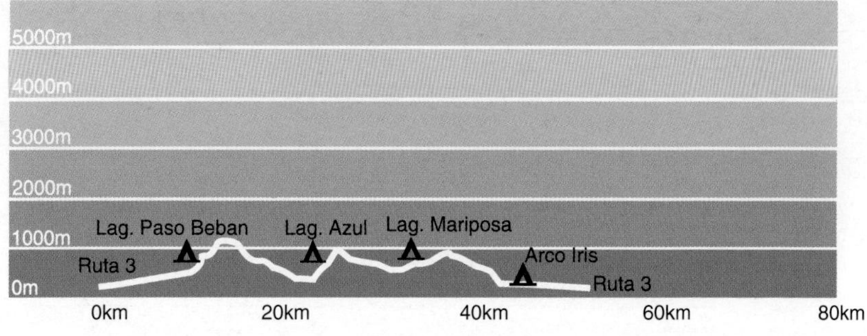

steep scree, then follow the right hand side of the first lake. Picking up the stream walk on over boggy ground to the Laguna Mariposa, **2 hours**. When you reach Lag. Mariposa back track 100 meters from the shore, there are two blue arrows indicating the start of the route around the lake. Strike up through dwarf lengas to the small bluff. From the rocky top walk 50 metres beyond the small pool to a well defined path which descends back to the lake shore and along to the upper bay where camping is possible by the inlet, **45 mins.**

4. 6-8 hours. From the south shore of Lag. Mariposa it is around **50 mins** to the Paso Mariposa, following the stream with a short section of dwarf lengas to tackle before you are back on open ground and rising gradually past a series of small lakes. There are nice views out to the large Lago Kami. A small glacier comes into view high on your right as you walk over the broad pass. Pick up the path again and descend towards the Carabajal valley skirting the larger Laguna Paso Valdivieso on the left hand side. Follow the stream down, keeping on its right bank once you reach the stunted lengas and trees. The Rio Carbajal is reached after **1½ hours.** Camping is possible in places by the river.

Follow the river down the valley, which although flat is tough going under foot and may take **4 to 5 hours** to reach Lag. Arco Iris. Keep to the left hand side where there are fallen trees and beaver pools to negotiate. There are occasional vague animal tracks to follow. Further down the valley the thick woods change to open ground but the going is still slow with spongy vegetation underfoot. Towards the end of the valley there is an area of higher ground in the middle of the valley where the going will get easier. This tree covered moraine leads towards Lag. Arco Iris. There is pleasant and dry camping at the end of this moraine amongst some trees.

5. 2½ hours. Retrace your steps to return to Ruta 3, **2½ hours** away.

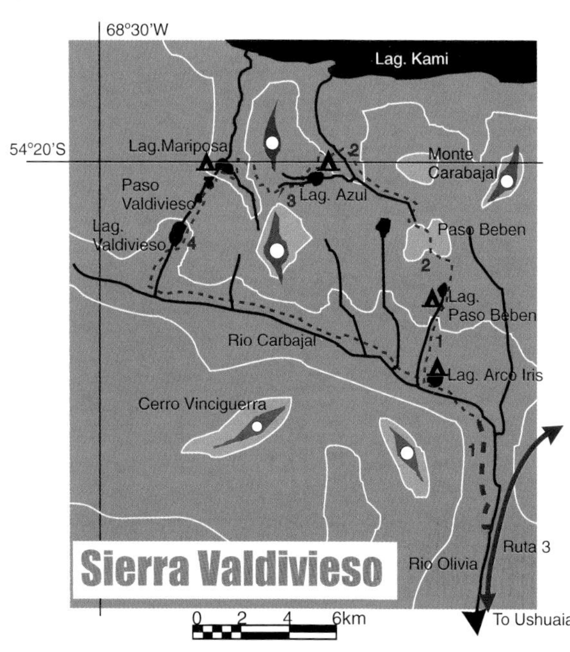

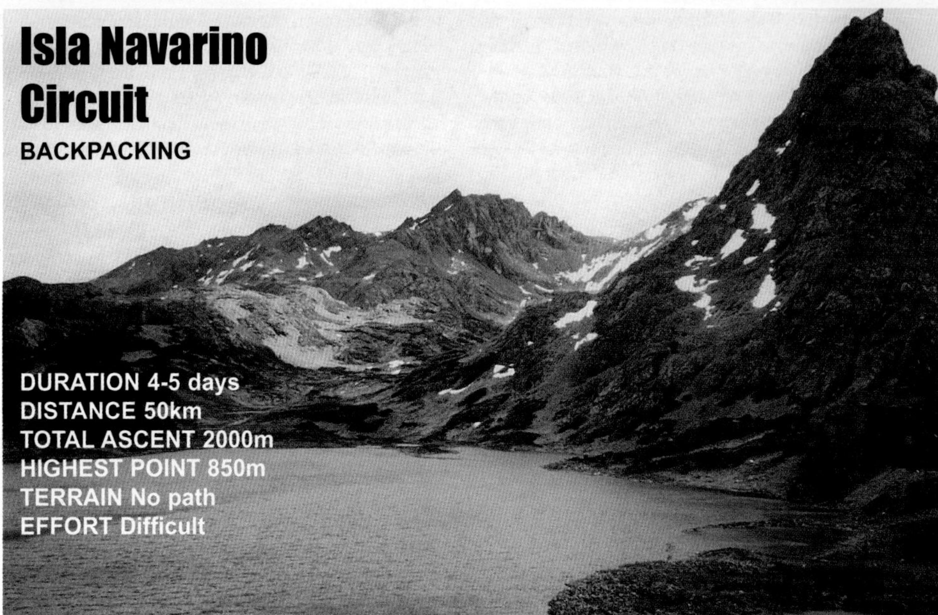

Isla Navarino Circuit

BACKPACKING

DURATION 4-5 days
DISTANCE 50km
TOTAL ASCENT 2000m
HIGHEST POINT 850m
TERRAIN No path
EFFORT Difficult

ISLA NAVARINO CIRCUIT

This walk circumnavigates the Dientes massif with peaks over 1000m on the Chilean island of Isla Navarino - a large island lying just south of Isla Grande in the Beagle channel. It offers some of the most southerly walking in the world. The walking is almost entirely off path passing through many valleys with small lakes and over many cols. In poor weather conditions route finding could be very tricky. There are no predators on the island so the guanaco and the introduced beaver are often seen.

PERMIT

Registration is necessary at the Carabineros office in Puerto Williams. No fee.

PUERTO WILLIAMS

This small naval port does not offer a great deal for tourists. There is a post office and 2 or 3 small shops. There is a friendly new backpackers lodge in town and you can go for a pleasant drink in the Club de Yachts in the harbour.

ACCESS

From Punto Arenas (travel information page 183) it is possible to fly or take the Cruz Australis, a small rusty passenger ferry to get to Puerto Williams. This is a spectacular 36 hour cruise through the Beagle channel passing the foot of the Cordillera Darwin with its glaciers falling into the sea. It can sometimes be possible to charter a boat from Ushuaia or hitch a ride on a tourist yacht.

Supplies can be bought in Puerto Williams. However, it would be advisable to bring some food from mainland towns as there is limited choice here.

MAP TO USE

Chilean IGM Puerto Williams (section L, 190) and Lago Windhoud (section L, 203) both at 1:50,000.

THE ROUTE

1. 4-5 hours. From Puerto Williams take the road, west, to Puerto Navarino. Just out of town take the left turn, at the statue of the Virgin, towards the forest and mountains. At the end of this road, keeping to the right at the next junction, there is a tiny dam where you can pick up a good track on the left hand side of the stream Rio Ukika. The path is flat at first but becomes steeper through the beautiful Fuegian forest up to Cerro Bandera above the tree line after **2 hours**. From there head south across a stony plateau (some cairns), keeping to the right hand side of the ridge.

Approximately 150m above the tree line, a good guanaco track leads southwest along the hillside towards the Dientes (a few paint patches). Follow this track as far as possible, almost to the head of the valley. A crag and big scree slope marks the end of the track, roughly 300 m above a lake. Walk down the scree slope, no path now, to good camping by the Laguna el Salto, **2½ hours**.

2. 8-9 hours. Walk around the shore of the Laguna El Salto and climb up a steep and wet grassy gully next to the small inlet stream. At the top of the gully the slope eases and becomes very much like an alpine valley, with meadows and snow fields. The impressive Dientes can be seen on the right. Head southeast towards a col marked by a big cairn, **2 hours**. On the other side of the col a dark glacier lake is visible - Laguna del Paso. From the col traverse downwards to the right through snow fields to reach a faint track (rock ledges and easy scrambling) that leads to another low col to the southwest after **45 minutes**. At this col, Paso de los Dientes, there are extensive views to the south of the island and beyond to Wollaston Islands and Cape Horn in clear weather. Head down south through snow fields to the first lake then on to a second smaller lake. Turn right below this second lake, skirting under a crag where some paint patches are just visible. Traverse to the west without dropping too much. Pick up a guanaco track to cross a forest that leads to the next big lake, Laguna de los Dientes. There is good camping here. Pass this lake by the north shore and head up a smooth valley to the next big lake **2½ hours** from the Paso de los Dientes. At this lake walk southwest for 10 minutes, crossing the outlet stream and climb a steep moraine over difficult vegetation to reach a large valley. Walk up this valley to the northwest first crossing shrub and then climbing a big scree slope to a col with a big cairn, **2 hours**. Pass the col without dropping but traversing to the right on a faint guanaco track on scree. The track disappears once at the vegetation line. Cross towards the west skirting lakes by the north to gain another col, Paso Guerrico, by a short steep climb **1½ hours**. From this col a new lake appears, Laguna Hermosa. Walk around the west side of this lake to reach the Laguna Martillo. Good camping on the shore.

3. 5-6 hours. Follow the right hand shore of Laguna Martillo and continue in a northeasterly direction following the outlet stream. Route finding can be tricky in this valley. After about 2 km make your way up the slope to the north. The crest is very flat but there is a faint col almost at its northwest end. Once at the bottom of this col climb steeply through the forest, pass the tree line, then continue on easy terrain to the large Paso Virginia, **2½-3 hours.** A long flat area of scree leads to the edge of a vast cirque and cairn. Here a valley opens to the northeast with Laguna Guanaco. An impressive snow cornice must be skirted by walking to the extreme right (east) of the cirque, and then down a steep scree slope. A very good guanaco track runs along the left of the lake. At the end of the lake go down northwest through the forest, steep at first, to a flatter area with another smaller lake, **2 hours** from the pass. There is good camping in the forest.

4. 3-4 hours. Continue down the valley of the Estero Virginia staying on the slopes to the right through the thick forest, aiming for the fishery on the road below by the Beagle Channel. Head east along the road to Puerto Williams.

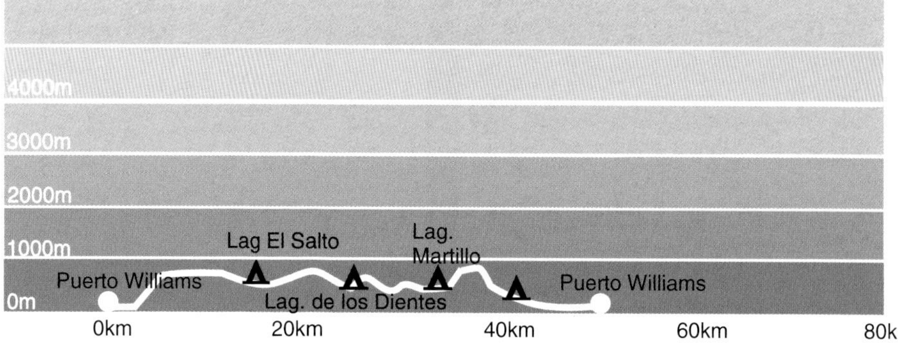

Beaver dam, Isla Navarino

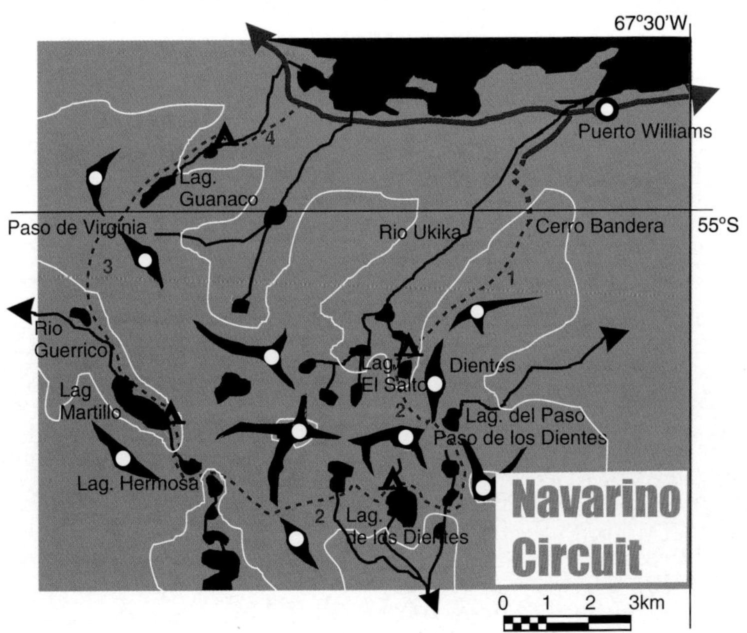

The Wildlife and Plants of the Andes

Only a selection of the more interesting or commonly seen species are described in this chapter. See the 'Natural History' section of the bibliography on page 187 for a list of more comprehensive titles on the Flora and Fauna of the Andes.

Habitats

The Andes can be divided into three very broad habitat regions with differing fauna and flora in each.

In the north there is the **Paramo**, a high altitude moorland of Venezuela, Colombia and Ecuador, with a generally wet climate and a less pronounced dry season.

South of the Equator the high valleys of northern Peru and the **Altiplano** in southern Peru, Bolivia and in northern Chile and Argentina has a generally drier climate. Here there is a pronounced winter dry season (May-August) when there are colder temperatures and almost no rain. There is a lot of semi-desert vegetation with isolated patches, usually in valleys, of more lush vegetation (known as bofedales).

Finally the mountains of **Patagonia** have a temperate climate and a strong rainfall gradient from west to east. There can be heavy winter snowfalls and the summers are usually warm and dry. There is a lot of dense forest in this area.

PARAMO

The Andes of Venezuela, Colombia and Ecuador are characterised by high and wet moorland known as paramo. These are often mist shrouded and a number of unusual plants including the bizarre espeletias grow in this habitat along with several species of shrub such as the chuquiragua.

ALTIPLANO

The high plateau of the Andes is known as the Altiplano in southern Peru and Bolivia and the Puna in northern Chile and Argentina. Similar habitats, with a slightly wetter climate are also found in the Cordilleras Blanca and Huayhuash of northern Peru. This is the most typical Andean habitat that trekkers encounter.

Rainfall is low everywhere in this region and exceptionally low in the Puna de Atacama. Because of the high altitudes temperatures can be very cold at night and in the winter months. The vegetation varies from dry grasslands in the east and in the highlands to totally barren deserts on the western side of the Andes above the Pacific Ocean. Vegetation growth also varies with altitude. Between 3500m and 4500m there can be considerable vegetation growth particularly in the wetter areas of northern Peru, with a mixture of grassland, scattered shrubby forest and areas of cacti and similar plants. In the valley bottoms there are often very swampy areas with a peaty soil, known as bofedales. There is little or nothing growing above 4800m because of perpetual frost and little or nothing grows below 2000m-3000m on the western (Pacific) side of the Andes because of the extreme aridity. Below 3500m on the east side the altiplano vegetation gives way to cloud forest, as seen on the Inca Trail to Machu Picchu.

Paramo

Bolivian Altiplano

PATAGONIA

In the Patagonian Andes, south of about 40°S, rainfall varies dramatically because of the high barrier the Andes present to the prevailing moist westerly winds. There is one of the most pronounced rain shadows in the world and the vegetation changes from thick mixed temperate rain-forest around the western fjords in Chile to dry grassland and scrubland on the eastern (Argentine) side of the mountains in less than twenty kilometres. Vegetation grows to about 1500 or 2000m in most areas with trees growing to between 600m (in the south) and 1400m (in the north). The western slopes are characterised by wet beech forests with a very dense undergrowth of bamboo and evergreen bushes. Higher up the trees grow as thick shrubs, often very difficult to walk through.

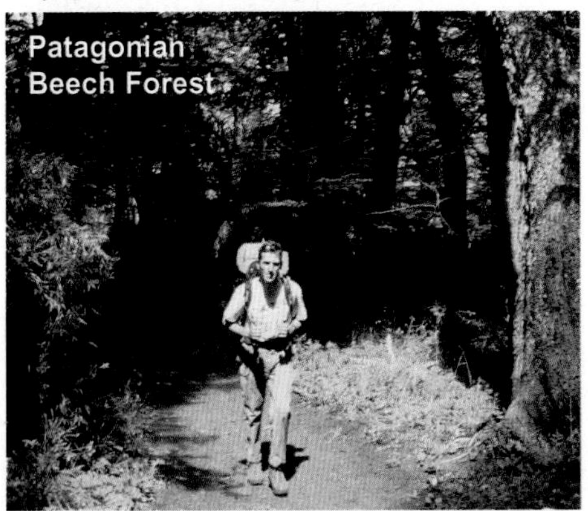

Patagonian Beech Forest

THE EVOLUTION OF SOUTH AMERICAN SPECIES

For many millions of years South America was an isolated continent and animal life developed very differently there to the rest of the world. There were all sorts of strange creatures such as giant ground sloths, giant armadillos and giant anteaters. Many important groups of animals found elsewhere were not present, particularly the sheep, cattle, antelopes and the carnivores. About a million years ago South America became joined to North America via the isthmus of Panama and there was an invasion of new (and usually better evolved) species, particularly cats, dogs, deer, the llama family, and of course humans. Since then many of South Americas wierdest species have been killed off by this new and more vigorous competition. One of the most remarkable of these, the giant ground sloth died out just a few thousand years ago.

Peruvian Altiplano

Patagonian Monkey Puzzle Forest

Animal types particularly common in South Amercia today include large and unusual rodents, carnivores such as foxes and cats, edentates such as sloths, anteaters and armadillos and of course the llama family. Animal types common elsewhere but not native to South America include the family Bovidae (sheep, goats, cattle, antelopes) and the Insectivores (moles, shrews, hedgehogs). There are no large mammals like elephants, rhinos and hippopotamuses and no native rabbits or hares.

Some typically South American animals are not found in the harsh climate of the mountains: anteaters, sloths, monkeys, the jaguar and the spectacled bear.

Mammals

VICUÑA

Vicuñas are a smaller and more slender relative of the Llama and Guanaco. Vicuñas (Vicugna vicugna) are pale brown on top and white underneath, up to 1m tall and weighing about 50kg. When alarmed they give a single high pitched whistle. Though they have never been domesticated Vicuñas are still rounded up by the Indians and sheared for their extremely fine wool in some parts of the Andes. They came close to extinction when it was found to be easier to shoot them, but are now undergoing a recovery in many areas, particularly where they are protected. They are found from the Cordillera Blanca in Peru to the northern Puna de Atacama. They are particularly common and easy to see in the Cordillera Vilcanota of Peru and the Cordillera Apolobamba of Bolivia

Vicuña

GUANACO

This wild relative of the Llama is found from the Cordillera Blanca of Peru to Tierra del Fuego. Guanacos (Lama guanicoe) can be up to 1.5m tall and weigh up to 75kg. They live in small herds of young males or females led by a single male. They are brown with white undersides and often a greyish patch on their head.

Guanaco

LLAMA AND ALPACA

These are the two domesticated species of camelid, thought to have been bred from the guanaco. Like cows at home they can be any colour or combination of colours from white to black and brown. Alpacas are woollier and more heavily built than llamas and are kept mostly for their fine wool and meat. Llamas (Lama glama) are also used as beasts of burden though they can carry only about 25kg. Both species are commonest in the high plateau areas of southern Peru, Bolivia and northern Chile and Argentina. The Llama family are all well adapted to high altitude, typically having two to three times the density of red blood corpuscles as man.

Llama

GUEMUL (HUEMUL)

This small short legged deer occurs as two species. Only the Peruvian species (Hippocamelus antiensis) is found in the High Andes. It occurs from Ecuador to north Chile up to 3000m or 4000m, usually in grassy or partly forested areas. It is known locally as the Taruca. Their body is 1.5m long Only the males have small antlers.

PUDU

The Pudu is a very small deer. The southern species of Pudu (Pudu pudu) is found in the Aisen region of Chile in thick rainforests. They are much smaller than the Guemul, being only about 90cm long, 30cm high at the shoulder and weighing only 7-10kg. Their coat is a slightly reddish shade of brown. They are very shy and only rarely seen.

Pudu

ANDEAN FOX

The Andean fox (Dusicyon culpaeus) or Culpeo fox is the commonest of the foxes seen in the Andes! From 50-70cm long, and weighing up to 8kg, they look more like a small dog than a fox at home. Their back is grey and the flanks are reddish. They are found commonly from southern Ecuador to Tierra del Fuego. Also seen and very difficult to distinguish is the Paraguayan fox (Dusicyon gymnocercus) which can be up to 60cm long. Their back is grey and their legs are yellowish red. They are found from the Equator to the Magellan Strait in more open ground - pampas and deserts to 4000m. Both species eat carrion, lizards, rodents and fish.

Andean Fox

PUMA

The Puma (Felis concolor) is known in North America as the Cougar or Mountain Lion. These large cats can be up to 1.5m long, with a long black-tipped tail. Despite their size Pumas are classed as small cats because they cannot roar but can purr! Pumas are found throughout the Andes and although they are relatively common they are rarely seen. They prey on rodents, vicuña and sheep and even, in Patagonia, on sea-lions. Very occasionally they attack people - there have been several documented incidents in North America in recent years. In the Andes they are often known as Leon (Lion) or Tigre (Tiger).

Puma

SMALL CATS

There are several smaller species of cat found in the Andes though all are now very rare in the wild. All are 50-75cm long and they can be difficult to distinguish. The Mountain Cat has thick silvery grey hair with orange-brown spots and tail rings. They are found up to 5000m from the Cordillera Occidental in southern Peru to the Maule region of Chile. The Kodkod is found in Chile from Arica to Puerto Montt, living on the ground among shrubs. Geoffroys cat, is found in rocky terrain and amongst trees and shrubs throughout Argentina. The Pampas cat is found on the east side of the Andes, from Ecuador to the Magellan Straits, in open country. This cat has pointed ears and silver grey fur with reddish hues on the back and skull and red-brown stripes on its flanks.

LITTLE GRISON

The Little Grison (Galictis cuja) is related to the stoats and weasels. They are about 40cm long and weigh about 1kg. They are grey on top with black undersides and face and a short bushy tail. They are found throughout South America over 1000m in forest and open country. They eat rodents and birds. They were used by Chinchilla hunters to ferret out the chinchillas and are still often kept as pets.

WEASELS

The long tailed weasel (Mustela frenata) is found in Peru and Bolivia. They are up to 20cm long and are very similar to the European stoat but are a darker brown. The Patagonian Weasel is a carnivorous animal (Lyncodon patagonicus) up to 20cm long and very similar to the Little Grison with a grey back and black undersides and face.

SKUNKS

The Andean Skunk (Conepatus rex) shares with other types of skunks the ability to drive off attackers with a foul smell. They are up to 50cm long with a white back and black undersides. Skunks are omnivorous and will even attack snakes. They are found from Peru to northern Chile up to 5000m. The Patagonian Skunk (Conepatus humboldti) is found further south.

COYPU

The Coypu or Nutria (Myocastor coypus) is a large (up to 60cm long) aquatic rodent found in southern Patagonia and up the Chilean coast about as far as Santiago. They eat shellfish as well as plants and breed very rapidly. Introduced to Britain, they can now be found wild in East Anglia!

Beaver Dam

BEAVER

Introduced from North America to Tierra del Fuego the beaver has done considerable environmental damage, felling trees and building dams. Though these large aquatic rodents are not often seen their dams are easily seen in the Sierra Valdivieso and on Isla Navarino.

MARA

The Mara (Dolichotis patagonum) is sometimes known as the Patagonian Hare, or Patagonian Cavy. They are a large rodent actually related to the Guinea Pig. They are bigger than hares (50-70cm long and weighing up to 15kg) and live on the open pampas country of Patagonia. Like rabbits they dig burrows. They are now suffering through competition for food with the introduced European Hare.

Mara

CHINCHILLA

The Chinchilla is a small rodent very similar in appearance to the Vizcacha, but only about 30cm long. There are two species, both of which have almost been killed off for their soft silvery fur. The Short-tailed Chinchilla (Chinchilla chinchilla) of Bolivia and southern Peru is now practically extinct in the wild. The Long-tailed Chinchilla (C. laniger) of the Puna area of Chile and Bolivia is commoner but rarely seen. They live like the Vizcacha amongst rocky areas high in the Andes, but are mainly nocturnal. Many are now bred for their fur on farms.

MOUNTAIN VIZCACHA

These commonly seen rodents look a bit like a cross between a grey squirrel and a large rabbit, with large ears and long furry tails. They live normally amongst boulders high in the mountains (up to 5000m) filling the same ecological niche as the marmot does in Europe. There are two closely related species; the Peruvian Vizcacha (Lagidium peruanaum) found from the Cordillera Blanca to around Lago Titicaca and the Common Mountain Vizcacha (Lagidium viscacia) found from Bolivia south to the Aisen region of Chile. Both are about 40cm long and weigh up to 1.5kg.

Vizcacha

WILD CAVY

The Wild Cavy (Cavia aperea) is the ancestor of the domestic guinea pig. These small rodents can still be seen in the wild in Peru, Ecuador and Bolivia. In the pure wild form they are always an olive or greyish shade with no white patches. Otherwise they look much like the domestic guinea pig. They eat a diet of shoots, seeds and plants. They live in burrows and are largely nocturnal. The Mountain Cavies (Microcavia spp.) are very similar and are found from Bolivia as far south as the Aisen region of Chile.

OCTODONTS

There are many species of these small rodents in the family Octodontidae. Degus are found from Copiapo to Santiago are 15cm long and live in burrows. The Cururo (Spalacopus cyanus) a similar size, is found from Copiapo to Valdivia. The Viscacha Rat (Octomys mimax) is found from Bolivia to the Puna and the Bori (Octodontomys gliroides) is found from southern Peru to the northern Puna. Also found in this area is the South American Rock Rat (Aconaemys fuscus). All these species are generally easy to confuse with each other and with the wild guinea pig.

ARMADILLOS

There are about twenty species of Armadillo found in South America. They are small insect eating animals which do a lot of burrowing. For defence they have a back covered in horn like hard skin. When threatened they roll up into a ball. The common Hairy Armadillo (Euphractus villosus) is 40cm long and weighs up to 3kg. It can be seen from southern Peru to northern Patagonia. The closely related and very small Pichyciego is found in two species from Bolivia to the Aconcagua area.

Armadillo

LEAF-EARED MICE

There are about fifteen species of these large but cute mice from the family Cricetidae found from Ecuador to Patagonia.

BATS

Many species of bats are found in South America though because they eat insects they are relatively rare at high altitudes. They are very difficult to identify becuse they only come out at night and fly rather fast. Just hope that it isn't a Vampire Bat bothering you (Desmodus rotundus) which is found in South America and does indeed come out at night to draw blood from its victims.

Birds

The Barn Owl and Peregrine Falcon are the only two species of bird widespread in South America which are also found at home.

FLAMINGO

There are three species of flamingo found in the High Andes, the Chilean flamingo (Phoenicopterus chilensis) the James' or Puna flamingo (Phoenicoparrus jamesi) and the Andean flamingo (Phoenicoparrus andinus). The three species are hard to tell apart except from very close up. Flamingos are unmistakable tall (over 1 metre) stork like birds with white, pink or red plumage. They live in salt lakes and lagoons in large flocks. Their beaks are large and curved and are used to filter microscopic animal life from the waters of the lagoons in which they live. The three species eat different diets and so can feed together without competing.

Their pink colour comes from eating a particular type of shrimp.

Flamingo

GIANT COOT

If you know what a coot looks like then you'll recognise the Giant Coot. It is a big dark grey or black bird with a distinctive white streak above its beak. The Giant Coot (Fulica gigantea) is up to 70cm long and are found on the fresh water lakes of the Altiplano at up to altitudes of 5000m. There are several other similar species of smaller stature such as the red-fronted, white-winged and horned coots.

BLACK NECK SWAN

The Black neck swan (Cygnus melancoryphus) is an unmistakable bird which needs no further description than its name! Normally found on rivers near the coast or on the sea itself from central Chile to Patagonia.

Black Neck Swan

DUCKS

Many species of duck are commonly seen in the Andes. The Torrent Duck (Merganetta armata) is often seen in or near fast flowing mountain streams. They are very powerful swimmers which eat insects and larva. The males have an easily recognised black and white striped head and red beak but is otherwise an unremarkable grey brown colour. The Puna Duck (Anas puna) can be seen in rivers and lagoons of the high mountains. They have a distinctive black cap and blue beak, a white neck but are otherwise a fairly drab brown.

Torrent Duck

GEESE

The Andean Goose is found near lakes and bogs and is very common throughout the High Andes, from Peru to Argentina. They are almost always seen in pairs. They have a pure white head and body with black wing tips.

Several closely related species of medium sized geese are found in Patagonia. There are two species of Canquen, the Red-headed and Ashy-headed. Both have browniush bodies with black barring. The Ashy headed has some white underneath and is found throughout Patagonia. The Red-headed is found only in southern Patagonia south of the icecaps. Both these species are found in meadows and by water. The male Caiquen has a pure white neck and white and black barred body, the female is very like the Red-headed Canquen. The Caiquen lives in more open, arid country.

Andean Geese

PYGMY OWL

The Pygmy Owl or Chuncho (Glaucidium nanum) is a small owl (20cm). They are found in the forests of southern Chile and Argentina and are distinguishable by their small size. They are banded pale brown and buff and have a yellow beak and feet.

Pygmy Owl

TINAMOU

These birds of the genus Nothoprocta are very similar to the partridge and indeed are known in Spanish as Perdiz. They are flightless and live on the ground amongst clumps of grass, and eat seeds and shoots.

RHEA
There are two distinct species of Rhea in South America but only Darwins Rhea (Pterocnemia pennata) sometimes called the Lesser Rhea, is found in the Andes. The subspecies found in the Puna is known as the Puna Rhea or Ñandu. These are unmistakable birds. They are large (about one and a half metres tall) grey and flightless and related to the ostrich, they are normally seen running away at high speed across the scrubland of the high Puna. They are also commonly seen in the Torres del Paine area. Rheas live in small groups. They lay 20 to 30 eggs in one large nest; these are hatched and the young are reared by the male.

Rhea

CACHAÑA
The Austral Parakeet or Cachaña (Enicognathus ferrugineus) is common in the more open areas of Patagonia and the Lake District and particularly in the Torres del Paine park. These noisy parrots are a dark green colour with dark red stains and are about 35cm long. They often live in large raucous flocks.

Cachaña

COMETOCINO
This brightly coloured finch often hangs around campsites in forest areas and Beech shrub in Patagonia and the Lake District. They eat almost anything, but are particularly fond of cheese! Also known as the Patagonian Sierra Finch.

Cometocino

Condor

CONDOR
With a wing span of over 3m the Condor (Vultur gryphus) is the worlds largest flying bird. Males can weigh up to 12kg. They are beautiful birds when seen soaring over a distant mountain but closer up they are pretty ugly - big black vultures with wrinkled bald heads. Apart from their sheer size they are most easily distinguished by a white neck collar. Condors eat mainly carrion. They are found throughout the Andes and are seen fairly often, but they are most easy to see in the Torres del Paine in Chilean Patagonia and at the Colca Canyon.

CARACARA
Several species of these common carrion eating falcons are found in the high Andes. They are about the size of a buzzard. The Mountain Caracara (Phalcoboenus megalopterus) has a black back and neck but white undersides. They have a pinkish face and orange coloured legs. The Crested Caracara (Polyborus plancus) has a white neck and pinkish face and distinctive black crest.

Caracara

ANDEAN HILLSTAR (HUMMING BIRD)

The Andean Hillstar (Oreotrochilus estella) is the commonest of the hummingbirds seen in the mountains. They are unmistakable when seen flying and hovering with their extremely rapid wing beat, which can reach 70 beats per second. Only 13cm long they are shiny grey on their backs with a shimmering green throat and white breast. The Andean Hillstar is found from the Cordillera Blanca to northern Chile above 3000m. The very similar White-sided Hillstar or Picaflor Cordillerano (O. leucopleurus) is found further south. Humming birds pollinate many of the flowering plants of the high Andes, partly because of the scarcity of insects at these altitudes. Their Spanish name is Picaflor, which means flower pecker.

Humming Bird
Chilean Flicker

CHILEAN FLICKER

The Pitio (Colaptes pitius) or Chilean Flicker is a medium sized (30cm) woodpecker. They live in semi-open land with scattered trees from central Chile to the Magellan strait and are commonly seen in the Torres del Paine park. The body is barred a dark and pale coffee colour, the front and neck are pale grey.

MAGELLANIC WOODPECKER

This large (45cm) woodpecker is deep black with a blue sheen. The males have an unmistakable crimson head and crest. They live in the woods and forests of Patagonia and the Lake District. In Spanish they are known as Carpintero Negro.

Magellanic Penguin

PENGUINS

The only Penguin seen from the Patagonian mainland is the Magellanic penguin (Spheniscus magellanicus) which is about 70cm high and with a black back and black stripes down a white chest. Other species like the Macaroni and Rockhopper live on the more remote islands of Tierra del Fuego.

Bandurrias

BANDURRIA

The Bandurria or Buff-necked Ibis are commonly seen, and even more commonly heard in Patagonia and central Chile. They have large grey bodies, beige necks and unmistakable long curving bills. They are insectivourous.

CHILEAN PLOVER

These large plovers are often seen on grasslands in southern Patagonia around the Torres del Paine and on Tierra del Fuego. They are greyish with black and white patches on their undersides.

Plants

ICHU GRASS

Many of the higher areas of the Andes are covered in the clumpy brown Ichu grass. This is the staple food of several species such as guanacoes and vicuñas. It is a dry and spiky plant best avoided when sitting down.

Ichu Grass

LLARETA

This commonly seen plant (Azorella yareta) looks exactly like clumps of bright green moss growing over the rocks, but they are in fact brick hard. They are seen from Peru south to the Lake District, normally up near the vegetation line and often as high as 5000m. Unfortunately they are dry and woody and burn easily in areas where other firewood is scarce and this may threaten their long term survival.

Llareta

CACTI

Many species of Cacti grow on the slopes of the High Andes from about 2000m to 4000m, depending on how much water is available. They are commonly seen around Arequipa, Arica and Salta. Particularly beautiful is the Candelabra Cactus found inland from Arica.

Cactus
Puna de Atacama

COIHUE - BAMBOO

A common plant in several areas of the Andes, species of bamboo grow to several metres tall and can form impenetrable thickets. Bamboo species are most often seen in the wetter forested areas such as northern Patagonia, where they are known as Coihue and grow at about 1000m and in Venezuela and Colombia where they grow at higher altitudes of between 2500-3500m

Bamboo

FRAILEJONES

These distinctive plants are also known as espeletias. They are found on the paramos from Venezuela to northern Ecuador and are members of the espeletia family. They have beautiful soft leaves to insulate themselves from the cold paramo nights. These plants are members of the daisy family of plants. They have bright yellow flowers.

Frailejones

PUYA

This rare plant, known only by its scientifc name of Puya raimondi, has the honour of producing the worlds tallest flower, often towering to over 10m. They are pollinated by moths and hummingbirds. Puya which are members of the bromeliad family, are found only in Peru and Bolivia growing in small pockets in high valleys from the Cordillera Blanca to La Paz and also in the Cordillera Occidental. They grow very slowly and flower only once before dying.

Puya

LUPINS
Several species of lupins are native to the high valleys of Peru. Their flowers look very like the flowers seen in gardens at home, usually purple or bluish, but the plants themselves come in a variety of sizes and shapes.

Lupins

Fuchsia

FUCHSIA
The fuchsia is a common sight in southern Patagonia, growing well in the damp climate there. This is another plant that has been imported in to British gardens.

CHAURA
The Chaura plant produces small edible berries which taste very like raspberries. It is an evergreen bush which grows only very low to the ground. They are common all over Patagonia and the Lake District.

Chaura

CALAFATE
The Calafate is a thorny perrenial bush which can grow as high as 4m. It has deep yellow flowers between October and January. The fruit, ripe in January or February, is a small blue-black berry which is edible and very tasty. There is a saying that if you eat Calafate berries in Patagonia you will have to return.

Calafate

PAN DE INDIO
The Pan de Indio (Cyttaria darwinii) is a distinctive parasitic tree fungus. This bright orange fungus grows in the trees in Tierra del Fuego and Torres del Paine. The name means 'Indians Bread', because they were eaten by the natives.

Pan de Indio

EUCALYPTUS

Eucalyptus trees, introduced from Australia, are commonly seen in cultivated parts of the High Andes, particularly in Peru and Ecuador. They are tall thin trees, characterised by their long thin grey leaves and pale smooth, patchy bark, The leaves and seeds have a strong distinctive smell. It is a hardy and fast growing tree and therefore it has become important locally for its use in providing fuel. There are large plantations on the slopes of the Cordillera Blanca.

Young Eucalyptus

QUEÑOA

These small trees (Polyepis spp.), with their beautiful papery red bark grow higher than any other species of tree, reaching altitudes of 4800m on the slopes of Sajama in Bolivia. They are found in small patches at high altitude from Colombia southwards to northern Chile.

Queñoa

MONKEY PUZZLE

A very distinctive sight in the southern Andes of Chile and Argentina are the areas of Monkey Puzzle forest. These beautiful umbrella shaped conifers trees, also known as Araucarias, can be found above about 1000m from Antuco south to Villarrica. They grow in very open forests often on steep hillsides. The trees get their name from their complicated looking branches, enough to 'puzzle a monkey'. The nuts were harvested and eaten by the Pehuenche indians.

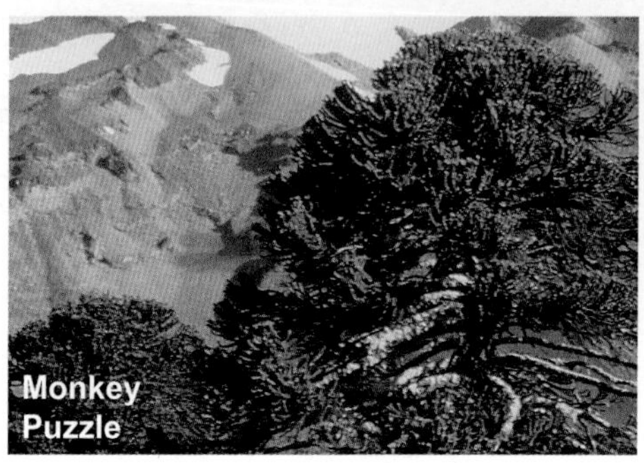
Monkey Puzzle

BEECH FOREST

Beech forests are found in the Andes of southern Chile and Argentina. They are often a mixture of evergreen and deciduous species. Three of the more common species are the Lenga, Guindo and Ñirre. The Lenga can be a tall and majestic deciduous beech tree which is also very often found growing as a shrub in thickets at altitudes above 600m. The Guindo or Coigue is an evergreen beech tree which can grow very tall, over 50m, but is also found growing as a bush on thin and rocky soils. The Ñirre is a low deciduous beech tree. All three trees are characterised by their small leafs.

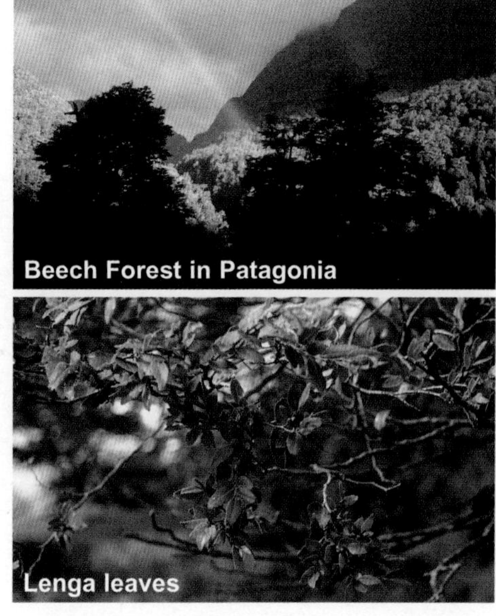
Beech Forest in Patagonia

Lenga leaves

Travel Information

In these pages we have compiled a list of useful travel information for the major towns you will need to pass through to reach the treks and walks. Smaller villages are generally not included as everything is usually easy to find and there may not be much choice!
The list is arranged from north to south.
Included is information of particular use to walkers such as supermarkets, camping equipment, mountain travel agencies and sources of information on mountain and trek routes. These have usually been used personally by us or been recommended to us by others. They will have given a good and reliable service in the past but we cannot however guarantee a good service in the future!
We have also included hotel recommendations in three different price levels. **Basic** up to $10, **Mid-grade** up to $40 and **Luxury** over $40 per room. Hotels have not always been used or checked by us (especially in the luxury category).

WARNING

The information below will assist your arrival in a town but can never be completely up to date. Prices go up, service standards may go down and businesses in South America close and change hands frequently.

Venezuela

Caracas

Telephone code (00 58) 2

The capital of Venezuela, you may pass through on your way to Merida.

MOUNTAIN INFORMATION

For information about national parks go to the Direccion de Parques Nacionales at the Parque del Este metro station.

MAPS

IGM maps can be bought from Edificio Camejo, 1st Floor, Avenida Este 6, (south side).

TRAVEL

Buses to Merida leave from the rather busy Nuevo Circo bus station near La Hoyada metro station. The airport is on the coast, 30km away, taxi $15-20.

LUXURY HOTELS

Las Américas, tel. 951 7387, fax 951 1717, C los Cerritos.
Atlántida, tel. 793 3211, fax 781 3696, Av. La Salle, Los Caobos.

MID-GRADE HOTELS

Savoy, tel. 762 1971, fax 762 2792, Av Francisco Solano y Av Las Delicias.
El Condor, tel. 762 9911, Av Las Delicias.

BASIC HOTELS

Guarapiche, tel. 545 3073, Este 8, Zamuro a Pájaro.
Hospedaje Torreiro, tel. 577 2148, Sur 11, Bolivar a Sucre.

Macuto

Telephone code (00 58) 31

This town on the Caribbean coast is closer to Caracas airport and more convenient if you are travelling straight on to Merida.

TRAVEL

'Por puestos', a kind of communal taxi, run regularly to the airport and Caracas from the main street.

MID-GRADE HOTELS

Macuto, tel. 461310, fax 461854, Av. La Playa y Calle 3.
Las Quince Letras, tel/fax 461432, Av. la Playa.

BASIC HOTELS

Plazamar, tel. 44271, beside the Contraloria.
Corona, tel. 44631, Calle La Iglesia.

Merida

Telephone code (00 58) 74

The city at the foot of the Sierra Nevada.

TREK FOOD

There are plenty of supermarkets in the central area. The most convenient is the chinese run one on Av. Las Americas opposite the viaduct.

FUEL

Gas canisters and white gas (bencina blanca) can be bought from the climbing and trekking agencies at the end of C24 near the teleferico station.

OUTDOOR EQUIPMENT

Several shops near the cable car (teleferico) station sell a good range of camping equipment, 'Expedicion Andina' seems to be the best of these.

TRAVEL

The airport is very near the middle of town, taxi $2. Buses to Caracas leave from the bus station, 3km from centre.

LUXURY HOTELS
Park Hotel, tel. 637014, fax 634582, Parque Glorias Patrias. Chama, tel. 521011, 521224, Av 4 con C 29.
MID-GRADE HOTELS
Hotel Mintoy, fax 526005, Ayacucho 8-130, mintoy@ing.ula.ve.
Hispano Turistico, tel. 528019, Av 3 Independencia No 27-51.
BASIC HOTELS
Alemania, tel. 524067, Av 2 y C 18.
Glorias Patrias, tel. 638113, Plaza Glorias Patrias, Av 2, No 35-64.

Colombia

Bogotá

The capital of Colombia.
Telephone code (00 57) 1

TREK FOOD
The Metropolis shopping centre on Av 68, No.75A-50 has a good supermarket opposite.
MOUNTAIN INFORMATION
For up to date information on trekking try the Central Nacional de Montaña, at Transversal 10 number 106-35, Bogotá. There's a nice cafe here too. Or try asking at the 'Cafes y Crepes' cafe at Carrera 16, No. 82-17.
OUTDOOR EQUIPMENT
Both the above places are also possible sources of any camping or walking equipment you might need and there is also a shop called Almacen Aventura at Carrera 13, No. 67-26, or Carrera 7, No.116-22.
MAPS
To buy topographic maps go to the national map office at Agustin Codazzi, Carrera 30 # 48-51.
TRAVEL
The airport is 20 mins. from the centre, taxi $10. The long distance bus station (Terminal de Transportes) is west of the centre, near Av. Boyaca.
LUXURY HOTELS
H. de la Candelaria, tel. 342 1727, Calle 9, No 3-11.
H Nueva Granada, tel. 286 5877, Av Jiménez 4-77.
MID-GRADE HOTELS
H. Planeta, tel. 284 2711, Carrera 5, No 14-64.
H. Bogotá International, tel. 341 9513, Carrera 7, No 21-20.
BASIC HOTELS
H. Platypus, tel. 341 2874 Calle 16 No 2-43.
H. Las Nieves, tel. 334 8181, Calle 20 No 7-27.

Valledupar

Access city for the Sierra Nevada de Santa Marta.
Telephone code (00 57) 55

TREK FOOD
Reasonable supplies can be bought in stores in the middle of town.
FUEL
Ask at the fuel station for kerosene. A source of camping gas is not known.
TRAVEL
The airport is 15 mins south, taxi $5.
LUXURY HOTELS
Hotel Sicarare, tel. 722 137, Carrera 9, No 16-04.
MID-GRADE HOTELS
Apartamentos Éxito, tel. 732 140, Calle 17, No 7A-19.

Manizales

The access city for the Los Nevados range, set spectacularly on a high ridge.
Telephone code (00 57) 68

TREK FOOD
Reasonable stores in the centre of town, though none are very big.
FUEL
Kerosene can be bought from some fuel stations. Try at the agencies below for camping gas.
TRAVEL
The airport is about 20 mins. out of town, taxi about $5. The bus station is on Calle 19 between Carreras 15 and 17.
AGENCIES
Tourist office, tel. 846 211 on the Plaza de Bolivar. Or try Turcaldas, tel. 848 124, Calle 20A between Carreras 21 and 22.
LUXURY HOTELS
H. Las Colinas, tel. 842 009, Carrera 22 No. 20-20.
MID-GRADE HOTELS
H. Amaru, tel. 843 560, Calle 20, No. 20-19.
H. Escorial, tel. 847 696, Calle 21, No. 21-11.
H. Europa, tel. 822 253, Av Centenario No. 25-98.
BASIC HOTELS
Residencias Bonaire, tel. 821 936, Carrera 22 No. 18-38.
Pensión Margarita No. 2, Calle 17 No. 22-14.

Ecuador

Quito

The capital of Ecuador.
Telephone code (00 593) 2

TREK FOOD
There is a good choice of supermarkets in Quito. Look for 'Supermaxi' in the new part of town, e.g. in the Multicentro on 6 de diciembre or in the Iñaquito and Jardin shopping malls near Parque Carolina.
FUEL
Bencina blanca (white gas) can be bought from 'Los Alpes' on Reina Victoria near Baquedano. Gas canisters can be bought from various sports and mountain equipment retailers around the new town (see below). Buy kerosene from petrol stations or ferreterrias in the old part of town. If you are going to any of the peaks its worth knowing that most refuges have gas stoves.
MOUNTAIN INFORMATION
For up to date information on trekking conditions and safety ask at the South American Explorers Club at Jorge Washington 311 or the Nuevos Horizontes Club at Colon 2038.
MAPS
IGM maps can be bought from the office on the hill by the astronomical observatory, Av. T. Paz y Miño, off Av. Colombia.
TREKKING AGENCIES - OUTDOOR EQUIPMENT
For private transport and to hire or buy equipment try one of the following agencies:
Safari Tours at Calama 380, fax 220 426, admin@safariec.ecuanex.net.ec,
Alta Montaña at Jorge Washington 425, tel.
Sierra Nevada at Pinto 637, tel. 553 658.
Ecuador Alpine Institute tel. 565 465, fax 568 949 EAI@ecuadorexplorer.com
TRAVEL
The airport is about 20 min. north of the centre of the new town. The bus station (Terminal Terrestre) is in the old town just beneath the Panecillo hill with the large statue on it.

LUXURY HOTELS
H Sebastian, tel. 222 400 fax 222 500, Almagro 822.
Hostal Villantigua, tel. 545 663, Jorge Washington 237.
MID-GRADE HOTELS
H. Plaza Internacional, fax 505 075, Plaza 150 y 18 de setiembre, hplaza@uio.satnet.net
H Embassy, tel. 561 990, fax 563 192, Presidente Wilson 441.
BASIC HOTELS
Residencial Italia, tel. 224 332, 9 de Octubre 237.
Loro Verde, tel. 226 173, Rodriguez 241.

Cuenca

A small city in the southern highlands of Ecuador.
Telephone code (00 593) 7

TREK FOOD
There is a good supermarket behind Res España on Colombia and Américas.
TRAVEL
The airport and bus station are both on Av. España, very near the centre of town.
AGENCIES
Try Ecotrek, tel. 842 531 fax 835 387 on Cordero.
LUXURY HOTELS
Crespo, tel. 827 857, fax 835 387, on Larga 7-93.
MID-GRADE HOTELS
Catedral, 823 204, Padre Aguirre 8-17.
BASIC HOTELS
El Cafecito, tel. 827 341, Vásquez 7-36.

Peru

Lima

The capital of Peru, on the coast.
Telephone Code (00 51) 14

TREK FOOD
There are a number of big supermarkets in the affluent central area of Miraflores with a good choice of dried foods etc. (a much better choice than in the provincial cities). In the old part of town there is a huge supermarket at the corner of Calles Venezuela and Ugarte, in the area of Breña.
FUEL
Try at the fuel stations for kerosene. Try the shop mentioned below for camping gas.
MOUNTAIN INFORMATION
For up to date travel and mountain information go to the South American Explorers Club, Portugal 146, just off Ugarte in the suburb of Breña. The staff are helpful and are a good source of information on trekking and a very good source for travel in general and for up to date information on trouble spots. It is also a good place to contact other trekkers in Lima if you're looking for a partner.

MAPS
Topographic IGM maps can be bought at the national map office at Av. Aramburu 1190 in the suburb of San Isidro. (best to take a taxi)
OUTDOOR EQUIPMENT
'Alpamayo' at Larco 345 on the central park in Miraflores, has a good range of camping equipment.
TRAVEL
The airport is on the coast near Callao, taxi about $10-$15. Most of the bus companies have their own terminals in the area around the Plaza San Martin. There are many different offices. Cruz del Sur at Quilca 531 can be recommended.
AGENCIES
Victor Travel Service, tel/fax 431 0046, Belen 1068
LUXURY HOTELS
Gran H.Bolivar, Plaza San Martin, fax 428 7674, tel. 427 2305.
H. Crillón, Nicolás de Piérola 589, fax 432 5920, tel. 428 3290.
MID-GRADE HOTELS
H. San Martin, fax 423 5744, tel. 428 5337, Nicolas de Pierola 882. hsanmartin@goalsnet.com.pe
Hostal Victor fax 568 9570, tel. 567 5107, near the airport.
BASIC HOTELS
Hostal Malka, fax 442 0162, tel. 442 0162, Los Lirios 165, San Isidro.
Familia Rodriguez, tel. 423 6465, Nicolas de Piérola.

Huaraz

The base town for treks in the Cordillera Blanca.
Telephone code (00 51) 44

TREK FOOD
There are no great one-stop shops in Huaraz. The small supermarket on the corner of Luzuriaga and Raymondi has the best choice and there are a number of others in this area. The indoor market and surrounding area west of Luzuriaga has a reasonable choice of fresh fruit and vegetables. It's also a good place to look for good quality imported food like chocolate and muesli.
FUEL
Camping Gas is usually available from the climbing and trekking agencies on Luzuriaga, but isn't cheap. The fuel station ('Grifo' - in Peru) on Raymondi just west of Luzuriaga sells petrol and kerosene and the hardware shop next door sells bencina blanca. Bencina blanca is also sold on Cruz Romero near the market.
MOUNTAIN INFORMATION
The best place to go for information on conditions is the Casa de Guias (guides office) in a quiet square called Plaza Ginebra just east of Luzuriaga behind the bank. Peruvian IGM maps can usually be bought here. Some of the trekking agencies along the main street of Luzuriaga are quite good for information, particularly if you're buying something from them. Lobo Adventure Shop and Baloo Tours are two of the best for information.
OUTDOOR EQUIPMENT
Several shops along the main street (Luzuriaga) sell and rent equipment - you'll trip over the tents pitched on the pavement. As most of this is second-hand or dumped equipment don't expect good quality - make sure you check everything before you rent.
MOUNTAIN TRANSPORT AND AGENCIES
Many tour agencies up and down Luzuriaga will provide private transport and arrange donkey or porter services but try Pablo Tours, Luzuriaga 501, fax 721145, or ask at the Casa de Guias, Plaza Ginebra. On Lucar y Torre by the river you can hire a rusty old pick-up truck for short journeys up to the mountains.
GUIDES
Professional IFMGA mountain guides can be contacted through the Casa de Guias, Plaza Ginebra 28-G, (just east of Luzuriaga)
TRAVEL
Bus companies each have their own terminals in or near the centre of town. Cruz del Sur are good.

LUXURY HOTELS
Hostal Andino, fax 722 830, tel. 721 662, Pedro Cochachin 357, Casilla 24.
andino@mail.cosapidata.com.pe
Hotel Colomba, fax 722 273, tel. 721501, Zela 278
colomba@cosapidata.com.pe
MID-GRADE HOTELS
Hostal Yanett, tel. 721 466, Centenario 106,
Hostal Tumi, tel. 721784, San Martin 1121,
BASIC HOTELS
Hostal Oscar, tel. 721145, José de la Mar 624.
Edwards Inn, tel. 722 692, Bolognesi 121

Chiquian

The base town for trekking in the Cordillera Huayhuash.
Telephone code (00 51) 44

TREK FOOD
There are several small grocery stores round the centre of town, but there is a much better choice of food for using on the trek in Huaraz (or even Lima).
FUEL
Kerosene can be bought from shops in town. If you need Camping Gas it is better to buy it in Huaraz.

BASIC HOTELS
Hostal San Miguel, tel. 747 001, Comercio 233

Huancayo

A large highland town in central Peru.
Telephone code (00 51) 64

TREK FOOD
There are several quite good supermarkets in the centre of town.
FUEL
Bencina blanca and kerosene can be bought from the ferreterrias at the south end of Calle Real. A source for camping gas is not known.
AGENCIES
Huancayo is so far off the tourist trail that it is hard to find much help or information, but Lucho Hurtado at La Cabaña, Giraldez 652 knows a bit about the Cordillera Central and can help with private transport.
MID-GRADE HOTELS
H. Santa Felicita, tel. 231 431, Plaza de Armas.
BASIC HOTELS
Residencial Huancayo, tel. 233 541, Giráldez 356.
La Casa de mi Abuela, Giraldez.

Cuzco

The chief city of southeast Peru and a base for some of the best treks in the country.
Telephone code (00 51) 84

TREK FOOD
There are several big grocers shops near the centre of Cuzco. Try the supermarkets on the north side of Plateros and on Matará.
FUEL
Petrol and kerosene can be bought from the petrol stations on Saphi. Camping Gas and bencina blanca can be bought from several shops around the Plaza that also sell and rent camping equipment.
MOUNTAIN TRANSPORT AND AGENCIES
There are numerous agencies in and around the Plaza de Armas who can arrange mountain transport, donkeys and or porters. Most are set up for trekkers, and particularly those doing the Inca Trail. Ask around for the best prices. Southern Cross, fax 239 447, tel. 237 649, Portal de Panes 123. PO Box 612. chpaullo@titan.amnet.com.pe.
Peruvian Andean Treks, Pardo 705, tel. 225 701.
OUTDOOR EQUIPMENT
There are many shops around the centre of town renting and selling camping equipment, but check the quality carefully.

GUIDES
Casa de Guias, 226 844, Urbanizacion Cerveceros #2

TRAVEL
The airport is just 10 mins from the centre, $5 in a taxi. The station for Machu Picchu is just behind the market five blocks from the Plaza de Armas. Bus travel in or out of Cuzco is not recommended.
LUXURY HOTELS
Royal Inka 1 and 2, fax 234 221, tel. 231 067, Plaza Recocijo 299.
MID-GRADE HOTELS
H. Los Portales, tel. 223 500 fax 222 391, Matara 322
Hostal Cristina fax 227 233, tel. 227 251, Av. de l Sol 341 hcristina@protelsa.com.pe.
BASIC HOTELS
Hostal Suecia II, tel. 239 757, Tecsecocha 465.
Hostal Tumi II, tel. 228 361, Maruri 312.

Tinqui

Access town for the Cordillera Vilcanota
no phone line

Only very basic food is available. Kerosene can be bought if you ask around. There is no supply of camping gas.
AGENCIES
The owner of the Hostal Ausangate, Cayetano, also provides a guide and mule service.
BASIC HOTELS
Hostal Auzangate as you enter the village and a newly opened hostal opposite.

Arequipa

The chief city of southwest Peru, access city for Misti and the Colca Canyon
Telephone code (00 51) 54

TREK FOOD
There is a good supermarket on the southwest corner of the Plaza de Armas.
FUEL
Camping gas has not been seen. Kerosene can be bought at south end of Calle La Merced. There are many petrol stations around the central area.
MOUNTAIN TRANSPORT AND INFO
A good source of information is Carlos Zarate. Also try the Casa de Guias of the AGMP at Desguadero 126, San Lazaro. For trek support or logistics try tour agencies towards the north end of Calle Jerusalen or the Zarate family. zarateexpedition@hotmail.com

TRAVEL
The airport is 10km north of town. The bus station (Terminal Terrestre) is on Av. Caceres south of the centre.

LUXURY HOTELS
H. El Portal, fax 234 374, tel. 215 530, Portal de Flores 116.
H Posada del Puente, fax 253 576, tel. 253 132, Bolognesi 101.
MID-GRADE HOTELS
H. Maison Plaza, tel. 218 929, Plaza de Armas.
H. Jerusalen, fax 243 472, Jerusalen 601.
BASIC HOTELS
H. Regis, tel. 226 111, Ugarte 202.
Hostal Colca Tours, tel. 211 679, Victor Lira 105.

Bolivia

La Paz

The capital of Bolivia.
Telephone code (00 591) 2

TREK FOOD
There are good markets in the budget hotel area around Sagarnaga and Santa Cruz or try the Mercado Lanza near the bottom of Calle Graneros. For supermarkets try the affluent suburbs a long way downhill in the area around Avenida Arce.
FUEL
Bencina blanca can be bought in the Ferreteria at the foot of Calle Santa Cruz. Kerosene can be bought on Calle Gallardo, directly uphill from Sagarnaga or at the neighbourhood pump on Plaza Alexander. There are several petrol stations in the middle of town. Expensive gas cannisters can be bought from the trekking agencies mentioned below.
MOUNTAIN TRANSPORT AND INFO
For information, trek support and transport try Guarachi, located upstairs at Camacho 1377 or the Club Andino Boliviano, Calle Mexico 1638. There are also several agencies in the 'Galeria Doryan' at Sagarnaga 189 - of these Andean Summits, can be recommended. In the neighbouring building Juan Villaroel at Azimut Explorer is also very helpful fax 329 464, azimexbo@caoba.entelnet.bo
MAPS
IGM maps can be bought at Edificio Murillo, Calle Murillo. The entrance is round the back in a dirty alley off Calle Diagonal.
OUTDOOR EQUIPMENT
The best shop seems to be Condoriri at Sagarnaga 339, with tents, rucksacks, ropes, karabiners etc. There are also several places in the shopping centre at Sagarnaga 189 which have rented or second hand gear.
TRAVEL
The airport is high above the city in the suburb of El Alto, taxi about $15. The bus station is on Plaza Antofagasta but for small mountain villages many buses (or more often trucks) leave from the market area around the cemetery.
LUXURY HOTELS
H. Presidente, tel. 368 601, Calle Potosi 920.
Rey Palace, tel. 393 016, Av. 20 de Octubre 1947.
MID-GRADE HOTELS
Residencial Rosario, fax 375 532, tel. 325 348, Illampu 704.
H. Sagárnaga, tel. 350 252, Sagárnaga 326.
Estrella Andina , fax 367 914, tel. 350 001, Illampu 716.
BASIC HOTELS
H. Austria, tel. 351 140, Yanacocha 531.
H. Andes tel. 323 461, Calle Manco Capac 364.

Chile

Santiago

The capital of Chile.
Telephone code (00 56) 2

TREK FOOD
There are plenty of big supermarkets in Santiago selling a good range of food. Near the centre of town try those down San Diego, or near Estacion Central.
FUEL
Most petrol stations sell kerosene. White gas (bencina blanca) can be bought from some farmacias. Camping Gas is available in most camping shops round town, e.g Casa Italiana at Prat 169.
MOUNTAIN TRANSPORT AND INFO
Casa del Andinista at Almirante Simpson 77 or 'Mountain Service' at Paseo Las Palmas 2209 #016.
MAPS
To buy IGM maps go to the office at Dieciocho 369 (Metro station Los Heroes).
OUTDOOR EQUIPMENT
Try Patagonia Sport at Almirante Simpson 77 or at Santa Victoria 0220. There are also several reasonable climbing and camping shops in the shopping centres up in Providencia. The best are near the Los Leones metro station at Providencia 2198 #14 or on the opposite corner, Paseo Las Palmas 2209 #016.

TRAVEL
The airport is about 1 hour out of town, taxi about $15-20. The main bus station is on the Alameda at O'Higgins 3712 (metro Univ. de Santiago). Bus services are very comfortable and reliable.
AGENCIES
Azimut 360, tel. 777 2375
LUXURY HOTELS
Santa Lucia, tel. 634 5753, San Antonio 327.
H. Ducado, fax 6951271, tel. 696 9384, Agustinas 1990.
MID-GRADE HOTELS
Vegas, fax 632 5084 , tel. 632 2514, Londres 49 Londres 49.
Santa Victoria, tel. 6345753, Vicuña MacKenna 435.
BASIC HOTELS
Res. del Norte, tel. 696 9251, Catedral 2207.
San Patricio, tel. 695 4800, Catedral 2235.
H. Rihue, Tarapaca 1037.

Calama

A small city in the north of Chile.
Telephone code (00 56) 55

TREK FOOD
Two large supermarkets can be found on Vargas.
AGENCIES
Nativa tel 319 834 fax 340107.
TRAVEL
Airport taxi $8. Buses leave from various company offices, all fairly near the centre of town.
LUXURY HOTELS
Hosteria Calama, tel. 341511, Latorre 1521.
MID-GRADE HOTELS
El Loa, tel. 311 963, Abaroa 1617.
BASIC HOTELS
Luxor, tel. 310 292, Vargas 1881.

Temuco

Access city for the Lakes region of Chile.
Telephone code (00 56) 45

TREK FOOD
Supermarket on Carrara 899.
FUEL
Try at the fuel stations for kerosene. Camping gas source not known, nearest supply known is in Pucon.
TRAVEL
The airport is just across the river, south of town, taxi $8-10. Buses leave from various offices around town.
LUXURY HOTELS
H. Nicolas, tel. 210 020, fax 213 468, Mackenna 420.
MID-GRADE HOTELS
H. Continental, fax 233 830, tel. 238 973, Varas 708.
BASIC HOTELS
Hospedaje Espejo, 238 408, Aldunate 124.

Pucon

A small town in the Chilean Lake District at the foot of Volcan Villarrica.
Telephone code (00 56) 45

TREK FOOD
There is a big supermarket on the main street.
FUEL
Camping gas, white gas and kerosene are all available.
MOUNTAIN TRANSPORT AND INFO
There are numerous agencies on the main street offering ascents of Villarrica. They don't know much about any other walks but you may be lucky and find someone who does know.
OUTDOOR EQUIPMENT
Due to the large numbers of tour groups climbing Villarrica renting and buying equipment is very easy. As always in South America the quality is a bit suspect. Some recent reports are that if you are not an 'officially guided' party you may find it hard to hire kit to climb the volcano.
TRAVEL
Buses leave from various terminals in town.
LUXURY HOTELS
H. El Principito, tel. 441 200, Urutia 291.
MID-GRADE HOTELS
H. Casablanca, tel./fax 441 450, Palguin 136, marlysacuna@yahoo.com.
H. Millarahue, tel 441 904, O'Higgins 460
BASIC HOTELS
Casa Eliana, tel. 441 851, Pasaje Chile 225.

Puerto Montt

Telephone code (00 56) 65

TREK FOOD
Good supermarket opposite the bus station
FUEL
Try at the agencies below for camping gas.
AGENCIES
Tourist office, tel. 253551, Anexo 2307 at Varas and O'Higgins. Travellers, fax 258 555, Angelmo 2270 Casilla 854, travlers@chilepac.net.cl
MID-GRADE HOTELS
Res. Millantu tel. 252 758, Illapel 146.

BASIC HOTELS
Res. Urmeneta tel. 253 262, Urmeneta 290.

Punta Arenas

A small city at the southern end of Chile, airport access for the Torres del Paine.
Telephone code (00 56) 61

TREK FOOD
Choice of supermarkets at 21 de Mayo 1133, Lautaro Navarro 1293, and at Zenteno 0164.
FUEL
Try asking in the agencies in town.
AGENCIES
There are many agencies in the centre of town.
TRAVEL
The airport is just about 20 mins. north of town, bus \$3, taxi \$10. Buses to Puerto Natales leave from various offices around the centre of town.
LUXURY HOTELS
Cabo de Hornes tel/fax 242 134, Plaza Muñoz Gamero.
MID-GRADE HOTELS
Carpa Manzano, tel/fax 248 864, Lautaro Navarro 336.
BASIC HOTELS
Hostal Dinka's House, tel. 226 056, fax 244 292, Caupolicán 169.

Puerto Natales

The gateway town for the Paine national park.
Telephone code (00 56) 61

TREK FOOD
There are a number of small supermarkets in the middle of town, but nothing great. They also run frequent and convenient public bus services in the summer months. Basic equipment such as tents and gas stoves can be rented or bought.
FUEL
White gas (bencina blanca) is available from several chemists in the middle of town and kerosene can usually be found by asking around a lot of houses! Camping gas from several of the agencies listed.
AGENCIES
Turis Ann, fax 411 141, Esmeralda 556.
Knudsen Tours, fax 411 819, Blanco Encalada 284, knudsen@chilesat.net
Andes Patagonicos, fax 411 594, Blanco Encalada 226
TRAVEL
Buses to the Torres del Paine, Calafate and Punta Arenas leave from various locations.
LUXURY HOTELS
H. Glaciares, tel/fax 412 189, Eberhard 104.
MID-GRADE HOTELS
H. Melissa, tel. 411 944, Blanco Encalada 258.
BASIC HOTELS
There are many 'casa de familia' lodgings round town.

Argentina

Buenos Aires

The capital of Argentina.
Telephone code (00 54) 11

TREK FOOD
A supermarket can be found in the Paseo Alcorta shopping mall on Figueroa Alcorta and Salguero.
MAPS
The IGM sales office is at Cabildo 301, Casilla 1426, (metro - take Subte D to Ministero Carranza).
OUTDOOR EQUIPMENT
Outside Mountain Equipment on Donado 4660. Cacique Camping at Arenales 1435 Barrio Norte and San Lororenzo 4220, Munro, Provencia Buenos Airres.
Try also stores at Guatemala 5908 and 5451.
TRAVEL
The central bus station is at Retiro, just north of the centre and on the Subte C metro line. The domestic airport 'Aeroparque' is by the river near the city centre (taxi \$10). The international airport is at Ezeiza, taxi \$35. Regular buses connect the two airports for \$15.
LUXURY HOTELS
H. Phoenix, tel. 4312 4845, San Martin 780.
H. Waldorf, tel 4312 2071, fax 2079, Paraguay 450.
MID-GRADE HOTELS
San Antonio, tel. 4312 5381, Paraguay 372
Gran Orly, fax 4312 5344, Paraguay 474.
BASIC HOTELS
H Maipu, tel. 4322 5142, Maipu 735.
H. Bahia, Yrigoyen 3062.

Salta

The nearest city to the Nevados de Cachi.
Telephone code (00 54) 87

TREK FOOD
A good supermarket can be found at Alberdi and Leguizamon.
FUEL AND OUTDOOR EQUIPMENT
Camping gas and very basic camping supplies can be bought at 'Maluf' on San Martin.

TRAVEL
Salta as a single main bus terminal below the hill at the east end of San Martin. Airport taxi about $10.
LUXURY HOTELS
H. California, tel. 216 266, Alvarado 646.
MID-GRADE HOTELS
Res. Elena, tel. 211 529, Buenos Aires 256.
BASIC HOTELS
Hospedaje Doll, Pasaje Ruiz de los Llanos 1360.

Catamarca

The nearest city to the central Puna de Atacama.
Telephone code (00 54) 3837

TREK FOOD
There is a good 'Tia' supermarket in the pedestrian street south of the main plaza.
FUEL
Try at fuel stations for kerosene. Camping gas supply not known.
AGENCIES
Contact Hugo Jonson Reynoso, fax 496154, FM Fiambala, in Fiambala.
andestravesias@hotmail.com
TRAVEL
Catamarca has a central bus station at Güemes 856. The airport is a long way out of town, taxi $15
MID-GRADE HOTELS
H. Colonial, tel. 423502, Republica 802,
simonamado@uol.com.ar
BASIC HOTELS
The area around the bus station has lots of residenciales for cheap accommodation.

Mendoza

The nearest city to the Aconcagua area, and a gateway if travelling to or from Chile.
Telephone code (00 54) 261

TREK FOOD
There are many good quality supermarkets in the centre of town, usually open long hours and Sundays.
FUEL
Petrol and kerosene as usual from most petrol stations. Bencina blanca (white gas/coleman fuel) is available in some pharmacies and ferreterias. Camping Gas can be bought at the outdoor shops on Las Heras.
MOUNTAIN TRANSPORT AND INFO
Try Andesport fax 4235 992 andesport@cpsarg.com or Turismo Aymara, tel/fax 4200 607 or 4205 304, 9 de Julio 1023. aymara@satlink.com.
Daniel Alessio, tel. and fax 4962 201, aconcagua@alessio.com.ar

For information on the Aconcagua Provincial Park go to the 'Subsecretaria de Turismo' at San Martin 1143 (this is also where you currently buy the necessary trekking permits, although be warned that every few years the location to do this changes).

OUTDOOR EQUIPMENT
Several shops on Las Heras sell camping and outdoor equipment (Pire reccomended). There is also a good camping, climbing shop 'Orviz' at Juan B. Justo 532.
TRAVEL
The airport is a $10 taxi ride out of town. The bus station is at Av. Videla, 1km from centre.
LUXURY HOTELS
H Balbi, tel. 4233 500, Las Heras 340.
H Royal, tel. 4380 675, Av Las Heras 145.
MID-GRADE HOTELS
H. Argentino, tel/fax 4254 000, Espejo 455.
H San Martin, tel/fax 4380 677, Espejo 435.
BASIC HOTELS
H Montecarlo, tel. 425 9285, General Paz 360.
H Galicia, tel. 420 2619, San Juan 881.

Bariloche

The main town in the Argentine Lake District
Telephone code (00 54) 2944
TREK FOOD
There is a good supermarket on Moreno.
FUEL
Camping gas can be bought from outdoor stores and bencina blanca from ferreterias.
MOUNTAIN TRANSPORT AND INFO
The best place to go for information is the Club Andino Bariloche (CAB) at 20 de febrero 30, open every day and selling maps and local guidebooks. They can organise transport to Catedral and Pampa Linda. It's also worth trying Datos next door and some of the other tour agencies around town.
OUTDOOR EQUIPMENT
There are several good shops in town catering for trekkers and climbers as well as skiers. Try those at Juramento 184 or Urquiza 248.
LUXURY HOTELS
H Bella Vista, tel. 422 435, Rolando 351.

MID-GRADE HOTELS
Hosteria El Radal, tel/fax 422 551, 24 de setiembre 46.
BASIC HOTELS
Hosteria del Inca, Gallardo 252.

Rio Gallegos

Telephone code (00 54) 2966

TREK FOOD
Tia supermarket on Au-Roca.
TRAVEL
The bus station is a few km out of town, so take a taxi. Buses to Calafate usually meet incoming flights so you may be able to connect straight through.
LUXURY HOTELS
H Costa Rio, tel. 423 412, Av San Martin 673.
MID-GRADE HOTELS
Santa Cruz, fax 420 603, Roca 701, htlscruz@infovia.com.ar
BASIC HOTELS
H Cabo Virgenes, tel. 422 141, Rivadavia 259.

El Calafate

Access town for Los Glaciares national park.
Telephone code (00 54) 2902

TREK FOOD
There are several supermarkets on the main street with a better choice of food than you will get in Chalten.
FUEL
White gas is available from several chemists in the middle of town and kerosene can usually be found at the YPF petrol station on the way into town. Gas canisters are also available from several shops in town.
TRAVEL
The bus station is up on the hill above town.
LUXURY HOTELS
H Los Alamos, tel. 91144, Moyano 1355
MID-GRADE HOTELS
Los Lagos, tel. 491 170, fax 491 348, 25 de Mayo, loslagos@cotecal.com.ar
BASIC HOTELS
H La Loma, tel. 491 096, Av Roca 849.

El Chalten

Access town for Los Glaciares national park.
Telephone code (00 54) 2962

TREK FOOD
Some supplies can be bought but there is more choice in Calafate.
FUEL
Kerosene can be bought from the YPF station, White gas, known locally as 'solvente', can usually be bought if you ask around.
AGENCIES
Alberto del Castillo, Fitzroy Expediciones tel. 493 017,. Oscar Pandolfi, tel and fax 493 043, expedpat@internet.siscotel.com.
LUXURY HOTELS
H. Robert, tel. 461 452, Av San Martin 2151.
MID-GRADEHOTELS
H Capri, tel. 461 132, José Hernández 1145.
BASIC HOTELS
Residencial Las Vegas, tel. 461 177 on Yrigoyen.

Ushuaia

Access town for Tierra del Fuego.
Telephone code (00 54) 2901

TREK FOOD
There are several very good supermarkets in the middle of town. e.g. on the 12 de Octubre.
FUEL
White gas is difficult to get in large quantities but may be available from several hardware shops (ferreterias) in town. Kerosene can be bought from the YPF petrol station. Availability of gas canisters is not known.
AGENCIES
There are many tour agencies in the middle of town who will provide private transport.
OUTDOOR EQUIPMENT
There are some reasonable outdoor clothing and equipment shops in the centre. The tourist office is also very helpful.
LUXURY HOTELS
H Cabo de Hornos, tel. 422 187, Av San Martin.
MID-GRADE HOTELS
H Maiten, tel. 422 733, Avenida 12 de Octubre 140.
BASIC HOTELS
Hospedaje Torres al Sur, Gobernador Paz 1437.

Further Reading

OOP = Out of Print

ENGLISH LANGUAGE WALKING AND CLIMBING GUIDEBOOKS
Guide to the Worlds Mountains, **Kelsey**, Kelsey Publishing, 4th edition 2001
The Andes - A guide for Climbers, **Biggar,** BigR Publishing (Andes), 2nd edition 1999
Aconcagua, **Secor**, The Mountaineers, 2nd edition 1999
Peru and Bolivia - Backpacking and Trekking, **Bradt**, Bradt Pub., 7th edition 1998
Chile and Argentina - Backpacking and Hiking, **Burford,** Bradt Pub., 4th edition 1998
Trekking in the Patagonian Andes, **various,** Lonely Planet 1998
The Inca Trail, **Danbury,** Trailblazer 1999
Climbing and Hiking in Ecuador, **various**, Bradt Publications, 4th edition 1997
Trekking in Bolivia, **Brain, North, Stoddart**, Cordee 1997
Mountaineering in the Andes, **Neate**, Expedition Advisory Centre, RGS, 2nd edition 1994
South America Ski Guide, **Lizza**, Bradt 1992 (OOP)
The Peruvian Andes (Cordillera Blanca and Huayhuash), **Beaud**, Cordee 1988 (OOP)

SPANISH LANGUAGE WALKING AND CLIMBING GUIDEBOOKS
Peru - La Cordillera Blanca de los Andes, **Gomez Bohorquez y Tome Ñacle**, Ed. Desnivel 1998
Trekking en Chalten, **Miguel Alonso**, Zagier and Urruty, 1998
Alta Colombia, **von Rothkirch**, Villegas 1998
Ecuador - Montañas del Sol, **Serrano - Rojas - Landazuri**, Ediciones Campo Abierto 1994

GENERAL TRAVEL GUIDEBOOKS
South American Handbook, Footprint. A detailed travel guide to the whole continent, revised annually.
Rough Guides - Good general guidebooks to the individual countries of South America, revised every few years.
Insight guides - General guidebooks to the Andean countries, less informative but with better pictures!

MAPS
The best maps for use in the mountains are usually those published by the national IGM's but these are only available in South America (see page 16).
A few good maps are normally available in Europe and the US. These include:
ITMB South America - Northwest (Venezuela to Bolivia), 3rd edition 1999
ITMB South America - Southern (Chile and Argentina), 3rd edition 1998
ITMB Ecuador, 2nd edition 1997
Alpenvereinskarte, Cordillera Real sheets 0/8 and 0/9
Alpenvereinskarte, Cordillera Blanca sheets 0/3a and 0/3b
Alpenvereinskarte, Cordillera Huayhuash sheet 0/3c

MEDICINE
Healthy Travel - Central and South America, **Lonely Planet,** 2000
The High Altitude Medicine Handbook, **Pollard and Murdoch**, Radcliffe, 1998
Altitude Illness, **Bezruchka**, The Mountaineers 1994
Medicine for Mountaineering, **Wilkerson**, The Mountaineers 1992

NATURAL HISTORY
Andes to Amazon, **Bright,** BBC books, 2000
Mammals of the Neotropics (3 volumes), **Eisenberg et. al.** , 1989-1992
Guia de Campo de las Aves de Chile, **Araya + Millie**, Ed. Universitaria, 1991
South Americas National Parks, **Leitch**, The Mountaineers 1990
The Flight of the Condor, **Andrews**, Collins 1982 (OOP)

ANDEAN HISTORY
Ancient Kingdoms of Peru, **Pendle**, Penguin, 1997
Penguin History of Latin America, **Williamson**, Penguin Books, 1993
Sacred Peaks of the Andes, **Reinhard,** National Geographic magazine #181, 1992
Kingdom of the Sun God, **Cameron**, Facts on File 1990
Exploring Cusco, **Frost**, Nuevas Imagenes, 1989
Conquest of the Incas, **Hemming**, Macmillan 1970

BACKPACKING, CAMPING AND WALKING TECHNIQUE
Mountaincraft and Leadership, **Langmuir,** MLTB, 1999
The Backpackers Handbook, **Townsend,** Ragged Mountain Press, 1997
Mountain Hazards, Mountain Navigation, Mountain Safety, **all by Walker,** Constable
Mountain Navigation, **Cliff Cordee, 1991**

MOUNTAINEERING TECHNIQUE
Handbook of Climbing, **Fyffe and Peter**, Pelham Books, 2nd edition 1997
NOLS Wilderness Mountaineering, **Powers**, Stackpole Books 1993
A Manual of Modern Rope Techniques, **Shepherd**, Constable 1990
Glacier Travel and Crevasse Rescue, **Selters,** Diadem Books, 1990

Websites

www.andes.org	An index site with a huge number of links to other sites on archaeology, language, music, history, travel, etc.

TREKKING AND CLIMBING IN THE ANDES

www.info.andes.com	Information and trips - Trekking, skiing and mountaineering in the Andes.
www.andeantrails.co.uk	Trekking and Mountain Biking in Peru, Bolivia and Patagonia.
www.mtsobek.com	US tour operator
www.wildernesstravel.com	US tour operator

GENERAL TRAVEL INFORMATION

www.samexplo.org	South American Explorers Club. Good for up to date travel and security advice.
www.fco.gov.uk	Foreign Office (UK). Up to date travel advisories.

MAPS

www.omnimap.com	US map retailer.
www.itmb.com	US/Canadian map maker.
www.themapshop.co.uk	UK map retailer.

BOOKS

www.chesslerbooks.com	US retailer of walking and climbing books.
www.mountainbooks.co.uk	Jarvis Books, a UK retailer of specialist walking and climbing guidebooks.

Equipment List

This is a general equipment list which should be found suitable for most treks and backpacking routes in this guidebook with just minor variations.

ESSENTIAL EQUIPMENT FOR ALL ROUTES

Wind and waterproof jacket
Wind and waterproof overtrousers
Warm hat and gloves
Comfortable walking boots
3 or 4 season sleeping bag
Foam or inflatable camping mat
Torch with spare batteries and bulbs
Sun cream, sun hat and lip protection stick
Trekking poles (walking sticks)
One litre water bottle x2
First aid kit

GENERAL EQUIPMENT

Mug and penknife
Sleeping bag liner
Camera and plenty of film
Washing kit, toothbrush etc.
Books to read

SUGGESTED CLOTHING

Personal underwear
Thermal underwear
T-shirts and at least one long sleeved shirt
Mid-weight fleece and warm fleece jacket
Fleece or similar warm trousers
Trainers or lightweight canvas boots
A change of clothes for around town after trekking

FOR MOST PEAK ASCENTS

Ice-axe (50-70 cm shaft)
Crampons
Harness and rope if there is a glacier
Karabiners, prussik loops etc.

FOR HIGH ALTITUDE TRIPS ONLY

Down jacket

CAMPING EQUIPMENT

The following extra equipment will be needed where an agent is not providing all camping services
Lightweight tent
One stove for every 3 or 4 people
Fuel and (for multi-fuel stoves) fuel bottles
Pots, pans, bowls, plates and cutlery
Trowel (for burying toilet waste) and a simple repair kit for stoves and tents

RUCKSACKS

On treks it is a good idea to have both a small rucksack (30-40 litres) for carrying waterproofs, camera etc., during the day and a big rucksack (60-70 litres) to put all the rest of your gear into for transport by mule or donkey. For backpacking trips you will obviously need to get everything into one 60-70 litre rucksack. With careful packing, good choice of food and using lightweight tents and efficient stoves even the longest (7 or 8 night) backpacking trips can be done with just 17-18kg on your back.

DON'T FORGET ALL THESE ESSENTIALS

Maps, guidebooks, passport, some spare money, credit card and insurance.

Abbreviations

Co.	Cerro	hill
Cord.	Cordillera	mountain range
Hac.	Hacienda	farm, small village
Ref.	Refugio	hut, mountain refuge
Lag.	Lago, Laguna	lake, lochan, lagoon, tarn
Q.	Quebrada	ravine, valley
Ao.	Arroyo	stream, river
E.	Estero	stream, river
mins.		minute(s)
tel.		telephone
b.c.		base camp

Acknowledgements

This guide could not have been compiled without the help of many people. In particular the following deserve special mention for their contributions:-

Damian Aurelio, Huaraz, Peru
Linda Biggar, Castle Douglas, Scotland
Ian Humberstone, Aberdeen, Scotland
Sergio Llano, Bogota, Colombia
Rick Marchant, Chamonix, France
James McLeod, London, England
Paul-Erik Mondron, Brussels, Belgium
Ingrid Matthews, Penrith, England

Photo Credits

All photographs are by the authors, John and Cathy Biggar except as follows:-
Damian Aurelio pages 55, 57, 58, 60 and 61
Linda Biggar pages 24, 27, 53, 64 and 103 (top)
Rick Marchant pages 18, 99, 101, and 103 (lower)
Ian Humberstone pages 17, 62 and 90
Ingrid Matthews pages 5, 84 and 85
Sergio Llano pages 39 and 44
Paul-Erik Mondron pages 162 and 164
James McLeod page 93
Gordon Biggar page 117
Andrew Owen page 122

Geographical Terms and Mountain Features

Most of the geographical terms listed here are translated from Spanish but a few words are of Indian language origin, either Q = Quechua, A = Aymará . Words relating more specifically to walking and trekking appear in the walkers vocabulary below on page 193.

ESPAÑOL (Q,A)	ENGLISH	DEUTSCH	FRANCAIS	ITALIANO
abra	pass	pass, joch	col	passo
acequia	aqueduct, ditch	graben	rigole	fosso
altiplano	high plateau in Peru and Bolivia	plateau	plateau	altipiano
arista	ridge	grat	arete	cresta
arroyo	stream	bach, strom	ruisseau	corso
baños	thermals		source chaude	
bofedal	bog, marsh	sumpf, moor	marecage	pantano
camino	path	fussweg	sentier	sentiero
campo de hielo	ice-cap	eiskappe	calotte glaciere	calotta di ghiacciaio
carreterrra	road	strasse, weg	route	strada, via
casa	house	haus	maison	casa
cascada	waterfall	wasserfall	cascade	cascata
cerro	hill, mountain	hugel	colline	collina
cocha, cota (Q, A)	loch, lake	see, lagune	lac	lago
collado	col	joch, scharte	col	forcella
cordillera	mountain range	gebirge	chaine	catena
cresta	ridge	grat, kamm	arete	cresta, spigolo
cueva	cave	hohle, grube	caverne	caverna
cumbre	summit	gipfel	sommet	cima
embalse, represa	reservoir		reservoir	
estancia	large farm (often a village)	bauernhof	ferme grande	fattoria grande
este	east	ost	est	est
estero	stream	bach, strom	ruisseau	corso
filo	ridge	grat	arete	spigolo, cresta
glaciar	glacier	gletscher	glacier	ghiacciaio
grande	big	gross	grand	grande
grieta	crevasse	gletscherspalte	crevasse	crepaccio
hacienda	ranch, farm	ranch	ranch	ranch
hierba	pasture	weideland	pature	pastura
hito	cairn, marker post	steinhugel	cairn	ometto
janka, hanca (Q)	snow peak	schneeberg	montagne de neige	montagna nevoso
jirka (Q)	mountain	berg	montagne	montagna
lago, laguna	lake, lagoon	see, lagune	lac, lagune	lago, laguna

ESPAÑOL (Q, A)	ENGLISH	DEUTSCH	FRANCAIS	ITALIANO
llanos	tropical plains			
loma	hill	hugel	colline	collina
macizo	massif	gebirgsmassiv	massif	massiccio
mina	mine	bergwerk	mine	mina
monte	mount	berg	mont	monte
morrena	moraine	morane	moraine	morena
nevado	snow mountain	schneeberg	montagne de neige	montagna nevosa
norte	north	nord	nord	nord
occidental	western	westlich	occidentale	occidentale
oeste	west	west	ouest	ovest
oriental	eastern	ostlich	oriental	orientale
pampa (Q)	plateau, plain	ebene	plaine	altipiano
paramo	moorland	heidemoor	lande	landa
paso	pass	joch	defile	sella, colle
pata (Q)	summit, hill	gipfel, hugel	sommet, colline	cima, collina
peña	boulder	block	rocher, bloc	masso
pico	peak	gipfel, berg	pic, cime	cima
piedra	rock, stone	stein	pierre	pietra
pirca	cairn	steinmann	cairn	ometto
portachuelo	pass	pass, sattel	col	passo
portezuelo	pass	pass, sattel	col	passo
puca (Q)	red	rot	rouge	rosso
puente	bridge	brucke	pont	ponte
punta	point	punkt	point	punta
quebrada	ravine-gorge-river	klamm	ravin, riviere	burrone
razo, raju (Q)	snow summit	schneeberg	montagne de niege	m. nevosa
refugio	mountain hut	hutte	cabane, refuge	rifugio
rio	river	fluss	riviere	fiume
riti (Q)	snow peak	schneeberg	montagne de niege	m. nevosa
salto	waterfall	wasserfall	chute d'eau	cascata
sendero	path	fussweg	sentier	sentiero
sierra	mountain range	gebirge	chaine	catena
sur	south	sud	sud	sud
termas	thermal springs		source chaude	
valle	valley	tal	vallee	valle
yana (Q)	black	schwarz	noir	nero
yungas	high tropical valley			
yurac (Q)	white	weiss	blanc	bianco

Walkers Vocabulary

This vocabulary is intended to help trekkers and walkers translate useful words relating to trekking and walking into Spanish. It will also be useful for foreign users of this guidebook to translate any unfamiliar English language walking and mountain terms used into their own language. See also the geographical glossary above on page 191 for more general mountain terms such as ridge, valley, river, etc.
The list below is in alphabetical order in English.

ENGLISH	ESPAÑOL	DEUTSCH	FRANCAIS	ITALIANO
above	arriba	über	au dessus de	sopra
altitude	altura	hohe	altitude	altitudine
altitude sickness	soroche	hohenkrankheit	mal d'altitude	
ascent	subida, escalada	beisteigung	ascension	salita
avalanche	avalancha, alud	lawine	avalanche	valanga
below	abajo	unten	au dessous de	sotto
bivouac, bivvy	vivac	biwak	bivouac	bivacco
boots	botas, zapatos	stiefel	bottes	scarpone
(to) bypass	desviar	umgehen	devier	deviare
camp (base)	campamento base	basis lager	camp de base	campo base
climb	escalada	klettern	escalade	scalata
(to) climb	escalar	ansteigen	grimper	scalare
cook (person)	cocinero	koch	cuisinier	cucinare
(to) cook	cocinar	kochen	cuisiner	cucinare
crampons	grampones	steigeisen	crampons	rampone
crevasse	grieta	spalt	crevasse	crepaccio
(to) cross	atravesar	kreuzen	traverser	attraversare
degrees	grados	grad	degres	grados
(to) descend	bajar	absteigen	descendre	scendere
distant	lejos	fern	lointain	distante
dog	perro	hund	chien	cane
donkey	burro	esel	ane	asino
(to go) down	bajar	absteigen	descendre	scendere
driver	chofer	fahrer	chaufeur	conducente
field	campo	feld	champ	campo
food	comida	essen	alimentation	sciocco
gloves	guantes	handschuhe	gants	guanti
grass	hierba	gras	herbe	erba
guide	guia	bergfuhrer	guide	guida
hail	pedrisco	hagel	grele	grandine
hat	gorra	hut	chapeau	cappello
horse	caballo	pferd	cheval	cavallo
house	casa	haus	maison	casa
ice	hielo	eis	glace	ghiaccio
ice-axe	piolet	eispickel	piolet	piccoza
jacket	abrigo	jacke	veston	giacca
kerosene, paraffin	kerosina	kerosin, paraffin	kerosene, petrole	cherosene
(to) leave	dejar	lassen	laisser	lasciare
ledge	cornisa, terraza	leiste	corniche	cornice
left	izquierda	linke	gauche	sinistro

ENGLISH	ESPAÑOL	DEUTSCH	FRANCAIS	ITALIANO
lightning	relampago	blitz	eclairs	fulmine
map	mapa	landkarte	carte	carta, mappa
mist, fog	neblina	nebel	brouillard	nebbia
mountaineer	andinista, alpinista	bergsteiger	alpiniste	alpinista
muleteer	arriero	eseltreiber	muletier	carrettiere
near	cerca	naher	pres de	vicino
normal route	ruta normal		voie normale	via normale
pack animals	asemillas	saumtiere	animaux a charge	animale de soma
path	sendero	fussweg	sentier	sentiero
petrol, gas (Am.)	gasolina	benzin	essence	benzina
(to) pick up	recoger		ramasser	prendere
pick-up truck	camioneta	lieferwagen	camionette	
poles	bastones	stock	baton	bastoncino
porter	porteador	trager	porteur	portatore
rain	lluvia	regen	pluie	pioggia
(to) rain	llover	regnen	pleuvoir	piovere
right	derecha	recht	droit	destro
rock (substance)	roca	fels	rocher	roccia
rockfall	caida de piedra	steinschlag	chute de rochers	frana
roof	techo	dach	toit	tetto
rope	cuerda, soga	seil	corde	corda
(to) rope up	encordar	anseilen	s'encorder	mettersi in cordata
route	via, ruta	führe, weg	voie, route	via
rucksack	mochilla	rucksack	sac a dos	zaino
sleeping bag	esleeping	schlafsack	sac de couchage	sacco a pelo
sleeping mat	colchoneta			
sleet	agua nieve	graupeln	pluie gelante	nevischio
snow	nieve	schnee	neige	neve
(to) snow	nevar	schneien	neiger	nevicare
steep	pendiente	steilhang	raide, abrupt	ripido
stone	piedra	stein	pierre	pietra
storm	tormenta,tempuesto	sturm	tempete	temporale
stove	cocina, estufa		rechaud	cucina, stufa
straight on	derecho		tout droit	dirito
tent	carpa	zelt	tente	tenda
toilet	baño	toilette	toilette	gabinetto
traverse	travesia	traverse	traverse	traversa
(to) traverse	atravesar	überschreitung	traverser	traversare
(to go) up	subir	hinaufgehen	monter	montare
valley	valle	tal	vallee	valle
(to) walk	caminar	gehen	marcher	camminare
wall	muro	mauer	mur	muro
(to) walk	caminar	spazierengehen	randonner	escursionismo
water	agua	wasser	eau	acqua
white gas	bencina blanca			
wind	viento	wind	vent	vento